DATE DUE FOR RETURN

- 9 MAY 2013

0 1 OCT 2018

Renewals
www.liverpool.gov.uk/libraries
0151 2

D1380424

About the author

Tracey Cox is an international sex, body language and relationships expert as well as a bestselling author and TV presenter. She also has her own range of pleasure products developed exclusively with Lovehoney. She has two weekly columns in Closer magazine, has appeared on Oprah, CNN and was a regular on the Today Show in the US. In the UK, she was a presenter on BBC`s *Would You Like to Meet?* as well as Channel 4`s *The Sex Inspectors*. Born in the UK, Tracey spent many years in Australia before moving back to London. She currently lives in Notting Hill, London.

Tweet Tracey Cox at @TraceyCox or
follow her on facebook.com/TraceyCoxSexpert

Find out more about Tracey, her books or product range or
write to her at www.traceycox.com

Dare

What happens when fantasies come true

TRACEY COX

HODDER

First published in Great Britain in 2013 by Hodder & Stoughton
An Hachette UK company

1

Copyright © Tracey Cox 2013

A CIP catalogue record for this title is available from the British Library

Paperback ISBN 978 1 444 76992 0
Ebook ISBN 978 1 444 76994 4

Typeset by Hewer Text UK Ltd, Edinburgh
Printed and bound by CPI Group (UK) Ltd, Croydon, CR0 4YY

Hodder & Stoughton policy is to use papers that are natural, renewable
and recyclable products and made from wood grown in sustainable
forests. The logging and manufacturing processes are expected to
conform to the environmental regulations of the country of origin.

Hodder & Stoughton Ltd
338 Euston Road
London NW1 3BH

www.hodder.co.uk

To all the women who dared

Contents

Before You Dare . . .

Just about everyone has sexual fantasies – and there are lots of reasons why. What happens in our heads is completely private. If no-one can see or hear what we're thinking, there are no rules. We're free to be totally honest. No-one can read our minds, so we can't be condemned for being slutty, immoral, 'dirty', depraved, kinky, degenerate, or horribly (*delightedly*) politically incorrect. Because we're directing the films that play in our own 'sexual cinemas', everything runs exactly to plan. Our lovers are handsome, tall, muscular and sexually skilled. They're able to predict exactly what type of kiss, touch, lick or thrust we're longing for. We are perfect, air-brushed versions of ourselves: wildly desirable, impossible to resist. No matter where the fantasy takes place, real-life distractions disappear. Mortgage payments, cramped commutes, sickly children, sulking husbands, irate bosses, cellulite, stress – they're all banished from fantasy land. Given these idyllic conditions, is it any wonder ninety per cent of women (and ninety-six per cent of men) have daily sexual fantasies? Or that some of us decide they're just *too* delicious to be left in our imagination?

Most fantasies, we'd never want to try in reality. Many would have us not only running for the hills but calling the police along the way. But others . . . others stay with us long after the arousal and orgasm has faded. We can't stop thinking about them and somewhere, somehow, they transform from erotic entertainment into possible real-life scenarios. The focus shifts from titillation to what might happen if we took them through to reality. They start to seem so appealing, so *doable*; 'Could I get away with it?'

turns into 'When and how can I get away with it?' Before we know it, we are actually doing it and, almost inevitably, dealing with situations and consequences we didn't quite bargain for.

Dare is about what happens when women take something that existed perfectly in their heads, into the stark and sometimes brutal reality of their beds. It is about what happened when they went that one step further and turned their wildest sex dreams into reality. Some of their stories are deliciously steamy and lustful, many are laugh-out-loud hilarious, and others are embarrassing, disappointing or plain disastrous. But all are endlessly fascinating – because they're real.

This isn't erotica, fiction or porn: it's real life. The women who've dared to take a risk are just like you and me. (In some cases they *are* you and me, depending on who is reading!) The ages, professions and stories are true but everyone's identity is protected. Any names, circumstances or identifying details have been changed for this reason, but the sense of the story remains true to life. The stories have been collected from friends, acquaintances and women who've contacted me via my website and columns, happy to share their secrets. All contributions are anonymous but my written versions of their fantasies and experiences have been approved.

Dare can be read on two levels. If you want a guaranteed raunchy read, go straight to the fantasy sections. Turn to the decision and reality parts and it's a collection of fresh, original stories that will arouse, amuse and also entertain.

I loved writing this book so much, I didn't want to finish it. I hope it gives you just as much pleasure.

Each story is written in three parts:

The fantasy is the glossy version of what each woman imagined the encounter would be like: electrifying, tantalising and risqué. It's the idealised, perfect scenario. You'll notice that the fantasies don't always match the reality. But they all, in some way, inspired the real life event.

The decision is when the story switches from fantasy to reality. We get a sense of who the woman is – her personality, motivation, personal circumstances – and why she decided to act out the fantasy.

The reality details what actually happened when she brought her sexual dreams to life.

Why Do We Fantasise?

Think of your fantasies as a vibrator for the mind. There are a finite number of possible physical combinations of what we can do with our bodies, but our minds are limitless.

Your imagination is the single, most potent engine driving sexual desire. Tap into your imagination and you've turned on nature's built-in aphrodisiac. Fantasies are what keep sex fizzy when your sex life – or your partner – goes temporarily pear-shaped. They're what can make sex with someone we've slept with hundreds of times seem not only remotely appealing but exciting. One of the quickest ways to arouse yourself is to fantasise. Even better, fantasies are a form of foreplay we can access in an instant – anywhere, any time – because we carry them with us always.

Some fantasies are fleeting. Others start off small then develop over time into rich, complex formats. Often they'll start the same or feature the same characters but have different endings, designed to suit the mood we're in. They generally last as long as it takes us to orgasm and we become adept at timing them so the climax happens when we do. Just like sexual positions, most of us have three or four favourite fantasies we return to time and time again.

Our fantasies tend not to change in theme terribly much, though women's tend to be more involved than men's are. Women read more, are generally more imaginative and need more varied stimulation to arouse them. Our fantasies almost always have a plot. There is scene setting, character development, a narrative arc ... Men go for instant action. They fast forward straight to the naughty bits – often sliding straight into bits in graphic detail. They'll often have one simple image rather than a 'video' – usually of someone they could pull in real life. This is why amateur porn sites and live webcams with 'normal' looking girls are so popular with men. They like to think they've got a chance of the sex actually happening.

Women, on the other hand, have no problems picturing Bradley Cooper frothing at the mouth for the chance to slide a hand up our skirts. It's one of the few times we allow our egos to run rampant and our self-esteem to soar!

Another significant difference between the two sexes is that women are more likely to fantasise when we're having lots of sex. Men do it more when they're not. Which backs up the 'use it or lose it' theory about female sexuality: we need stimulation, physical or mental, to kick start ourselves.

But for all the similarities about fantasies, there's one thing that's abundantly clear on reading *Dare*: they're highly person-alised. This is because our fantasies are influenced by everything from genetics, libido, childhood and parental upbringing to religious beliefs and the resulting moral codes and 'erotic blue-prints' we form as a consequence. A desire to want to strip on stage might stem from something as simple as catching a glimpse of our mother undressing at a time when our sexual thoughts and feelings were first being formed. The act of taking clothes off, someone watching and our sexual arousal get, albeit innocently, linked.

Most of the time we're not conscious of where our fanta-sies originate from and – somewhat wisely – don't rummage around our subconscious searching for answers. This is mainly because most fantasies seem harmless and we're aware of making them up, constructing them from things we know turn us on and adding a few fictional flourishes along the way to turn them into an even more appealing scenario. Scenes from books, films or porn are also great fantasy fodder, though even then we'll tweak them to suit our individual preferences.

However we get there, the end result is rather marvellous when you think about it. Homemade movies, tailor-made for every single one of us, *and* we get a front row seat in all of them. If only we could customise the rest of our lives the same way!

'I slept with a stranger from craigslist'

Claire, 38, works in real estate

THE FANTASY

In my fantasy, I'm younger than I am now and a tarted-up, perfect version of me. I'm having lunch on my own at a place I go to often. It's a Japanese place in central London that has a counter for people eating solo, so attracts lots of stressed-looking businessmen. Most of the 'suits' don't appeal: men with big egos and beer guts who I find repulsive and impossibly smug. As I'm eating my sashimi, I'm checking everyone out and thinking this but then a guy walks in who really gets my attention. He reminds me of Don Draper, a character from 'Mad Men' (played by Jon Hamm). Draper is classically good-looking and perfect on the outside but flawed and damaged on the inside. He's the ultimate bad boy: cheats constantly but women forgive him everything. It's not just his looks; it's the combination of vulnerability and masculinity that I find fascinating. The man who sits down next to me for lunch reminds me so strongly of Draper that he morphs into him almost immediately and I find it hard to separate the two. This suits me just fine.

He's tall, mid 30s, wearing an expensive suit that's modern and sexy without looking like he is trying too hard. His eyes flick over me when he sits down and spend just that little bit too long travelling over my legs and breasts. I know he finds me attractive. I'm wearing a tight pencil skirt with a slit up the thigh, a white fitted shirt tucked in at my waist and unbuttoned to show

9

cleavage, and towering high heels. I'm multi-tasking, reading the paper and news on my phone simultaneously, and I shift over slightly to give him space. He nods and smiles, saying 'Thanks'. His voice is deep and friendly and he speaks to me the way men speak to attractive women. There's direct eye contact that lingers. If I looked like a middle-aged frump, he wouldn't even glance in my direction.

I watch him surreptitiously while adjusting my position on the stool. I push my breasts out, arch my back and cross my legs prettily, pressing them together to make them look thinner and more toned – all the stuff girls do to attract men. I do all this while still reading, frowning now and then to look as though I'm doing it subconsciously and I'm really engrossed in my paper. He notices and does the same. He takes some papers out of a smart, leather wallet and puts them on the counter. Then he loosens his tie and takes off his jacket to show broad shoulders. His eyes flick in my direction whenever I preen or move or flex so much as a muscle. A smile twitches at the corner of his mouth. His lips are thin, slightly cruel. Don Draper has lips like that which makes me want him more. Neither of us acknowledges it but we are flirting outrageously without even saying a word. He's good at the game.

As the waitress gives him a menu, he sees an opening and starts a conversation.

'So how's the sashimi here? It looks good,' he says. His eyes flick over my body rather than the raw fish on my plate, letting me know it's me he finds scrumptious, not the food.

I haven't had sex with a man for years (through choice – I had a bad break-up) and I suddenly long for the sheer physicality of having a big, well-hung penis inside me. There's nothing like it and nothing can simulate that feeling. Dildos are great but I crave the rock-hard, hot, real thing. I am horny, short on time and brazen. I don't want a relationship with this man. I don't want a conversation. I just want to be pounded hard and preferably for at least 20 minutes by a man who looks like he would oblige without asking too many questions.

There's a big, spacious disabled loo hidden around the corner from the main toilets in the restaurant. I know it's there but not too many others do and the staff are being kept busy by the lunchtime crowd. I might have to make do with ten minutes instead of twenty, but it will do and I am now desperate to be fucked and am practically panting in public.

'Do you want more than that? Because I do,' I say simply. 'Wait two minutes then follow me downstairs. Go past the toilets and you'll find a disabled loo. I will be in there.'

I watch as shock, disbelief, some type of moral mental wrestle (a girlfriend/wife he's going to cheat on?) play across his face, then – of course, he's a man and men never say no to no-strings sex, never – he nods. A curt, no-nonsense nod. Perfect.

I slide off my seat as he pretends to study the papers in front of him. I consider taking my handbag with me but figure that's too obvious. No-one's going to steal it in full view of the staff and chefs in the restaurant. 'Fuck it if they do', I think. I leave it behind me and walk calmly downstairs. No-one's lining up for the main toilets. Excellent. I walk around the corner, see the other loo is free – thank God – step inside and lock the door. I take off my thong underwear and wrap it around my wrist. There's a knock on the door. I open it and he comes inside.

I knew he'd get what this is about and he does. There's no talking. He grabs my hair and we kiss roughly but only for a second or two. I don't want to kiss him. Kissing is intimate and this is lust, nothing else. I turn around to face the wall and yank my skirt up around my waist. He sucks in his breath at the sight of my bare ass. I push my bottom in the air and he puts his hand between my legs instantly. He knows I'm going to be soaking wet and ready for this and he slides his fingers between my lips, manipulates my clitoris expertly and goes for a quick grab of my breasts, squeezing my nipples hard. I like it. I don't want tenderness. I hear rather than see him unzip himself, then turn around to see what I'm in for. This is the moment of truth. If he's small or only semi-erect, I'm out of here!

I'm not disappointed. He's perfect. Big and throbbing and it's lying nearly flat against his stomach. He's younger than I figured and so excited, it's pointing to the sky. He's circumcised and I can't wait to have him inside me. He takes his hand away and I'm aching from the loss. Every nerve ending is on full alert, waiting and expectant. I want him so badly, what takes him a second feels like hours. He holds himself at the base and guides that incredible penis inside me. I am so wet and so ready for him, he slides in easily and his first thrust is so satisfyingly deep, I come immediately. I am highly orgasmic and so turned on by what I've done – picking up a stranger – the flirting at the bar was my foreplay. I feel myself contract around him, pulsing against the rigid, hardness buried so deep inside me.

'Oh baby,' he groans. I back my hips up to meet him and grind against him hungrily as he thrusts inside me, deep and slow, trying to control himself, pace himself. When he's as deep as he can go, he circles his hips to make sure every part of me can feel him, that all areas are explored. I'm relishing the union of penis and pussy. He's holding me by my hips and I have my hands on the wall in front of me. It's hot and sexy and I know I am going to orgasm again and I can't even see how good this must look, so he'll be about a minute away if I'm lucky.

So I give into the feeling of being fucked. God, how I have missed this! I climax around him and have to stop myself shouting, it's so bloody intense. I can feel him tense and then he's ramming into me hard, fast, before he stops and holds still. He's so hard and so deep inside me when he comes, my last few contractions get extra life and we're both transported into a place where all we can feel is ecstatic, primitive pleasure.

When we're both done, he collapses onto my back. I allow him to stay there for a minute while we both return to reality.

Then I move and he instantly gets the message and straightens up.

'That was . . . unexpected and extraordinary,' he says.

It's just the line Don Draper would have come out with which makes me smile. But even so, I'm bored with him now and want him to leave. We both busy ourselves with adjusting clothing. He wins the race and stands there, a little awkwardly. I say 'You leave first' and undo the door for him and he leaves, grateful I didn't want anything else from him. I put my panties back on, smooth down my skirt, check my hair and emerge cool as a cucumber. I feel powerful, liberated but, best of all, sated.

THE DECISION

My long-term partner is much older than I am (by 20 years), and his sex drive isn't high. I don't think he's bothered by the infrequency of our sex but I'm young and sexual and need an outlet. I've always fantasised about a whole heap of things while masturbating but one theme in particular is my favourite: picking up a stranger and having sex. After a particularly barren period with my partner, I decided to act on it.

I'd never have pursued this if I was having great sex at home and it would have been far more dangerous to my relationship if I'd chosen to cheat with a man I know or worked with. Choosing a stranger was my way of staying faithful, as well as getting to live out something I'd always wanted to do.

I read somewhere that craigslist 'casual encounters' was where people went if they wanted sex on the side, so I had a look online. There's a lot of shit on there that you have to wade through and it took me days to find anyone remotely suitable. I was very specific in my search: I wanted a young guy, under 30, who was educated and of a certain class. I might just want sex but I still had standards! I wanted him young because I thought there'd be less chance of erection problems. When my partner does sleep with me, his erection is as half-hearted as he is about sex. I wanted a good, hard, long fuck with a man who really wanted me. I was desperate.

The guy's ad said he was a musician, visiting from Boston, on tour with an orchestra and 29 years old. He said he enjoyed sex but had never met anyone who allowed his passion to be 'unleashed'. This was a rather pleasant request, compared to the illiterate, vulgar stuff that I had seen on craigslist. There was a picture of him as well and he was very hot! He had a black suede jacket on and a hat – it doesn't sound sexy but the way he wore it was. I was incredibly nervous answering the ad, let alone meeting up with him! I mean, how do you really know if the person's going to turn out to be a nutter? I worried I'd be putting myself in danger but even answering the ad turned me on so much, I was typing with one hand and using my vibrator with the other.

I told one friend what I was doing for safety reasons. She seemed a bit surprised but was more worried about my safety than objecting morally. I agreed I'd text her once I'd met him in a public place and then also text details of wherever we ended up going onto (if he turned out to be OK). I'd do a further check-in one hour after that. This made me feel more secure but I was still absolutely terrified on the night. What if he didn't fancy me? Would it feel erotic in real life or would I simply feel sleazy – and not in a good way?!

THE REALITY

We met in the bar of a hotel in Mayfair. He looked just like he had in the picture, which I was relieved about, except he was shyer and almost other-worldish. He looked out of place in London, like an Amish guy suddenly transported to a modern place. He had on a cream shirt with ruffles on the sleeves. Again, it sounds bonkers but it suited him and for some reason, made me feel safer. I couldn't imagine someone dangerous choosing to wear something like that. I wanted to take off with him right then and there but we had a drink first and made small talk, then he asked if I'd like to hear him play the piano. I said yes and we got into my car and drove to where he and the orchestra were staying. At the lights, he took one of my hands inside two of his and moved his fingers over mine. It was like he was playing the piano on my hands. No-one had ever got me so aroused just by doing that, I was nearly sliding off the seat at this point. I really, really wanted him and would have done it in the car if he'd suggested it.

He was staying with all the other musicians in some halls of residence. It was really late, after midnight, and he took me to this big room that had a grand piano in it and lots of chairs. I guess it was the practice room. There was no-one inside – I guess everyone was in bed – but he locked the door behind us anyway. This snapped me back to reality quick smart. I suddenly felt panicked but he picked up on it and told me not to be worried and offered to unlock it. I calmed down and said no, it was fine. Then he got a chair and put it behind the piano stool and made me sit behind him while he played. I sat there with my knees pressing against his hips and undid his shirt, my hands moving all over his chest. He played Chopin faultlessly, didn't miss a beat, even though I was pinching his nipples and kissing the back of his neck. God, it was all so erotic.

Then he told me to sit on top of the piano. I'm only tiny so figured why not? I took off my heels and he said, really quietly, 'Take off your panties as well'. I swear I nearly came when he said that. So I did and I sat up there in front of him and crossed my legs, brazenly, so he could see everything. But he kept play-ing the piano the entire time. He'd stare intensely at my face, never smiling, and then he'd look at my legs spread wide in front of him, with everything on display. It was so intense, I was dripping wet. I felt like I was in a film, like in *Pretty Woman*, when Richard Gere lifts Julia Roberts up and shags her against the piano. I was absolutely entranced by the way he was looking at me, so seriously. Sitting there so exposed, I felt wanton and alive and couldn't wait to be pushed further.

Which made what happened next so bloody disappointing . . .!

He stopped playing after about 10 minutes of this unbelievably arousing foreplay, stood up and half lifted, half pulled me off the piano onto the floor. This sounds a lot sexier than it was! It was much harder than I had hoped and what was meant to be masterful, ended up awkward. Once we were both lying on the floor, it was kind of like he didn't really know what to do next. I think playing gave him confidence but without the piano as a distraction, he suddenly turned into a fumbling adolescent. So I took over, straddled him and unzipped his jeans. Within a second of me freeing and caressing his penis – which was beautifully hard and long, damn it! – he came all over my expensive dress, spurting what seemed like copious amounts of semen all over me. I was shocked and a bit pissed off because the dress was silk and possibly ruined. But I figured he was nervous and assumed he'd make me come with his fingers and tongue, get another erection and all would be fine. But he didn't. He just sat up, zipped up his pants, muttered about having to get up early and that was my cue to leave.

I felt embarrassed for him: he'd come after only a second's contact with my hand and didn't seem interested in continuing, so I pulled on my knickers and got ready to leave. We said goodbye and at the door he gave me a huge cheeky grin which really annoyed me! He didn't seem at all perturbed about his performance so I guess it happened to him all the time. It clearly hadn't even occurred to him to look after my needs.

I don't regret doing it because, up until the rather unfortunate ending, the whole experience was a huge turn on. But I did leave feeling unfulfilled and horny as hell. My tips for anyone wanting to try this would be don't leave anything to chance and don't assume people will behave the way you expect. If I did it again I would do it differently. I'd hire a hotel room so we had somewhere private to go back to – I assumed he would do that, but he didn't. I also should have taken more control and told him no, the session wasn't over until I'd had an orgasm as well.

I also forgot to keep my word to check in via text with my friend once we'd gone to his place and when I checked my phone, which I'd had on silent, there were increasingly worried calls from her. She was furious that I hadn't rung her. I don't know what it says about me, but I felt more guilt over that than I had over cheating on my partner. Was it cheating? All I did was touch the guy's chest and penis for about a second and expose myself. It wasn't even full sex. Personally, I don't think it counts.

'We joined the mile high club – and got caught'

Madison, 24, works in sales

THE FANTASY

I'm travelling with a work colleague who I have always lusted after. We're both single and we travel together a lot for business. We get on really well but I've never been able to tell if he fancies me or just likes me as a friend. The night before our flight, we were up late schmoozing clients, so we're both a bit hungover and in silly moods. He looks even hotter than usual because he hasn't shaved and I love the stubble – his jaw line is square and the stubble just accentuates it. He's got long, dark eyelashes and gorgeous blue eyes, and every time we work together half of me works while the other fantasises about the two of us getting it on. We both line up to board the plane and are delighted to find we've been bumped up from Business to First-Class. It's an eight hour flight and we're both looking forward to having a glass of wine and then passing out on the flat beds. We settle in, chat a bit, then both start watching movies while enjoying our wine.

In First-Class, there are about a zillion films to choose from and I end up watching an old movie: *8 Mile* starring Eminem and Brittany Murphy. There's an incredibly hot sex scene in it that's explicit and looks really real, like they're really having sex, not just acting for the cameras. The combination of the hangover (I'm always up for sex the day after drinking), the wine, the sexy luxury of being in First and my hot colleague sitting next to me, makes me feel really turned on. I surreptitiously play the same sex scene over and over, rewinding and replaying. My colleague is blissfully unaware of my high state of excitement because I've angled the screen so he can't see what I'm watching. (Well, that's what I think, anyway!)

Eventually, I get to the point where I'm desperate for release and it just so happens, I have a small bullet vibrator in my hand luggage. I discreetly get it out of my bag, pocket it and get up out of my seat, smiling at my friend and pointing to the loo to explain where I'm going. He looks at me intently and we lock eyes. I flush. For a moment, it feels like he's reading my mind and knows exactly what I'm going to the loo to do . . .

As I move through the cabin, I see nearly all the passengers are asleep. Brilliant. I won't have to rush and won't be disturbed. The flight attendants are eating their meals and have the curtain pulled back. But I've barely had time to pull up my skirt and turn the vibe on, when there's a discreet knock at the door. What the fuck? Annoyed, I say loudly 'Someone's in here' and am astonished when I hear my work mate say, 'I know. Let me in'. My stomach flips and I'm genuinely shocked. What does he want? Is something wrong? I don't dare hope for what seems obvious: he wants to join in!

I get myself together and pocket the vibe. When I open the door he's standing there with a huge naughty grin on his face. He looks directly into my eyes and says 'I know what you're up to. I could see what you were watching. Let me in.'

I'm tipsy enough not to be embarrassed and all those years of pent-up lust render me incapable of resisting him. I reach out with my arm, grab him around the neck and pull him inside. We're kissing before I've even locked the door behind us and it feels glorious. We're biting each other's lips and there's lots of tongue. He starts moving his tongue inside my mouth suggestively, mimicking oral sex, so I push his head down and he immediately moves to my breasts and pulls open my top, sucking and squeezing my nipples.

There's not much room so I end up sitting on the closed loo seat with my skirt hiked up and him kneeling on the floor between my legs. He takes my panties off and then his deliciously slippery tongue is teasing me and I come in about two minutes. He pulls back and looks at me – his face is wet from licking me and he looks so aroused, it makes me crazy. I tell him to stand up then I unzip him and take his lovely erect penis into my mouth. It's big and thick and exactly as I'd imagined. I'm great at giving head – all of my boyfriends have told me – so he doesn't last very long either. The whole thing only takes about five minutes, so when he comes out of the loo, the coast is clear. I wait a few minutes then come out myself. There's only one guy awake in the cabin and he either didn't notice both of us missing or didn't care. Back at our seats, my sexy colleague leans over and gives me a slow, sexy kiss and says 'I've wanted to do that for years.'

THE DECISION

My boyfriend of two months and I went on our first dirty week-end and were at that 'can't keep our hands off each other' stage. We arrived at the airport a bit early so went to a bar to have some celebratory champagne. Then the flight was delayed, so we had another glass and by the time we got on the flight, we were pretty tipsy. The plane was full up the front and empty down the back so once we'd taken off, we headed down the back for some privacy. The staff could see we were a bit away with the fairies but we were so obviously smitten with each other, I think they found it quite sweet. They more than happily gave us more alcohol, which made us even soppier and then more and more daring. We were snogging like mad and started getting quite het up: my boyfriend started fondling my breasts when the flight attendants were up the front of the plane serving drinks, and safe to say we were both up for anything.

THE REALITY

My boyfriend went to the loo, which was literally right next to our seats, and after he'd had a pee he opened the door and said 'Quick, come inside here with me'. On the spur of the moment I went to join him, more as a bit of a laugh. It wasn't premeditated but becoming a member of the 'mile high club' was a favourite fantasy of mine. He pulled me inside and locked the door and we were giggling away but then we started kissing and the mood changed. I unzipped him, knelt down and took him in my mouth, which wasn't quite as sexy as it sounds because there's no space in there and it's bright as hell with the automatic lighting. It's not exactly romantic or erotic and it smelt a bit! So I've got my mouth wrapped around his penis but am eyeballing the flush lever and tissue dispenser, and he was looking at a plastic door. It was a turn on but not as hot as everyone makes out!

His penis was as hard as rock though so I thought *Sod it, we might as well go for it.* We swapped positions (easier said than done in a tiny space), so he had his back to the door and I turned around so my bum faced him, held onto the toilet seat for balance, lifted up my skirt and pulled my knickers to the side so he could slip inside. *That* felt amazing and clearly it did for my boyfriend as well because he was groaning way too loud. I turned around to tell him to *shhhh* but he put his fingers in my mouth and made me suck them and we fucked for a few minutes, hard and intensely, both loving every second.

But then we heard voices outside the door. It was the flight attendants chatting away – our seats and the loo were right next to their station. He pulled out and we got ourselves together ready to exit (neither of us had orgasmed but I don't think we really expected to – we figured it would be more of a tease than anything else) and waited for them to get whatever they'd come back for and then disappear back to the front of the plane. Except they didn't disappear and it soon became obvious they weren't going to because they were getting the trolley ready to serve the meal. *Shit!* We both stood there, locked inside the loo, our hands clapped over our mouths to stop us laughing, looking at each other with wide eyes because the realisation we probably weren't going to get away with it was starting to hit.

After a few minutes, we heard two other voices that weren't the flight attendants. A woman said 'Have you knocked on the door? Maybe there's no-one in there'. We froze. Next thing, there's a knock and the flight attendant says 'Is anyone in there?' We both looked at each other, willing the other to deal with the situation. I felt horribly drunk and didn't trust myself to speak because I knew I'd sound slurry. We hadn't thought this through at all so it wasn't like we had a back-up plan. My boyfriend finally said 'Just a moment!' I had a brain wave and said 'Say you came in here with me because I felt sick'. We both thought that was amazingly inventive but apparently that's the standard excuse every couple gives when caught.

Unlocking that door was the worst. My boyfriend opened it to see a queue of about three or four people, standing there with arms folded and looking really fed up. Our sense of time was obviously skewed from all the drink and I got the horrible feeling we'd been in there for a lot longer than we thought we had. They looked mighty pissed off when they saw my boyfriend and glared at him. Then they clocked that he wasn't in there alone.

'My girlfriend isn't feeling well,' he said, but absolutely no-one was buying it. The flight attendants kept stacking the trolley, pretending nothing untoward was happening but they looked highly amused. They'd obviously seen it all before! The woman at the front of the queue was stroppy and furious. 'She's drunk, not sick,' she said and gave us a withering look as we slunk out of the loo and slid back into our seats. That was the other problem: we then had to sit there while the other three people waiting for the loo smirked and giggled and whispered to each other because our seats were right where they were standing!

Even worse, they all went back to their seats and spread the word because suddenly everyone was craning their necks and turning around to look at us. It was mortifying! When the flight finally landed, we waited until everyone else got off the plane before leaving. The flight stewardess said 'That'll teach you' when she saw us hiding in our seats but at least she laughed. When we got off we hid until most of the people had got their luggage, then sheepishly went to get ours.

Despite the embarrassment, it was worth it. We laughed about it the whole weekend and although the actual sex was rubbish and we didn't even orgasm, the thought that you're having sex and there's only a flimsy door separating you from the other passengers is undeniably erotic.

'We hired a high-class hooker for some girl-on-girl action'

Michelle, 44, works in the media

THE FANTASY

The first time I see her, I'm lying by the pool, wearing a gorgeous blue mini-kaftan over my new Heidi Klein bikini. My hair is pinned up in a sexy, tumbly kind of way and my legs look toned and tanned, all stretched out on the sunbed. I'm in Morocco, at a five-star hotel that's really worth six stars. It's so luxurious, it's bordering on ostentatious and I love it. The weather is hot and I'm drinking an ice-cold vodka tonic and lazily flicking through a magazine when I see a girl walk up to the edge of the pool, drop her towel and bag and strip off to her bikini. She has long dark hair, olive skin and the most glorious body I have ever seen: tall and athletic but with curves. I try to guess her age and decide she's older than 17 but younger than 25. Maybe 19? 22? I stop looking at her face because her breasts are extraordinary. They're definitely real, judging by the way they jiggle and move when she leans forward to unbuckle her sandals. I can't decide if I want to be her or fancy her but judging by the way I'm getting wet just watching, it's the latter.

The girl is wearing a Missoni string bikini that barely covers anything. It can't contain her full, pert breasts that spill out of the sides of the tiny triangular top and I can clearly see the outline of her nipples. She feels my eyes on her and looks up, and I realise I am openly staring at her. I've dropped my magazine onto my lap and lifted my sunglasses for a better look, sitting up and leaning forward. Jesus! I couldn't be more obviously checking her out! But instead of looking annoyed or self-conscious, she looks straight at me and locks eyes. She's close enough for me to see hers are dark brown and sultry, lined with thick, black lustrous lashes. Mine are blue and I think just a little embarrassed, but I smile at her and she smiles back.

It's not a friendly smile, not a girly 'I know you're looking at me and I bet you're having body and bikini envy' type of smile. This smile is blatant and sexual, spreading slowly and sexily across her face. Her lips part slightly and I see straight, white teeth and a little pink tongue as it flicks over her full lips. She continues to stare back at me, still leaning forward, one hand hovering near her ankle where she was unbuckling her sandals. Then she finishes the job and straightens up, still with her eyes fixed on mine, and lifts up her long hair with both hands, allowing me a full frontal view of those glorious breasts moving, lifting. As she gathers her hair up, she subtly caresses the sides of her breasts, but I know it's deliberate and it's all for me. She looks up to meet my eyes again. I couldn't move my eyes even if I'd wanted to. And so I don't – I could watch her forever. She smiles another secret smile that makes me wetter than I already am, and then her long fingers disappear under her bikini top briefly and graze her nipples which are now erect. She does it discreetly and no-one is watching but me.

And, perhaps, my boyfriend.

'Do you want her, my darling?' he says, having watched the whole thing in amusement, stretched out beside me and peering over his iPad. He lifts my top to expose my brown belly and bikini bottoms and trails his hand teasingly over my lower abdomen. I push it away because I don't want the girl to know that I'm with him. I want her to think I'm here alone. Alone and available to her.

'Because I can buy her for you,' he continues, unabashed. 'The hotel lets high-class escorts come to the pool during the day for free. The men like to look before they buy. I'm not certain she's for sale but I'm guessing she's too young to afford to be a guest. And if she's here with her rich banker lover, where is he?'

My boyfriend, also rich and a CEO, looks at me enquiringly. Well, that explains the Missoni bikini. They're about £250.

'Do you want me to find out?' he says. 'Discreetly of course. You always promised me you'd let me watch you with another woman. So prove you're not just teasing. You know I won't touch, just watch.'

I look at his handsome face and wonder how I'll feel watching him look at another woman, naked. Will I like it or loathe it? He's incredibly hot to look at: tall with a swimmer's body and broad, muscled shoulders tapering down to a lean abdomen. He's got just the right amount of hair on his chest, and his usual great tan in evidence. I can see him starting to spring to attention through his shorts, just by watching our little episode by the pool. I like him. He's funny and we have brilliant sex. I don't see myself with him long-term though. He's too pretentious to settle with but perfect for play.

He whispers that he wants to see her lick me, touch me, and fuck me with her fingers. He tells me I'd be even sexier to him, watching her do that to me, if that's possible. I squirm in my seat and his eyes sparkle with lust. He knows I'm considering doing it, sleeping with a woman for the very first time, and he leans forward, using his body to shield us from other people sunbathing near us, oblivious to the sexual tensions playing out around them. He kisses me, hard and full on the mouth and slides his fingers along the side of my bikini bottoms to feel me quickly, to see if I'm wet. I'm soaking.

'Come on, you want to do this,' he whispers huskily in my ear. 'We're on holiday. No-one knows us. She wants you as much as you want her. Come on baby. Do it. Give into it.'

One part of me is bitterly disappointed that she might be a prostitute. I wanted to believe the girl was flirting with me for no other reason than lust, connection, chemistry. But knowing she might be bought, that there was a real possibility of me kissing that mouth, putting my hands on those breasts, pushing her head down, means lust quickly overtakes disappointment.

The girl was now in the water, swimming strongly, lapping the pool easily. I see glimpses of her gorgeous muscled body, sleek and wet and exquisite, with water rivulets clinging to places I want my mouth to be. She pulls herself up out of the water, showing off her athletic arms, toned back muscles, pert little bottom and long thighs and then flips herself around at the last moment so she's sitting on the side of the pool facing us. Water drips from her, she's panting slightly and she's looking straight at me. She's ignoring my boyfriend but she knows what's going on. The invitation is there. She smiles, I smile and my boyfriend seizes the moment and gets up, preparing to talk to her. He tells me to wait back in our room.

I walk back through the foyer, fast. The sooner I get to the room, the sooner she will join me. I have no doubt my boyfriend will persuade her to do as he wishes. He always gets what he wants. Inside the room, it's cool. I quickly change out of my swimsuit and run a cool, wet facecloth under my arms, over my swollen lips – even the act of washing myself is unbearably arousing. I quickly riffle through my lingerie, looking for the latest purchase from Agent Provocateur. It's a push-up bra in palest pink that's demi-cupped, so my breasts and nipples are hiked high and on display. The panties are cut to flatter and I know I look good in them. I look in the mirror. The last time I wore this was for my boyfriend but today, it's all for her.

There's a knock at the door. My boyfriend enters carrying champagne. I hold my breath then see she's following behind. She has her sundress on over her body and I want her to take it off immediately. No-one talks. Her eyes move from the room to my body and I can see her checking me out the way I was checking her out. She starts to speak, I guess to introduce herself but

I go up to her and put my finger across her mouth, silencing her. I ask her to put her arms in the air and lift the sundress over her head. I expect the bikini but she's changed into a transparent lacy bra and matching thong.

My boyfriend pours champagne and I lead her to the bed and we both lie down on our sides and look at each other. I run the back of my fingers along her skin. It's weird, touching a woman sexually like this. I'm used to the thicker skin of a man but her skin and body feel so delicate and soft. My fingers glide across it. She reaches behind her and undoes her bra, and her breasts are free and just as I'd expected: full and sensual with big nipples. She's lying back on the bed wearing nothing but those tiny, wispy panties, her mass of hair sprawling behind her.

I straddle her, grab her wrists and put her arms behind her, pinning them there. Then I lean forward and my breasts meet her breasts and rub against them and I kiss her for the first time. I hear a moan from my boyfriend, doing as he's told and sitting in the corner, but I know he's desperate to move closer, to see us. I know he can't see anything at all with us lying here kissing like this but oh God, it feels amazing kissing her with our bare breasts rubbing together so I don't care. Her mouth is soft but she kisses me back as passionately as I kiss her.

'Please,' I hear my boyfriend plead. 'I want to watch. Can I come to stand next to you?'

I pull back and sit up, still straddling the girl. I like that I don't know her name.

'You can come and stand by the edge of the bed. No closer,' I tell him.

He obeys. I can see he has stripped down to his Calvins and he roughly pulls them down, his hand wrapped around a massive erection, bigger and harder than I've ever seen before.

The girl looks at him, then back at me. She knows he's an observer, not a participant, and I like to think she wants me, a woman, not him.

29

'Let me undress you,' she says. It's the first time I've heard her voice and it's low and delicious with an accent I can't place. I nod and lie back on the bed. She takes off my bra, her hair brushing forward to caress my neck and breasts. I'm desperate for her to take off my panties. She crawls over me and I can't resist grabbing her by the hair, grabbing fists of it, and kissing her again. Her breasts and nipples dangle invitingly, so I put first one then the other in my mouth. It feels so erotic. Now I know why men love sucking breasts so much. I can feel hers harden as I flick my tongue across them, lick them, nip them lightly. 'Ahh,' she says, 'Mmmm.' She might be acting but if she is, she's doing a good job.

She pulls back and moves down the bed and slips my panties off. As they slide down my thighs, I think I'm going to orgasm just by watching her. My boyfriend exclaims, 'Fuck! Honey, if you could just see . . .' He trails off and goes back to watching, licking his lips.

She looks down at me, opens my legs wide and I'm completely exposed. She gazes down there, admiring me. Then she puts her fingers in her mouth, licks them and touches me just the right way. Enough so I can feel her, not too hard like men can be before you teach them what you like. When her fingers make contact with my clitoris, I moan loudly. She smiles and says 'Do you like that?' and moves the tips of her fingers over me in slow circles. I arch on the bed, pushing up against her hand, and she keeps one hand on me but takes off her own panties with the other. She has a strip of dark hair. A landing strip, my boyfriend calls it. Her eyes are misty with wanting, like mine are and I know my boyfriend's must be. I have never wanted anyone like this in my life.

'I want your mouth,' I say, and she nods and then she's between my legs. This is the moment I was longing for, been waiting for all my life. I love men but have always longed to feel a woman's mouth on me, a woman's tongue licking me, and she's so good at this, so much better than a man is. She knows exactly what I want because it's what she wants. Her tongue teases my clitoris, gentle but unrelenting. I push my pelvis up to her mouth, greedy, shameless, wanting more. She reaches around with her hand and puts two fingers inside me, plunging them in and out, all the while her tongue circles and licks. I am lost in desire so intense, I almost forget my boyfriend is in the room with us.

I open my eyes to watch him watching us. He is so aroused, he can't talk. His eyes plead with me.

'Lick my breasts,' I say to him roughly. He knows I'm about to come, so he moves forward and his ravenous mouth on my breasts tips me over and the sight and feeling of having my breasts sucked by a man and being licked by a women sends me spiralling into the deepest, fiercest orgasm I have ever experienced. I'm making animal noises I've never heard before. It's like they're coming from someone else but, Oh, the pleasure, the waves of pleasure that keep coming and coming and I don't ever want it to stop. I'm panting and begging the girl not to stop licking until the violent contractions start to fade and I can't take any more and, like only a woman can, she senses just the right moment to stop. Sitting back on the bed, she looks at me as she wipes her mouth, breathing heavily. I'm spent but I also know I want to do that to her, give her what she's done to me, drive her half insane with lust. This session's not over, it's only just beginning.

THE DECISION

I've always wondered what it would be like to sleep with a woman but felt too shy to suggest it to any of my boyfriends. Instead, I concocted all sorts of fantasies and masturbated to them privately. All the guys I'd dated, including my ex-husband, were quite 'vanilla' in their tastes and also not the types who'd want to share me, even with another woman. But then I started dating this guy who was really into talking dirty to me and one day, he started telling me what he'd like to see me do to another woman. It turned me on so much, I couldn't believe it!

It rapidly became the only thing we did whenever we had sex together: he'd detail all the filthy things we'd get up to with this girl. It was easily the best sex I'd ever had because I'd never explored this 'dirty' side of me with a partner before. Over time, our sessions got hotter and hotter and then he started suggesting us having a threesome in real life. In the heat of the moment, I was like 'Yes, yes, let's do it! Organise it!' The minute the orgasm was over, I'd rapidly go off the idea – but he never gave up trying to talk me into doing it.

I would *never* go to a swinger's club or have a threesome with friends – I honestly couldn't think of anything more embarrassing than sleeping with a female friend. It may sound odd but I knew if I did it, I'd want to control the situation and for it to be completely private which left us only one option in my eyes: hire a high-class hooker.

About two weeks later, my boyfriend booked a night in an upmarket hotel in London for my birthday, along with tickets to the ballet, and he joked that he'd throw in a high-class hooker as well. I laughed and said 'No way!' but the night before we were due to go, I went out with a girlfriend, laughingly telling her what he wanted us to do, and she confessed she'd had a threesome with another girl and loved it. I remember walking home from the restaurant thinking, *This is something I've always been curious about. When is this situation ever going to happen again? I'm with someone I completely trust but don't feel jealous with. Plus he has the money to afford a high-class hooker and a posh hotel room.*

I went to bed thinking about it and woke up at 5am having the most erotic dream I have ever had in my life about me kissing a woman and then burying my tongue between her legs. I was the most turned on I have ever been! I spent the next two hours, half awake, half asleep, imagining what it might be like – how soft she'd feel, what it would be like to kiss her, lick her – and then I got up at 7am and thought *Fuck it! It's today or never* and the decision was made. I sent my boyfriend an email saying 'Today is your lucky day. Let's do it!' Then I went to the gym!

THE REALITY

At the gym I thought the whole thing through. I have a high libido but I'm incredibly practical and a control freak so there was no way I was leaving anything to chance. The earliest we could book into the hotel was 3.30pm and our tickets to the ballet were for 7.30pm. I knew I'd never go through with it if we waited until after the ballet so it had to be before then. I also knew I'd chicken out unless I was sloshed, so had to factor in drinking time! I figured if we organised a hooker for 4.30pm, that would be about right. I'd have an hour in the bar, we'd have her from 4.30 to 5.30pm, and then have time to get ready for the ballet.

I came back from the gym at 9am to a stream of frenzied emails from my boyfriend saying 'What are you talking about? Do you mean what I think you mean?', so I called him and told him to organise a girl for 4.30pm. 'But where do I get a hooker from?' he kept asking me which was annoying. He was an ex-banker with a few 'interesting' friends, but he swore he didn't know so I ended up organising the whole thing, which wasn't exactly as I had imagined things to be.

I found an online site which seemed to have higher quality escorts on it than the others, but I had absolutely no illusions that the girl in the photo either looked like that in real life or would be the one who would turn up. I rang the agency but no-one picked up. It was 10am so I guess I was being naïve to expect them to be open! Ever tried to find a hooker for 4.30pm on a week day? It's not easy! It took another three calls to different sites before someone answered and the quality of the girls was dropping even though the cost of these girls was £800 for an hour. We had a choice of two girls, that was it! Any sane person would have just done it another day or when we got back from the ballet when there'd be loads to choose from but I was absolutely determined. It was then or not at all and I was really horny and excited about doing it that day.

I got in a cab when it was time to leave for the hotel, feeling so nervous I could hardly breathe. I picked up my boyfriend on the way and he was as edgy as I was. When we got to the hotel I felt even more paranoid because it was boutique and tiny! I imagined the hooker turning up in a mini and thigh-high boots and asking for our room and the front desk knowing exactly what was going on and who'd ordered her! I tried to cover by rattling on about expecting some friends later and asking for a champagne bucket and five glasses. Who knows if they bought it or not!

We put our overnight bags in the room and went straight to the bar where I proceeded to drink four BIG double gin and tonics in under half an hour. The bartender raised an eyebrow when I ordered my fourth but both of us were so jumpy, it was either get drunk or run away. I suddenly decided I didn't want the hooker to know my real name so I told my boyfriend he had to call me Jenny. He was like, 'Jenny? Really? Can't you choose something more exotic?' I told him his name was now James. We went through all the 'rules' about five times: he was to sit in a chair and watch until I felt comfortable about him joining us. I think he thought I was doing this to please him but it was always just about me. I wanted to try girl-on-girl and having him there gave me the courage to do it. Like I said, I didn't get jealous with him but even so, I told him I didn't want him to kiss her and to be guided by me about how much he should touch her. It was all done on my terms, right from word go, or not at all.

When my boyfriend's mobile rang to signal her arrival I seriously panicked. I had nice underwear on already but raced up to the room to open a bottle of champagne. I took my clothes off, leaving on the underwear and put on the bulky hotel towelling robe and sat on the bed waiting. I looked at myself in the mirror and decided I looked more like someone waiting for a massage than for hot sex. So I took the robe off and sat there in my underwear but suddenly felt very self-conscious about my body, so I put it back on again . . . and then there was a knock at the door.

I opened it to see an attractive blonde girl, late 20s, Eastern European, with a high pony tail wearing a mustard coat I'd had my eye on in Zara. She wasn't really my type but then I only fancy women in my head, rather than reality, so I'm not sure what my type is! My boyfriend was lurking behind, bright red and looking embarrassed.

The first thing I did was stick my hand out to shake hers and introduce myself by my real name and say 'I see you've met my boyfriend', calling him by his real name as well. He glowered at me and she looked a bit confused and said, 'Oh, I thought your name was Jenny for some reason'. I fought back the urge to laugh hysterically realising what I'd done and turned around to pour her a glass of champagne. When I turned back around she was naked, bar a tiny, plain, no-frills looking G-string. I was amazed! How the hell did she manage to take all her clothes off so quickly? Were hookers like strippers? Was everything held together with Velcro? I looked at her body and was relieved to see that while she had a good body, it wasn't threateningly good. Her breasts were a bit saggy. Big but saggy. She had a flat tummy but normal girl thighs – they weren't perfect at all. But I think had she been like the girl in my fantasies, I'd have hated it. I wanted to look better than she did, to give me confidence. I took the (deeply unflattering!) robe off, got on the bed and she asked if I'd ever done anything like this before. I said no and she said not to worry, she'd take over.

She kissed me for about one second, then started kissing my neck and moving south, all very lacklustre. I could see my boyfriend holding both his penis and his breath, his eyelids hooded with lust and suddenly I thought, *If you're going to do this, do it properly*, so I pulled her back up again and said, 'No, I'm in charge actually' and went for it.

I kissed her for a while which was, for me, the sexiest part. She was a great kisser and way better than most men. She tasted like toothpaste and her mouth was so much softer than a man's. She flicked her tongue inside my mouth and it was so soft and small. Totally different to how a man's tongue and mouth feels. I felt her breasts and they felt enormous compared to mine. I played with her nipples for a bit, doing what I like, but they didn't get hard which disappointed me a little. I'm competitive and I wanted to be good at sleeping with a woman, I guess! I tried sexily grabbing her hair but she told me not to. I asked if it was because she had hair extensions and she nodded and smiled.

The one thing I was really curious about was giving a girl oral sex. It's the way I usually orgasm with a partner but I'm quite picky about how I like it done and a few guys have told me as much and complained about how hard it is to do. I was interested to see whether I'd be any good at it or not. One reason why I think we have same sex fantasies is because we all secretly think we'll be great lovers since they surely like what we like having done to ourselves? In my imagination, I was brilliant at it!

We were on our knees, kneeling on the bed and kissing. My boyfriend's penis was so erect, I was amazed he didn't come all over the ceiling! His face was purple and he was looking hopefully at me, dying for me to say 'Come over and join in' but I wasn't ready yet.

I put my middle finger in my mouth to wet it, then gently slid it inside her. It felt odd, nothing like what I felt like inside. She stopped kissing, took my hand and removed my finger and said very matter of fact, 'Wrong hole. Put it in this one instead.' I was mortified! *Oh my God!* I thought, *I've just stuck my finger up her bum by accident!* I nearly burst out laughing again and completely lost it but managed to hold it together. I inched down the bed to take a closer look, confused, to see what was going on and then felt even more confused because the opening to her vagina was really high up. No wonder I'd put my finger in the wrong hole! I knew I was drunk but everything looked a bit, well, *wrong.* She didn't really have any outer vaginal lips. I figured she'd had labiaplasty and had them trimmed, like all the porn stars do. But even the inner lips seemed to look nothing like mine did. The hole to her vagina and opening to her anus both looked exactly the same. Both were the same colour, a light brown, whereas mine were pinkish and got redder the more turned on I was. And if I really *had* put my finger up her bottom, why didn't it feel tight and why didn't she flinch? I would have shot through the roof!

I was steaming drunk by this point though because, on top of the G&Ts, we were gulping champagne, so I sort of giggled and decided to hide my embarrassment by diving straight down there. The one thing I'd wondered about was how she'd smell. I think all women smell a little, especially when they're aroused, but this girl had no smell at all. Nothing! It was abnormal. I was thrown but again, I thought maybe she'd washed just before she met us to ensure she smelt fresh. I started licking where I thought her clitoris was but I couldn't find it! I pulled back to have a look but I couldn't see anything! Not even the tiniest bump! 'I can't find your clitoris,' I said and I heard my boyfriend laugh. (I never heard the end of this afterwards, as you could imagine!) She looked a bit embarrassed and said 'Yes you can, it's here' and shoved my head back there. I was ready to crawl under the bed at this point – I'd put my finger in the wrong hole, couldn't find the clitoris and was finding the whole thing more stressful than sexy but then it hit me: *this wasn't a woman, it was a man!*

She'd had a sex change and this is why everything looked so weird!

Now convinced she was a tranny, I surreptitiously looked for clues. I'd been to Malaysia and seen all the 'lady boys' up close and knew the signs: bum a little too high, big hands, giveaway 'Adam's Apple'. I kept looking and all looked fine. She *looked* like a girl but I was secretly convinced at this point that I wasn't, in fact, having a threesome with a girl but another man pretending to be a girl. For some bizarre reason – maybe because it explained why I'd been rubbish in bed – this cheered me up immensely. Maybe it gave me permission to let loose, knowing it wasn't a woman but suddenly I was snogging her ass off and feeling very hot and bothered.

I pulled back and told my boyfriend he could join us on the bed. He was there in about one second flat which made me want to laugh again. It was a bit wicked of me but I made him kiss her just because I wanted to see his reaction when he found out he'd perhaps kissed a man. Naughty I know! In my fantasy of how it would pan out, I'd imagined my boyfriend kissing me and playing with my breasts, watching while the girl went down on me. Whether it was a girl or a tranny, at this point I didn't really care. I told her to lick me and him to kiss me and they both did as they were told. It felt weird being licked by her. She had a tiny, tiny tongue. It was like getting oral sex from a mouse! Teensy weensy little flicks of the tongue. I'm not very good at coming once I've had a few and I'd had more than a few, so I really had to concentrate to orgasm. Ironically, what pushed me over the edge was closing my eyes and remembering how aroused I'd been in bed that morning, imagining it all, rather than having the real thing happen. I came really hard and intensely but the second I'd had an orgasm, I felt embarrassed.

I sneakily looked at the clock and this had all happened in about 30 minutes – we were only half way through! So we kissed in front of my boyfriend for a while, then he asked us both to lick his penis, which amused me no end because I was still on the 'tranny' theory. I have to say the girl was amazingly friendly. When we were licking him, we were looking at each other and smiling broadly at each other. She was incredibly careful to check everything with me before doing anything with him. I don't think she fancied him at all, to be honest. She'd do stuff with me enthusiastically but rush through things with him. There was a strong sense of sisterhood which I hadn't expected.

By this stage, we were onto our third bottle of champagne. She was drinking with us and it became all a bit giggly. When the time was up, she got dressed in a flash. I complemented her on her coat and we kept giggling and discussing clothes. She offered to give me her phone number and said she'd do it for half the price if we booked direct. I took it and she kissed me on the cheek, really sweetly, to say goodbye. My boyfriend took her to the door but then she came back again and gave me another impromptu kiss and hug. I liked her/him/whatever the hell she was. I swear if I ran into her somewhere on my own I would go up and say hello rather than want to sink through the floor.

After she left, my boyfriend wanted me to give him oral because he hadn't come but I was spent. I made him do it himself which I thought was ironic since he'd paid for every-thing and still ended up having to give himself a hand job! I was all set to jump in the shower but when I checked the time, there was no time left because I'd forgotten to allow for time to get to the venue for the ballet. So one minute, I had some hooker lick-ing me out, next minute, there we were watching the ballet and clapping and being all posh and saying 'Bravo!' like nothing had happened! It was surreal!

My boyfriend said he'd loved it but was relieved I seemed cool about it all. He said he'd worried we'd be watching the ballet in our own 'individual spirals of shame'! I briefly floated the idea that maybe something was 'odd' about her, given she didn't smell and I couldn't find her clitoris but he laughed and said I was imagining things to try to make up for being so shit at giving her oral. I've since told him I thought she might have been a 'he' but he won't have it. I still have my suspicions!

I didn't feel bad about what I did and I still don't. If anything, I'm proud of myself for giving it a go, though I have no real desire to repeat the experience and my fantasies were *way* sexier than the reality. What it did do though, was strip all the mystery from sex. It removed the taboo. I used to watch actresses kiss other women or hear stories about straight girl-on-girl stuff and think 'God, they're brave'. But now I know there's nothing to it. It's not a big deal at all. It's just sex. It made me think all women had done what I had. It *over*-normalised sex for a while, though it's worn off now. I'd also look at other women I didn't know and wonder if they were hookers. If I saw this girl in Zara, shopping for her mustard coat, I'd never in a million years know she was a sex worker.

'I seduced my hot, young flatmate who turned out to be a virgin'

Chloe, 35, is a journalist

THE FANTASY

I'm at a party of friends of mine who are very wealthy. They live in a beautiful three storey house in Prague and they always have a 'do' when I'm there because they know I love a good party and they love having me visit. They're a good-looking, sophisticated couple but much older than me. I entertain them with all my stories of life in London as a journalist who regularly interviews lots of celebrities. I'm wearing a gorgeous sparkly short dress that shows off my legs and holding court talking about what happened when I met a famous TV personality. I'm tall and lean and my dress is a plum-grey colour which looks fabulous with my long blonde hair. I'm making everyone laugh with how neurotic the celebrity was when I notice one of the waiters checking me out.

The couple always get their parties catered, even if there's only twenty or so people invited. I guess when you have pots of money, why would you do it yourself? The guy watching me is young – 18 tops. He's past the awkward stage when boys are all gangly with feet and hands too big for their body, but he's not yet a man. He's got broad shoulders but hasn't quite filled out yet. He doesn't lack confidence though: the eyes that meet mine have the self-assurance of a much older man. He waits until he's sure I've noticed him, flashes a broad, cheeky grin then disappears into the kitchen. 'He's going to be trouble when he's older', I think, then go back to telling my story.

I see him ten minutes later, walking around the party with a tray of champagne. Again, he makes lingering and deliberate eye contact with me and lets his eyes roam all over my body. Normally my friend's waiting staff are of the 'only speak when spoken to' variety but I'm betting this guy doesn't give a hoot about toeing the line. It's all a laugh to him and he's enjoying being part of the privileged crowd rather than taking his waiting job seriously. He makes his way through the crowd of people and comes to stand next to me. He offers me champagne, stares deeply into my eyes, then winks. It's a wink that says, 'I fancy you and you fancy me and something is going to happen tonight. I'll make sure of it'.

Dinner is served quite late and we're all giggly and tiddly and having a marvellous time when the hostess calls us into their spacious dining room. It's beautifully set up with little clusters of tables, four at each, floor-length white linen tablecloths, candles, glittering glassware and elegant flower arrangements. I wander around the room, looking for my place card and the waiter appears from nowhere and says, 'You're here'. How does he know my name? I have no idea but I like the fact that he does.

He leads me to a table that's on the side of the room, in a corner next to a doorway. There are three other guests on the table with me. They're quite old and a bit doddery and I'm slightly disappointed that I won't have vivacious company but the waiter says, 'I chose that seat for you for a reason'. I'm intrigued so I sit down and wait expectantly.

The first course is served: oysters with caviar, a perfect aphrodisiac. Not long after, the second course appears in front of me: lemon sole with new potatoes and green beans. I start to tuck in when I feel two hands on my knees, pushing them apart. I try not to look startled but my dinner companions probably wouldn't notice anyway. They're chatting amongst themselves about the economy. I sneak a peek under the table and see the waiter under there, on hands and knees. He snuck under the table from the doorway while no-one was watching and the long tablecloth means he can't be seen by anyone. No-one knows he's there but me.

He knows all I need to do is jump up indignantly, point under the table and blow his cover and he'd be sacked, frogmarched out of the room and down to the nearest police station. But I don't do that. Instead, I open my legs and allow him access and feel his fingers pulling my panties to one side and then his tongue is on me, gently and expertly and insistently. The lady to my left asks me what it is I do in London and I'm forced to tell her about my job while he's under there, bringing me closer and closer to an orgasm. I didn't think it was possible to orgasm while appearing perfectly normal and carrying on a conversation but I managed it. The waiter stops, realising I've come, and I point to someone across the room and direct the attention of the woman, giving him a little nudge with my leg to get the hell out of there. He slithers out from under the table and disappears into the corridor and no-one sees him but me. When he serves coffee later, he leans in so close I can smell myself on him. He smiles and winks again but I ignore him and pretend nothing has happened.

THE DECISION

I didn't set out to seduce my virgin flatmate, but I did know I was in trouble when he turned up in response to an ad I'd placed! I'd been renting this gorgeous house for a while but the rent was straining my finances. I already had one flatmate: a guy I worked with who was sweet but unattractive and a real geek. He put labels on his food in the fridge and wrote his name on everything, like I was going to steal it all! He was hardly ever there so I figured I might as well take on another flatmate and get extra cash in. The house had a couple of spare bedrooms, after all.

There was one problem with the design of the house though. The main bedroom on the first floor – my room – was open plan in that it only had three walls. There was a safety rail, but I could look down into the main living area from the bedroom. The place was architecturally designed and looked great but it wasn't a terribly practical design since whoever was sitting in the lounge room could also see into my bedroom – not to mention hear everything. I remember worrying about it at the time – more from the perspective of flatmates wanting to watch telly late at night or have people over while I was trying to sleep – but I'd fallen in love with the place and took it anyway. My geeky flatmate rarely stayed up late and was super private, so it hadn't been a problem so far.

I put an ad in the paper and was really busy with work so eager to find someone as quickly as possible. John was the first one I'd scheduled to see the place. He rang the bell and I went down to open the door and thought *Holy shit!* He was absolutely stunning to look at – tall, with broad shoulders and great features. He had on some faded jeans that hung really low and a tight T-shirt, so I could tell he was lean and fit underneath it. I should have known it was all going to get horribly out of control because I must have looked him up and down so blatantly that he went bright red. Then I realised I was staring at his crotch and that his fly was undone! He looked down and realised and said 'Shit, how embarrassing' and did it up quickly and then we both laughed. This had all happened before we'd even introduced ourselves!

I showed him around the house and he said how great it all was. I asked him how old he was and he said 20, then I told him I was 30 and he did the usual 'You don't look it' etc. He seemed to be checking me out more than the living quarters and I knew he fancied me. He said he was a builder (which explained the hot bod) and he seemed sweet and nice and had a good sense of humour, so I asked him if he fancied moving in. He grinned and said yes so we agreed he'd move in the following day.

We tiptoed around each other the first few days, both on our best behaviour. It was flirty from the start though. I'd say goodnight and be reading in bed, wearing my little boy shorts and a vest, and he'd be watching telly downstairs, the volume down really low, and you could cut the air with a knife. I couldn't concentrate on my book because I was acutely aware of him sitting looking all delicious in his sweat pants and vest that showed off his body. And he told me later, he didn't even know what he was watching half the time because all he could think of was me in bed. Even the geeky flatmate looked a bit disconcerted by all the obvious sexual tension and stayed away even more than usual.

One night I was reading a book in the living room and John walked in and asked what it was about, so I handed it to him and said 'Read the back, it's brilliant'. He flushed bright red and said 'I'll do it later' but there was something about the way he said it that made me wonder. I thought about it and realised I'd never seen him actually read anything. He never picked up the newspapers I'd leave lying around, nor did he have any books in his room. So I asked him if he liked reading and he looked at the floor then looked up at me and said simply, 'I can't read.' I tried not to overreact but I was pretty shocked as he told me he was severely dyslexic. He left school at 16 and went into the building trade and was too embarrassed to admit to anyone that he couldn't even read a signpost.

I immediately offered to help him. Who wouldn't? We started having reading lessons every night. He loved it and I really enjoyed teaching him. I was angry at his teachers for not making more effort and felt protective over him. It was also a brilliant excuse to sit close and hang around each other a lot too. I was so sexually attracted to him by this point it was awful. Whenever I masturbated, it was always to images of the two of us. I could tell he felt the same because I'd feel him watching me intently as I read to him and then he'd look down shyly when I caught his glance, like he didn't want me to see the longing in his eyes.

THE REALITY

The night it all kicked off, he was practising reading in his room down the hall and he kept shouting out questions to me in my bedroom. He came in to see me, under the guise of wanting to ask how to pronounce a word, and plonked himself down on the bed beside me. He had on boxer shorts but no shirt and holy crap he was hot.

I have always been a sucker for a great body, far more than a face, and his was divine. I could feel myself getting flushed, so after we talked for a bit I said, 'Come on you, it's late and I need to go to sleep'. But he looked at me and said, 'Can I just lie beside you for a bit? Please. I won't do anything'. He looked so innocent saying it, I sensed how important it was for me to say yes. And of course I secretly wanted him to so I said 'OK. But don't you move a muscle'. He grinned and nodded and I turned off the light and we both lay there – me under the covers and him on top of the covers, about a foot separating us. It was exquisite torture.

The room was dark but I felt him turn on his side and then he said, 'I have to kiss you. Please can I just kiss you.'

I'd been lying there with eyes wide open trying to resist pouncing on him. The logical part of my brain briefly resisted what was going to happen, reminding me this was a dreadful idea – the guy was ten years younger than me and my flatmate and, despite appearances, painfully shy. I had no illusions we'd end up together or anything but I hadn't had sex for about nine months and I hadn't wanted anyone this badly for years. Everyone knows sensible thought doesn't stand a hope against lust and temptation, so of course I said 'OK'. So he propped himself up on one elbow and leant forward and gave me the softest, sweetest kiss I have ever had.

'Was that OK?' he asked. I replied yes, thinking *Jesus, I was expecting a big tonguey snog and all I got was that,* so I grabbed him and gave him the snog of his life. He kissed me back, tentatively and a little clumsily. I was so turned on by finally being able to touch and kiss him, I'm ashamed to say all sense of coyness left and I straddled him, kissing him passionately, and literally grabbed his hands and put them under my vest onto my breasts.

Again, his touch was incredibly tentative. Most 20-year-olds would have had my top ripped off, one hand diving down below and their penis out by this point but he seemed shy to the point of ridiculous. I was just figuring it out for myself when he said into the darkness, 'I've never done this before. I've never been with a woman before' and I remember thinking *Bloody hell, he's a virgin. What the hell do I do now*!

In the world of fantasy, you can seduce a virgin without taking any responsibility for it. But even though John looked like a Calvin Klein underwear model , he was incredibly naïve and I wasn't sure if I wanted the responsibility of taking his virginity. I wanted hot sex not some guy mooning about the place like a lovesick teenager. Bugger! I was all hot and bothered but this was unexpected and I could feel desire leaving me, like a balloon deflating. I got off him and lay on my back beside him and he said 'Oh' and looked really disappointed.

I told him we needed to get a few things clear, so I turned on the light and as gently as possible, made it very clear that I didn't want a relationship and had I known he was a virgin, I'd never have let it get this far. He listened solemnly and didn't interrupt, just nodded and said yes he understood. I asked him how the hell he'd managed to get to 20 without some girl throwing herself on top of him because he looked like he'd fallen from heaven and he laughed and looked pleased. He said he'd never felt comfortable enough to make the first move and didn't have any female friends and he wasn't the most confident bloke. And then he said, 'I've wanted to kiss you from the moment I saw you. I know you don't want to take it further but can I just kiss you again?'

I know it sounds wrong and I should have resisted but I felt all horny again so I said yes and this time he got on top of me and kissed me confidently. He said, 'Teach me, like you taught me how to read' and his voice was deep and husky and thick with longing. I could feel myself getting wet again at the thought of being the first. There was no doubt it was appealing and he was becoming bolder and bolder in his advances. He kissed me again, then pulled back and, looking me straight in the eyes, unbuttoned my top. I put a hand up to stop him but he just pushed it out of the way, and him taking charge like that turned me on big time. He pushed my top open and looked down at my breasts, his breathing becoming hard and jagged. Next thing I know he's kissing them and groaning really loudly and I'm loving every second . . . and it was about then that we heard the front door open and realised geeky flatmate had come home.

We both froze. I recovered first and quickly turned out the light, just in time as our other flatmate strolled into the lounge room and turned on the telly, low enough for him to hear but not to disturb me. Fuck! He couldn't see my bed from the lounge room but if John got up to leave, he'd sure as hell spot that. Whether we liked it or not, we were stuck there for the moment. I suddenly had a fit of the giggles and I could feel John shaking with laughter beside me.

We laughed for about five minutes but then the mood changed. John went quiet and his hand reached across and started playing with one of my breasts. I held it and tried to stop him, whispering 'Stop it!' in a mock fierce voice but I really meant '*Don't* stop it' and he knew it. He was strong and grabbed my hand and held it out of the way while he fondled my breast with the other. Meanwhile, nerdy flatmate's innocently watching *Newsnight*, crunching on what sounded like a bowl of cereal, seemingly oblivious to what was going on upstairs.

Next thing I know John's hands are sliding down my pyjama bottoms. I try to resist but more to play the game of resisting than with any real intent of stopping him – nothing was going to stop either of us at this point. I found it interesting that he didn't try to put his fingers inside me but went down and licked me first. Like the kissing, he started out pretty clueless, licking with a poker-straight tongue, so I grabbed his hand and whispered, 'Do it like this', and demonstrated on the palm of his hand how to move with a relaxed tongue to cover more area and make it feel gentler.

He was a quick learner and I thought about how turned on he must be, pleasuring a woman for the first time, and I came hard but silently. I pushed him away and he looked hurt but I pulled him up to lie beside me and whispered into his ear, 'No, it's good. I just had an orgasm and it's sensitive afterwards'.

I felt rather than saw him smile and then I touched his penis for the very first time. I could feel how hard he was and how much he was trying not to lose control. 'Please can I put it inside you,' he whispered, and I didn't put up any fight. Then he was on top of me, penetrating a little roughly but by God, he was big. He was also young and inexperienced and while it felt absolutely delicious, I knew he was only going to last a few seconds before he ejaculated and sure enough he did.

I put my hands over his mouth to stop him making a noise and then he collapsed on top of me. He was bloody heavy, so I pushed him off and he nearly fell off the bed which made both of us laugh again. I could hear our other flatmate go still and I thought *Uh-oh, we've blown it*. He must have known something was going on because he turned off the telly and switched off the light. I heard him walking up the stairs and it was about then that we both realised John's car was in the drive and his bedroom door was wide open with the light on – it was going to take geeky flatmate about five seconds to figure out exactly who was in bed with me. Too late now though!

Once he was safely inside his bedroom and appeared to have gone to sleep, I sent John back to his room, practically bouncing along the hall, he was so happy. I lay in my bed alternating between shame at having seduced some poor innocent and still feeling turned on by the whole experience.

The next day, I ran into nerdy flatmate in the kitchen making breakfast and he gave me a strange look but didn't say anything. When John appeared it was tense and weird, and geeky flatmate took his breakfast into his room, rather than eat at the breakfast bar like he usually did. About a week later, he told me he'd found somewhere else to live. I don't think he approved at all!

I didn't regret what I did but, oddly, I had no real desire to do it again and I didn't want John reading anything into what happened. But he did, of course, and became really annoying. He'd pester me to come into my room and kept pleading with me to do it again. I was reminded of the huge age difference as he transformed from hot, desperately attractive young flatmate into whiney young boy that I, quite frankly, wished would leave. It was around this time that the lease came up for renewal so I rather gratefully gave notice. John seemed to think we'd move into a new place together which was *so* not going to happen. There was an awkward conversation but he eventually got the hint and I never saw him after we handed back the keys.

I feel a bit bad about it all in that sense and hope it was a positive experience for him rather than negative. But I was honest and he had to grow up at some point. It was still an extraordinary experience though and the image of me and him, knowing it was his very first time, still keeps me company on a lonely night!

'I hired a handsome male escort and slept with him'

Jo, 46, is a lawyer

THE FANTASY

I've been invited to my high school reunion which is quite traumatic for me. I was a real swot at school and used to be teased a lot about it. Boys don't really fancy brainy girls who wear glasses and they weren't exactly fighting over me. I've blossomed since then though and the schoolmates I have kept in contact with all seem terribly in awe of how well I've done professionally. All the popular pretty girls seem to have accomplished is popping out 2.4 children.

I've already decided to splash out on an expensive dress, get a great blow-dry and hire a make-up artist. The only thing missing is a gorgeous man on my arm to show off. I earn good money so, on a whim, I decide to hire a male model to accompany me. My friend does shoots for catalogues for all the big name fashion houses, so I asked him to approach one of the models he uses all the time and ask if he'd be prepared to act as my escort. I've met him once before and he is absolutely stunning and rather sweet. My friend says he'll ask and how much will I pay, so I say £300 but he has to pretend to be my boyfriend. He rings me straight back to say the guy said yes and I'm thrilled. I'll walk into the reunion looking great, having made it workwise and also having the hottest guy in the room on my arm.

I go from dreading the reunion to looking forward to it. I quiz my friend on how the model reacted to my request and he said he seemed quite chuffed to be asked. I don't know if that was because of the cash on offer or whether he secretly has a crush on me. I look at myself in the mirror just before he's due to arrive on the allotted night and think if he didn't before, he will now! I look fantastic in a long Armani dress that's cut to flatter. My make-up looks amazing and my hair looks sleek and sexy. The buzzer goes and the model says, 'Wow! You look fantastic!' when I answer the door. I'm ridiculously pleased. He looks good enough to eat and my tummy does a little flip when I wonder if anything will happen between us. I think he is amazingly sexy and would kill to kiss that gorgeous mouth of his.

When we walk into the reunion, everyone stops to stare. It's being held at my old school and it feels strange being back. I feel myself revert back to my old nerdy self and feel shy and insecure. My date squeezes my hand when I tell him I used to be geeky and whispers, 'Well you sure as hell aren't now' into my ear. Having his mouth close to my face is heaven. I grin at him and he grins back, his amazing teeth sparkling back at me.

We work the room and I make sure I speak to all the girls who used to be pretty and aren't now, and flirt with the men who didn't fancy me to show them what they missed out on. The model is having lots to drink and really getting into his role as my boyfriend. He's hugging me and kisses me on the cheek in front of a girl he knew I particularly wanted to show off to. I take a risk when we're next standing alone and plant one directly on his lips. He raises his eyebrows and looks quizzically at me, as if to say, what's going on here? But he doesn't object.

We dance to a few old tunes and I'm a bit bored, so I take him off to look at my old classroom and the gym. He holds my hand even though he doesn't need to because there's no-one around. When we get to the gym, we sit on one of the high benches and swig our beers and chat. Then, out of the blue, he kisses me. A long, hard, sexy, passionate kiss. He pulls back and looks me in the eye and says, 'If I really was your boyfriend, I'd take you right here and now.' I look back without flinching and cheekily say, 'But aren't you? Isn't that what I've paid you to be?'

A slow sexy smile with just the right amount of naughtiness and menace spreads across his face. Then he jumps off the bench and stands between my legs while I'm still sitting and then he's kissing me and biting my neck and my breasts and my God, it feels just incredible. I am so wet, I feel embarrassed. He licks his fingers before he touches me and when he puts his fingers there he says, 'God you're so wet. It's lovely,' and I nearly orgasm right there and then. Then his fingers are inside me but I want more so I reach down with my hands, unzip him and release his penis, which is exactly how I'd imagined it. Not too big but definitely on the large side and breathtakingly hard. I want it inside me and he takes no persuading, so the next thing we're fucking on the bench. We're both moaning and that's when I look across the room and see one of the girls from the party watching us open-mouthed through the little window in the door.

She sees that I've spotted her and disappears but I have no doubt at all, she'll go straight back to the party and everyone will know what we were up to. The model doesn't know we've been seen and I see no reason to stop now. It just makes the whole thing even hotter and tips me over into a phenomenal orgasm. He watches my face as I climax and it makes him do the same. I smile to myself when we walk back into the party and everyone's whispering and looking at us. I can't think of a more perfect way or time to exit the reunion in style.

THE DECISION

I was on the shortlist to be made a partner in a law firm who were traditional and conservative in their values. I knew they expected a woman of my age (46) to have a long-term boyfriend or husband and I also knew having a partner who was attractive and charming and able to dazzle clients would be considered a must. So whenever anyone at work asked me about my personal life, I'd vaguely hint at a long-term lover. Eventually – and inevitably I guess – there came a point when I had to produce him. I was invited to a stuffy dinner in an equally stuffy restaurant with the firm's partners and their spouses. It's not something I'd particularly relish but it was a significant invitation: I knew if I performed well at the dinner, I might be shortlisted as a partner and I wanted that badly.

I accepted the invitation and then went home and thought through my options. I didn't have a boyfriend and there were no prospective men on the immediate horizon. None of my male friends really fitted the bill and I had under a week to come up with someone. I toyed with the idea of pretending he was away or sick but I knew they'd just keep asking until they met him. They were old-fashioned and sexist and wouldn't look favourably on a single female for the job and, as much as I abhorred their value system and misogyny, it was a highly respected firm and I wanted the title on my CV.

I don't know where the idea for a male escort came from but it just seemed logical. I hire people to clean for me, cater parties, do my hair and give me massages and facials – what's so different about hiring a man to accompany me to a work dinner? I went online and after spending an hour or so sifting through the gay rent boys and slimy sex sites, I found a reputable agency that said it provided handsome and educated male escorts for businesswomen. I rang them to check they were legitimate and the woman who answered sounded cultured and completely understood what I was looking for. She directed me to three men she thought might be suitable, so I looked online and found one that looked suitable – early 40s, sophisticated and also decent looking, plus he was university educated. She assured me he was perfectly capable of holding his own in a smart restaurant, good at making small talk and charming. He cost £1000 for three hours and if I wanted to hire him for longer, it was £150 every hour after that. She said sex was not a service they provided but if I wanted to make private arrangements with him that was up to me. I was horrified she'd even suggested it and told her so in no uncertain terms. She apologised for offending me but said it was a question some clients wanted answered but found awkward to ask. I told her I understood, booked 'David' for the evening and was quite pleased with myself for thinking outside the box.

THE REALITY

I arranged for 'David' to meet me in a bar near the restaurant one hour before we were due at dinner. To be honest, I was feeling ambivalent about it all when he turned up. Part of me saw it as an intelligent solution to a business problem. The other part felt like a big, fat failure for not having a real perfect man to bring along. I've always been career-focused and while I've had boyfriends, relationships have never been a huge priority. I like sex when I'm having it but I tend to forget about it when I'm not.

But I'd be lying if I said it hadn't occurred to me to ponder if he'd be available for sex. I think that's why I'd reacted so indignantly when the woman mentioned it. My fantasy was one I came up with the night I booked him, when I masturbated for the first time in ages. My libido was low – I was in a weird place with my relationship with my body. I was getting older and my body was changing and not in a good way. I worked long hours, never got to the gym, grabbed food when I could get it and it was taking a toll on my looks. I'd made a special effort tonight though and thought I'd brushed up reasonably well.

When 'David' walked into the restaurant, I felt a bit sick. He was much better looking than I'd expected: taller, better built than in the photo and he looked great in a suit. I was the only one sitting at the bar so wasn't difficult to find but I half waved at him when he walked in, so he'd know it was me. He gave me a really nice genuine smile when he saw me and I kidded myself that maybe he thought I was attractive as well.

I did the usual thing of saying, 'I've never done this before' and he put me at ease immediately and said, 'Well, I'm not surprised, you're a very attractive woman and I'm sure you don't normally need to use the service. I'm flattered I could help you out on this occasion.'

It was a practised answer, one I'm sure he'd perfected over his years as an escort, but he made it sound genuine. I knew I wouldn't have any problems with him charming my musty old superiors and he didn't disappoint. I filled him in on some basics – where we'd met, how long we'd been going out, where I grew up and went to school – the type of thing they'd be likely to ask, and he assured me that if asked a question he didn't know the answer to, he was good at diverting the conversation.

I felt proud walking in with him. He was extremely handsome and showed just the right amount of affection, consistent with us having gone out for about two years but definitely leaning towards 'still in love' rather than 'bored shitless by each other'. He was attentive, complimentary and endeared himself to the partners and their wives. We had some wonderful wines and it went so smoothly, it was hard not to be swept up in the fantasy. I dared to imagine what it would be like if he really was my boyfriend and I wondered about his personal circumstances. Did he have a partner? What did she think about his job if he did? There was no way I'd let someone like him out of my sight!

The dinner was coming to an end and I could see he'd more than done his job in impressing my colleagues, so that put me in a good mood. Plus I was a bit tiddly and he'd made me feel really good about myself. His time was up and we'd already crept into the fourth hour, so I figured why not ask him home for a nightcap and get my money's worth by making him stay with me until the end of it. We sat on the sofa when we got back to my place and suddenly I really wanted to kiss him but I didn't know what the protocol was. Was kissing allowed? Was it extra? What a weird situation to be in. It made me giggle a bit and he asked what I was laughing about, so I told him.

He smiled and said kissing wasn't part of it but we could come to an arrangement if I wanted more, with sex costing another £400. I said what about just a kiss and he said he didn't charge per kiss because that was ridiculous. I wasn't sure and we chatted for a bit but he was so handsome and I knew I probably wasn't going to have sex for months, possibly years, so I thought why not?

He asked for the money up front, which I was expecting, and then he took charge. He stood up and led me by the hand into the bedroom and lay me down on the bed and started kissing me. He was a fantastic kisser and lover. The sex was very straightforward – he played with my breasts, went down on me and then we had intercourse missionary style – but his technique was outstanding. It sounds boring but it was heavenly. I worried I'd feel strange about it all and worry he was acting aroused when he really wasn't but the thing about having a penis is that's hard to do. It did occur to me later that he'd probably popped a Viagra but thankfully it didn't occur to me at the time. I had an orgasm during the oral sex part and he had one during intercourse – obviously he used a condom so I suppose he could have faked it – but it looked pretty real to me.

The only really embarrassing bit was that after sex, I went to snuggle up and you could see he didn't want that. He did it long enough to be polite and then said he needed to get going. I got the hint and got dressed as well. I know it sounds silly but I'd fallen for him a bit and didn't want him to go. I wanted to see him again but not as an escort. He gave me a cuddle at the door so I bit the bullet and said 'I don't know if you've got a girlfriend or wife but I'd love to see you again,' and he said, 'Do you mean as an escort?' which should have given me my answer but I stupidly continued and said, 'No, for a proper date'. He smiled and said, 'I can't do that I'm afraid, I have a partner' and I said, 'Never mind,' but felt like an idiot and like I was about to cry. I don't know if he really did have a partner or just didn't see me as a potential one. Either way, it didn't feel great. So I said good-bye and he left and smiled and said he'd had a great time but I pretty much shoved him out the door at that point because I'd just made a fool of myself.

I cried myself to sleep. Not because I hated the experience but because it made me realise how much I wanted a relation-ship after all. Plus, I was drunk and drinking always makes me emotional! The next day, I woke up and was more pragmatic. The experience was far more positive than negative and I would definitely use him again if I had to for work reasons. I didn't feel bad about myself for wanting to have sex with someone I'd only just met and the sex was good! It was purely the fact that I'd paid for sex that got to me.

Men don't feel strange paying for sex because I think there's a deeply ingrained belief in Western society that men will always say yes to sex and women will generally refuse it unless there's something in it for her (marriage, money, status). I remember having a discussion years ago when an Australian woman opened a brothel for women. It was set up to cater for women like me – professional females who were time poor, cash rich and had healthy libidos but no time for a committed relation-ship. I thought it was a brilliant idea but I remember my male friends thinking it was hilarious, saying a woman could walk into any bar in the world and get sex for free. And therein lies the difference between men and women because women don't want sex with just anybody, they want sex with someone they fancy. I know I could walk into a bar and get sex, even though I am middle-aged and not beautiful any more. But would I want to sleep with the guy who's offering? I suspect not. I know sex wasn't the purpose behind my evening but I did end up paying for it. Did it mean I was ugly or past it because I had to pay? Or did it mean I was a savvy, smart businesswoman who could afford to buy herself the best? I eventually decided the latter but I haven't told anyone about it for fear they'd think the former.

'I performed sex live on a webcam'

Lucy, 33, works in sales

THE FANTASY

He opens the door, leading me inside by the hand, and I see everything is already set up. The bed is made up simply with a black fitted sheet. The props sit on a small table next to it. I see a riding crop, a blindfold, a bottle of lube and some bondage ties. I've never done any of this, let alone in front of an audience. I can see the webcam waiting, like it's begging to be switched on. It sends an involuntary shiver down my back. He asks me if I'm sure I want to do this and I nod.

He stands by the computer and types. I wait, sitting perched on the edge of the bed dressed in my underwear, wondering what he's going to do to me and if I'll like it. Within minutes, he's back and standing before me, dressed only in his boxers. His body is extraordinary and he knows it. Perhaps that's why he loves being watched so much: there's no doubt in his head that people will be admiring rather than criticising him.

He takes my face in his hands and kisses me feverishly and passionately. The minute the camera went on, so did he. He loves showing off, loves playing to the crowd. His tongue is going wild inside my mouth, then he's licking my neck and pulling my hair back to get full access. I feel ravaged and aroused and groan loudly. He loves me making noise and moans in return. He was worried I wouldn't like this and would want him to stop or switch off the webcam and continue privately. But I do like it. I like it very much.

He takes off my bra and bites my breasts then lays me on the bed and I allow him to angle me for the best possible view. He pulls off my panties and licks me and I bury my hands in his hair, pulling him closer, holding him there. I could climax there and then but I don't want to, so push him away. He laughs then pins my hands behind my head, brings his face close to mine and says in a dangerous tone, 'I call the shots here, not you'. I shut up and obey. But only because it suits me.

'Do you want me?' he asks. 'Do you trust me with all of this?' he says, gesturing to all the props beside the bed.

'Yes,' I say, 'Yes'. I can't see the computer screen but he can. He glances towards it, then looks back to me and grins and whispers, 'they love you baby,' into my ear. I arch my back and tip back my head to let everyone watching know this isn't an act, this is real desire.

He makes me sit on the side of the bed facing the webcam, picks up the bondage ties and quickly binds my hands behind my back. Then he blindfolds me. It makes me less self-conscious having my eyes covered. I like not knowing what will happen next. He pushes me back onto the bed and makes me get on all fours. I'm guessing I'm side-on to the camera. He asks me to push my bottom in the air. I feel him pick something up and then a sharp sting as the riding crop hits my buttock cheek. I gasp from the pain and the shock of it but, inexplicably, the second the pain disappears – and it disappears quickly – I want him to hit me again.

I wasn't sure if I'd like it and it's a love/hate reaction to the pleasure/pain it causes. When he hits, it burns. When he stops, I ache for more. His fingers reach inside me to see how much I'm liking it and I push against his hand eagerly. I'm not wet, I'm soaking. He pulls me in a different direction so everyone can see what's going on and then pushes my legs wide open, holding them open with one hand, reaching for some love balls with his other hand. He pushes them inside me, slowly, so everyone can see them disappear, then picks up the crop again. It's mind-blowing having all these 'firsts': being spanked and blindfolded and balls pushed inside me and knowing all of it is being broadcast to whoever wants to see.

My bottom is raw when he finally stops and pulls the blindfold off. His eyes glitter with excitement and his breathing is ragged. He's so hard, he looks set to explode. He pushes me forward on the bed and straddles me from behind and then he's inside me and thrusting, pumping, hard and furiously. My buttocks are still raw and over-sensitive and he's leaning against them but it just adds to the sensations I'm experiencing. My body explodes and everything contracts and I have a mind-blowing, mind-bending climax like none before. I wish I could swap places with the people watching us to see how good I must look at this moment: debased, fulfilled, happy.

THE DECISION

I'm a huge fan of porn and love watching the amateur stuff, but then I discovered sites where people perform live on webcams. It's so much more exciting knowing people are doing it in real time – plus you can type comments to the person and ask them to do stuff especially for you. I've never told anyone that I liked masturbating to these sites – women aren't supposed to like things like that, are they? I get strange looks from people when I admit to even liking porn! I am up for anything at all sexually, so long as it doesn't involve other people there with the two of you. I'm not interested in swinging or threesomes – performing live sex on a webcam is completely different. I don't consider it being unfaithful if the person isn't able to physically touch me. I was going out with a guy who was really into sex and I thought he might be up for actually having sex live on a webcam with me. It's been a long-standing fantasy of mine and I thought we'd look really hot on camera together. But he went absolutely berserk when I mentioned it and called me a slut for suggesting it. I was so offended I dumped him. I think his reaction was ridiculous and one reason why women are nervous about coming up with anything remotely adventurous with guys.

I didn't date anyone for a while after I dumped my boyfriend – it really upset me how he'd behaved! I think it was being deprived of sex for a while that made me think about going on a webcam solo. When I first thought of it, I dismissed it instantly because what if someone I knew saw me? But then I figured those people wouldn't be on a website like that anyway and if I did it late at night, there would be even less chance of getting caught.

I logged onto my favourite website (CamMe) and looked up how to join as a 'model'. It seemed pretty straightforward, so I did it there and then. Just joining up turned me on so much! I decided to perform that night – about 11ish – and I was so excited getting ready. I did really nice make-up – smoky eyes, a slick of pink lipstick and piles of mascara – and blow-dried my hair so it was full and tousled, as men like it. When I put on my underwear, I felt really exhilarated but also nervous. People post comments on there while you're live on camera, commenting on what you look like and asking you to do things for them. The requests I could handle. But what if people said I looked ugly or fat? On the whole, the comments are pretty positive but you do get some guys being really nasty if the girl doesn't do what they want her to do.

THE REALITY

I set my laptop up on a chair at the end of the bed. Then I sat on the edge of it in my underwear and logged in. I could see myself on screen and I looked really hot, if a little apprehensive. It was weird looking at myself and knowing there were people out there looking at me. I wondered how long it would be before people would click on the 'free chat' button to see me. Nothing happened for a minute or two so I cupped my breasts in my hands and fondled them a bit. Immediately three people appeared as 'guests'.

The first comment was 'Wow you're hot', the next was 'Take off your bra and play with your titties'. I did as I was told and took off my bra and it was kind of freaky seeing myself topless on camera but instantly another four users clicked on me. There were about 10 or so people watching me in total and it made me feel sexy and beautiful to be admired.

I pushed my breasts together and got loads of positive feedback but they wanted more and I wanted to give them more. 'Rub yourself' someone asked, so I angled the camera lower and started rubbing myself through my panties. 'Take your panties off and put your fingers inside' someone typed. I wasn't ready for that. I wanted to tease for a bit longer to see how many more people would watch me so I made a deal with myself that when there were 20 people watching, I'd take my panties off.

It took about five more minutes to reach the target, then I was like 'Here goes!' I took my pants off and was stark naked which made me panic a little, so I angled the webcam so they couldn't see my face any more. It was safer that way. Once I knew I couldn't be identified, I felt much braver. I lay back, spread my legs and let everyone see me finger myself. It was wild watching the comments of people getting off on watching me get off! I did everything they wanted, nothing too original, and I even got a few requests for a 'private chat' which meant someone would pay me to do naughtier things solely for them but I didn't want that. The whole point of it was so a lot of people could see me.

Having an orgasm on camera while everyone watched was the hottest feeling I have ever had in my life. I loved it. But the thing about having an orgasm – well, for me – is that the second

I've had it, I'm not interested in sex any more. All desire vanishes. So the minute I'd had my fun, I switched the camera off immediately. It was probably a bit rude not warning everyone I was going offline but I felt suddenly embarrassed.

Weirdly, considering it was a positive experience, I only did it one more time after that and it wasn't as good. To be completely honest, I got a bit bored. I'd still like to have sex live on a webcam with a boyfriend while other people watch but there's no way I'm suggesting it to anyone else after what happened last time!

'My husband wanted to watch me have sex with another man'

Juliana, 29, is a hairdresser

THE FANTASY

I'm sitting at the bar of a popular hotel in London with my husband. It's a Friday night and we're both relaxing after a busy week, enjoying just hanging out together and drinking a few glasses of wine. We're kissing each other and laughing a lot and I can see people looking at us, perhaps because we look so happy. One man in particular keeps staring at me. He's also at the bar, a few stools up from me, and drinking a beer. He's on his own and stands out, not just because he keeps stealing glances at me and is handsome in an unusual way – blond hair, tall, strong features, his nose and mouth a little too big for his face – but because he's not fiddling with his phone. Few people can sit still while alone at a bar without texting or tweeting. I hate all social media, so always notice this stuff.

He stares at me again and this time I make eye contact and smile. He smiles back and looks happy that I've acknowledged him, rather than embarrassed to be caught checking out a girl who is already taken. With my eyes still gazing into this handsome stranger's, I put my arm around my husband's neck and whisper into his ear, 'Check out the man behind you. He keeps looking at us'. My husband turns around and looks him over. Rather than averting his gaze, the man lifts his beer and nods at my husband and smiles. It's an acknowledgement to him that he's with an attractive woman. My husband turns back to me and grins. 'He likes you,' he says, 'And why wouldn't he. You're beautiful!' I have a short dress on, with bare legs, and he leans over and lets his hand slide up my thigh, knowing the man at the bar can see. It's a proprietorial gesture – but also a sign that he doesn't mind a stranger admiring his wife.

We've played this game before. Once, when we were in Berlin, a man we got talking to in a club made it very clear he wanted to sleep with me and my husband was flattered. We were very drunk and in a secluded, dark corner of the club and I ended up kissing the man, then my husband, then the man again, and letting them both play with my breasts. It was the most risqué thing I have ever done and my husband loved it. He's always trying to get me to wear revealing clothing when I'm with him, and when we make love he whispers scenarios to me about giving me to another man for a night with him hidden behind a two-way mirror.

'Shall we see how much he really wants you?' my husband whispers. I nod nervously and he goes over to talk to him. The man bends his head to listen, all the while maintaining eye contact with me, then picks up his beer and comes to sit with us. I gulp. The thing with the guy in the club happened organically and we were drunk. This is pre-planned and feels more serious, like it might actually end in sex. I can't decide whether the thought is titillating beyond belief or scary as hell.

We drink and chat and my husband suggests the man joins us for a drink at our place, which is just around the corner. The bar is about to close and we're having such a good time, why do we want it to stop? I don't know what my husband told the man when he asked him to join us, but he knows he's not just coming back for a nightcap.

Next thing, we're in the flat and my husband claps and rubs his hands together in anticipation and offers to rustle up some drinks. He pats the sofa and invites me and the man to sit down and 'start getting to know each other properly'. I can hear my husband rattling around in the kitchen and boldly take the initiative, lean forward and kiss the man, straight on the lips. There's no doubt what that kiss means. He groans, takes a handful of my hair and kisses me back hard.

'Ah, splendid!' my husband says, appearing with drinks and putting them down on the table. He waves his hands at us and says, 'Don't let me stop you. I'll sit over here and amuse myself'. He's sounding flippant but I can see his erection straining against his jeans and his voice sounds thick.

'Are you sure about this?' the stranger says to both of us. I don't think he can believe his luck.

'Are you sure sweetheart?' my husband asks and I swallow and nod. I am indecently turned on by the thought of having this man inside me while my husband watches.

'Yes,' I reply, taking control. 'But let's move to the bedroom.'

'Undress me,' I say to the man. He lifts the dress above my head and says 'Fuck, you're gorgeous' when he sees me in my underwear which is lacy and sexy in a girly way. My husband stands a little way away from us. He's taken off his shirt, unzipped his jeans and taken out his penis. It's huge and erect and he sits in a chair in the corner and starts stroking himself.

The man is kissing my breasts and his hand is between my legs. His fingers push my panties to one side and he gasps at how wet I am. He slips one finger inside me, then two, then stops and pulls back to look at me. He removes my bra and attacks my breasts with his mouth, biting and licking like a mad man. It suddenly occurs to him that my husband might be bisexual because he whips around and says to him 'Nothing between us, right?' 'God no,' says my husband.

Once this is cleared up, he rips off my panties and we get down to it on the bed. My husband comes over and stands close to see all the action. As the man penetrates me, I maintain eye contact with my husband. It's so hot, I have orgasm after orgasm. At one stage, the man is licking me and I sit between my husband's legs and he fondles my breasts and kisses me and my neck saying 'Look how much he lusts after you'.

The guy senses that his role is to perform and enjoy but not try to engage me in intimacy. But he's really into me and while he's pretending this sort of thing happens all the time, I don't think anything like this has ever happened to him before. He comes the minute I put him in my mouth and my husband, who is touching himself, does as well. But the guy recovers fast and takes me from behind, pumping hard, and ejaculates for a second time.

Finally, after the man has explored every inch of me with his hands and fingers and penis, we are sated. We want the man gone now and he gets the hint and quickly dresses. He goes to kiss me on the cheek before he leaves but I'm having none of it. I'm not interested in any contact at all once it's over. The second the door clicks shut, my husband and I curl up in bed and he tells me how much he loved watching the whole thing but how he's glad the man is gone because he loves me and wants me to himself.

THE DECISION

I've only been married for two years and my husband and I are one of those couples who do everything together. My friends roll their eyes when I tell them what we're like. We sleep entwined in each other's arms and are close physically and emotionally. We're self-sufficient; sometimes it feels like we don't need anyone else. He's incredibly protective over me and gets jealous if men look at me – which is why I was a bit confused when he confessed that his fantasy was to see me with another man. It seemed odd: he hated men even looking at me, but found it arousing to imagine some other guy having sex with me? What was that all about!

I'm Brazilian and grew up with a permissive, relaxed attitude to sex so I didn't have the knee-jerk reaction most women would to his proposal that we turn it into reality. But it did take a while for me to get my head around the concept. I didn't ever interpret it to mean he didn't love me, which is what I think a lot of women would do. But I knew it was a dangerous thing to explore and that it could cause a lot of drama, so I did lots of research online to see what other people's experiences had been. Most were positive – but then I was mainly looking on swingers' sites. We started looking at the sites together, testing the water, and the thought that we might actually do it turned my husband on so much, I started getting all excited as well. I'm quite happy staying sexually faithful to my husband and don't have a desire to stray. There's nothing I want to do that I couldn't do with him. But there's something in all of us that likes new things, so being 'forced' to sleep with another man wasn't *un*appealing. Especially if he was hot!

My husband's motivation was simple: to him, I was the most beautiful woman in the world and he wanted to see other men intoxicated by me sexually. Part of the fantasy was also, I think, that he thought I was insatiable. I love sex and have a high sex drive and I think he likes to think it would take many men to satisfy me, not just one. I guess it made him feel powerful too, being man enough to 'share' his wife which was *his* 'property'.

But I was still cautious and made us take baby steps. We researched lots of websites and settled on one called Swingingheaven. The next step was posting an ad and some pictures, which freaked me out a bit. The pictures had to be tasteful but not reveal my identity. In the end we chose three: one of me with sunglasses on, all glammed up; another of us together – side-on so you could get a sense of what we looked like but not absolutely know it was us; and the third was sexier with me on the bed, face down, showing a tasteful view of my legs and bottom. The ad was really simple – it said, 'Couple seeking man for sensual fun.'

We got more than 30 responses but one stood out to us. The guy sounded like he'd done it before and he also sounded nice, bright and respectful. I know that sounds like an odd thing to be looking for, when you're looking for someone to have sex with you while your husband watches, but it was important to us. We might be adventurous in that sense but we're quite straight in others. Respecting that we were married was important. I tried not to be too enthusiastic, but the guy was hot as well. Great body, great face: if I was going to do this, I had to fancy the guy! But even then I was careful to let my husband know that I found him more attractive. We wrote back saying we were keen to explore it further and suggested meeting for a drink to see if we all liked each other before taking it further.

THE REALITY

Like most fantasies, the planning part and the anticipation was intensely sexual. Working out what to say in the ad, taking the photos, daring to post it live, watching to see if anyone would respond, knowing other men were looking at erotic pictures of me and lusting after me, planning what I'd wear on the night . . . that alone made sex more passionate than usual.

I also think it showed a sense of adventure on both our parts, and courage. It was brave to consider inviting another body into our bed. I know lots of people do it but we honestly love each other and the thought of it causing problems, or for us to split, was unbearable to both of us. That's why we did everything by the book and followed all the cautious advice we found. We'd worked out exactly what was allowed and what wasn't, like no involvement between the guy and my husband, no kissing, and we had a 'safe word' that meant no matter what stage we were at, we'd both stop everything and leave together (it was 'orange'). And we're both good at reading each other's body language: if he was hating it but keeping it going out of some macho thing, I'd be able to sense it. If I was hating it but going along with it to please him, he'd sense it. We had all the bases covered so when the night arrived to meet the guy, both of us were more excited than stressed.

We'd chosen a bar we knew of but didn't go to often, so we didn't have to worry about bumping into him in the future or ruining a favourite night spot. I was wearing a sexy, classic pencil skirt, gorgeous heels, a fitted shirt and looked sensational, if I say so myself. My husband has a fantastic body – big and muscular and he wore a shirt that showed it off coupled with some Levis.

We turned up first, deliberately, and we were both skittish, though my husband definitely more so. I was more worried that the guy would turn up and look nothing like the picture but he walked in and we both instantly recognised him because he looked exactly like he did online. He spotted us and came over and shook my husband's hand, sitting opposite us and seeming very laid back and confident. We all chatted for a bit and ordered some drinks but I could feel my husband was all stiff beside me – and not in a good way! I think the guy was a bit too good-looking and charming and while he flirted with me in a really mild way, it shocked my husband into realising exactly what we were planning on doing. At one point, the guy leaned forward to tell me something and laughingly touched my hand. And that tiny, non-sexual touch on the back of my hand – not even a sexual part of me – was enough to stop it right there and then. 'I can't do this,' my husband whispered to me, and so we wrapped the night up saying we'd contact him but he sensed the change in mood and parted graciously knowing we never would.

My husband had gone white and kept saying over and over, 'That was awful. He was flirting with you and he touched your hand!' He said it incredulously, like it was insane the guy would assume to touch my hand! Then we both laughed. I don't know what possessed either him or me to imagine he could possibly cope with someone else touching any part of me, let alone sexually, when he was so jealous of me generally and loved me totally. What had become his obsession was rapidly dropped once he was faced with the reality of it actually happening. It's quite amusing really.

How did I feel, having a hot man dangled in front of me and then not being able to fulfil the fantasy? I think I would have gone through with it, had my husband been OK with it. But I don't mind at all that we didn't. It was his fantasy not mine. That was a few years ago and lately, we've started talking, about going to a swinger's club but adopting the 'watch but don't touch' policy. That might just give us the kick we're looking for, without the jealousy kicking in. Or not. Knowing us, we'll plan the whole thing, get there, knock on the door and then run away. It's probably better that way. It's the fantasy planning part that's the hottest anyway.

'I gave myself a gorgeous 20-year-old for my 50th birthday'

Catherine, 51, is a journalist

THE FANTASY

I'm a sex education teacher visiting a boys-only sixth form college to instruct them on the facts of life. I haven't been there before but when I pull up in my sleek, black sports car, it looks quite posh. I swivel my body so my legs are out of the car, then lean down to put on my high heels (I always take my shoes off when I drive). My breasts spill out of the top I'm wearing as I bend over – I look professional but I'm definitely working the 'hot teacher' look. As I straighten up and smooth down the tight pencil skirt I'm wearing, I see some of the older boys eyeing me out of a classroom window, which looks onto the car park. They're all about 17 or 18 and walking erections: they can't believe their luck of seeing down my top.

I stand up and let them see how hot I am, then walk provocatively down the drive to the head teacher's office. I can see the boys all chatting excitedly when the head shows me into the classroom of all the older boys, clapping to get their attention, introducing me and asking them all to behave and not get silly because a woman is going to be talking about sex. The headmaster is old and musty and finds sex education incredibly embarrassing, so he's keen to leave me to it the second he can. I tell him not to disturb us for about an hour and to come back then. He leaves and I lock the door behind him. (It's a fantasy so classroom doors are lockable!) No-one can see in the windows, so it's just me and 20 young men and it's all completely private.

I start off fairly orthodox, talking to them about condoms and safe sex and how girls get pregnant. I write things on the blackboard and know they're checking out my bottom when I turn around. I sit on the desk and cross my legs as I explain things to them, letting my skirt ride high on my thighs. The students are transfixed. They wet their lips nervously and glance at each other, not sure if I'm being deliberately sexy or they're just permanently aroused and see every situation as sexual.

I like turning them on, it turns me on. I ask how many of them are familiar with the female body and anatomy and they all shake their heads. They're expecting me to refer to a chart to explain it all but instead I say 'I'll show you then. Come closer to have a look'.

They all hang back. I know it's because they have erections and don't want me to see. I tell them it's normal to get hard, because we're talking about sex, so they half reluctantly, half expectantly come out from behind their desks and crowd around me. I feel a surge of power that I am about to give them all their first sexual experience, even though I won't touch any of them.

I tell them I'll let them see me naked, if they promise not to tell their teacher or parents. They nod enthusiastically, and cross their hearts and jostle each other. Some of the boys can't help themselves and furtively touch themselves, hiding behind other boys to get away with it. I start to unbutton my top, all the while talking in a calm, professional 'teacher' way, explaining that they're about to see breasts. I take off my shirt and then remove my bra and touch my nipple with my finger, explaining that this is the most sensitive part of the breast and the dark part is called the areola. I tweak my nipples until they are hard and explain this is what happens if they're doing everything right to a girl. They can't take their eyes off me and their mouths drop open. They're astonished to be getting this live demonstration.

I reach behind me and unzip my skirt, leaving my heels on. It drops to the floor and I step out of it. I'm wearing a tiny G-string and I'm a total gym bunny, so my body is toned and taut. I like showing it off and I love seeing the desire etched on their young, innocent faces. The boys look straight at my panties, begging me with their eyes to take them off. None of them speak. They're scared if they say something, I'll stop the demonstration. I inch my panties down my legs. At the sight of me, some of the boys can't help but groan. I know this image of me will be masturbated to for many years to come. Maybe forever for some of them, depending on how sexy their future girlfriends and wives are.

I sit on the desk, naked, and open my legs and point to each part of me, showing them my clitoris and putting my fingers inside myself to show how women get wet when they are ready for sex and how they need to make sure this happens before they even attempt penetration. I remain matter of fact and don't reveal that I am getting my rocks off showing off to them. I tell them the best way to make a woman happy is to circle the clitoris with their fingers and as I show them exactly how to do it, I have a sneaky, secret orgasm. I can see most of them have already had one in their trousers and are looking sheepish, so I tell them the lesson is over. I calmly put my clothes on, instruct them to go back to their seats, and chat as though nothing has happened. The headmaster knocks on the door, right on time, and I wave goodbye cheerily and head back to the car, confident I've given them a lesson they will never forget.

THE DECISION

It's the weirdest thing, turning 50. No matter what you have achieved, how much you've accomplished, the brain hones in on the one thing you *haven't* done. Then it blows that up – your failing – in letters higher than the sky, puts them in flashing neon, and programmes the brain to focus obsessively on it every seven seconds for about six months preceding the dreaded day. Mine was not meeting the right partner; someone I would be happy with for life. Forget the career achievements, the fact I had a brilliant flat, great friends, looked good for my age, and (ironically) went on lots of dates. All I cared about was not having met 'The One', which is pretty funny because I don't even believe in the 'The One'! I think there are plenty of people who can make us happy. But that's the thing about milestone birthdays, they send you absolutely bonkers.

I knew things were really dire when two nights before my birthday I found myself simultaneously reading *The New Earth*, a spiritual 'what's the meaning of life' book, and watching *Eat Pray Love*, an equally deep 'I'm searching for answers because I don't have a clue what it's all about' film.

'For fuck's sake, this is ridiculous,' I said out loud to myself. I decided enough was enough – 50 was the new 40, as they say, and while I *would* still like to meet someone to share my life with, what I was doing just wasn't working. I had a serious think about why I might not have met my 'soul mate' and decided it was because I had a dreadful/delicious (depending on how you look at it) habit of dating men younger than me. That had to go. But as a compromise and to perk myself up a bit, I decided I was allowed one final fling with some young hot thing. I felt myself feeling ridiculously randy and happier than I'd been in ages. And that was my state of mind when I flew to Los Angeles on a work trip the following weekend . . .

THE REALITY

The hotel I was staying in was very LA – fab swimming pool, great view, more than the odd celeb hanging out. I had dinner with some friends who were also in town and it was one of those nights when everything works – you look great, you feel great, and the gin and tonics are sliding down your throat at a hell of a pace but you don't feel drunk, just vibrant and witty and alive. The restaurant overlooked the pool and we noticed the staff setting up a table for a private pool party that night, organised by some rich socialite who had parties for no reason other than to get 'super interesting rich and beautiful people' together. This was all compliments of our waiter, a struggling actor (of course) who was salivating at the prospect of the contacts he might make if asked to tend bar. We all thought it sounded pretty damn good as well and asked if all hotel guests were invited. He said 'Sure!', so along we went.

By this stage, the G&Ts had well and truly worked their magic. In my mind, my friends and I smoothly blended with the glossy, moneyed crowd, fitting in perfectly. In reality, we must have been obvious outsiders: all English, all a bit tipsy. I remember I had on a hot pink silk top with slit sleeves, denim shorts and high heels. It sounds ridiculous now but that's the thing about LA and days by the pool. A tan makes you brave enough to wear stuff you wouldn't dream of wearing in London and although I'm 50, my legs are still good. I felt glamorous and hot and, really, that's all that counts if you're in the mood for sex and open to being chatted up. And *God* did I feel like sex. I was like a dog on heat and one drink away from humping the leg of one of the waiters. The thing about being that aroused and that tiddly, is that all those sex pheromones don't just gently waft past men's noses, they practically drown the poor buggers, instantly alerting them to the fact that there's an up-for-it female within chatting up distance.

I don't remember how the conversation started, but I do remember talking to two guys with my friend who was way more sober than I was. God knows what I said but I have the ability to appear quite sober when I am, in fact, horribly pissed and this night was no exception. The other ability I have when drunk is to turn Quasimodo into Brad Pitt – my beer goggles are terrible! I could feel the guy I was talking to transforming before my very eyes! The next thing I know – and I still don't know why, maybe it's his party trick? – he picked me up and threw me over his shoulder. I remember thinking 'thank God I have shorts on and not a skirt', but it was all a bit of a laugh and I remember him walking around with me slung over his shoulder. I was massively impressed by his strength and the caveman masculinity of it all.

'You do realise he's 20, right?' my friend whispered when, at one stage, I found my head dangling next to her as my date for the night nonchalantly strolled around the party with me in a fireman's lift.

I can't remember what I replied because next thing I know, he walked out of the party with me on his shoulder, straight through the hotel lobby, bold as brass, and into the lift. I found it slightly alarming that no-one stopped him since he could have been abducting me. But then I guess if I was being abducted, I'd have shouted 'Help!' rather than asking 'Are you staying in the hotel?'

Next thing I know, I'm being plonked down on an enormous bed. I looked around and saw I was in a room much better than mine, and mine was reasonably flash.

'It's the penthouse,' he said.

'Are you really only 20?' I remember squeaking.

'Yes. Are you really 50?' he replied.

'Yes,' I said and then I remember snogging him senseless. He was a fantastic kisser, just the right amount of tongue, and I felt wicked and very, very naughty which made me want him even more.

He ordered a bottle of gin and extra tonic and I thought, if he's really 20 then he's either a drug dealer or has rich parents to afford all this. At that point though, I didn't really care.

For someone so young, he was incredibly confident, which backed up the rich Mummy and Daddy theory. I was loving the whole 'take charge' caveman stuff which continued. He pinned both my hands above my head with one hand, kissed me roughly, then put his hands under my top and started fondling my breasts. I was so turned on by him, I nearly came there and then. He undid my bra and took it off but left my top on and just pushed it up out of the way and started sucking my breasts. He let go of my arms but I kept them up there, above my head, because I liked the feeling of being helpless, while he undid my shorts and lifted my hips and slid them off. I had watermelon colour panties on and I remember him laughing and saying how cute they were. He took them off and put them on the sofa saying he was going to steal them.

I lay on the bed, bottom part of me naked but with my top still on and thought *Jesus! This guy is hot!* He told me to sit up and took my top completely off, then stood at the end of the bed and took off his shirt, looking at me like he wanted to eat me. He had my idea of the perfect body. He was lean but muscly, his jeans were super low cut and he had gorgeous hips and a washboard stomach. He could see me admiring him so he removed his jeans and pants and then suddenly his penis came into view and it was magnificent. A proper 20-year-old erection! It was big and hard, and so pumped full of blood, it was straining upwards and almost flush against his stomach. I wanted that hard, young penis inside me immediately. I said 'Do me' and so he did and it was the best intercourse I've ever, ever had.

He lay on top of me, and slid his fingers inside me and felt how wet I was. Then he penetrated slowly but deeply and settled into a rhythm: slow-and-deep, slow-and-deep. He'd grind his hips and pause to tease me now and then and he was reaching places no-one else had. The whole time he was kissing me and pushing back my hair to look at my face and saying, 'You like this don't you? Are you liking this?' And I'd say 'Yes, God yes' and then he'd say, 'You like my voice? You like my accent? It turns you on?' And I'd say 'God yes' and it went on like that for ages. And ages . . . And then I started to get paranoid. He was 20 and said this was his first time sleeping with an older woman, which is as much a fantasy for young guys as it is the other way around. Shouldn't he have the opposite problem and be ejaculating too fast? Suddenly I felt very, very sober. Was it drugs? I know that if guys do too much coke they can't orgasm. Maybe he was a drug dealer! Did he leave the room at any point to do drugs? I couldn't remember. Then it hit me: it was because I wasn't tight enough! A 20-year-old penis matched with 50-year-old bits! And there I was back at the bloody life-is-over-because-I'm-50 panic!

I asked him why he wasn't coming and he said 'I can last all night, don't worry about that'. 'Are you always like this?' I asked him and he said 'Yes, why don't you like it? Girls normally like it'. I felt relieved but snuck a look at my watch and it was 5am. We'd been at it for hours and I'd had enough. I asked him for a gin and tonic and while he made it in the kitchen, I got up, quickly got dressed, grabbed my watermelon knickers and shoes and snuck out, raced down to the lift, jumped inside and got out on my floor. He knew I was staying at the hotel but he didn't know my room number. Back in my room, I looked at myself in the mirror and I looked naughty and sexily ravaged and happy with myself. I didn't feel any shame because I don't make a habit of one-night-stands. But it was just what I needed and it was damn hot.

The next day I woke up so dehydrated that I wobbled to the bathroom and drank out of the tap for what felt like three hours. Then I stumbled back to bed and pieced the night before together in my head. My reaction was still 'Go girl! Why not!' and I felt sort of proud that I'd been able to pull a hot 20-year-old at the age of 50. I then took myself down to the poolside café and ordered a huge burger and fries and hid behind sunglasses, my brain still sodden with alcohol. About the moment I realised

I was perfectly positioned to view the balcony of the penthouse and had my mouth wrapped around the burger, ketchup dripping down my chin, he appeared. I recognised the body but couldn't see his face properly from that distance. He leant on the balcony and looked down at the poolside, looking long and hard at me. I don't know if he recognised me but I kind of liked the way I'd left without saying anything, so I just kept on eating my burger, safely behind my huge sunglasses, and didn't acknowledge him at all. Once he'd gone inside I smiled to myself and thought 'That was one hell of a birthday present' and I haven't worried about being 50 since!

'I stripped on stage in a strip club for my boyfriend'

Candice, 24, works in television

THE FANTASY

I'm on a resort holiday in Thailand with some girlfriends. We're supposed to be there relaxing at the spa, getting lots of massages and doing yoga, but we've been there a week and are pretty bored. So we go into Bangkok for the night and end up in a strip club. There are pretty Thai girls on stage shooting ping-pong balls out of their vaginas into the audience. The muscle control they have is damned impressive and there are women watching them and applauding, as well as men.

We decide to stay and watch for a while so order some champagne and get a buzz on. We've been 'good girls' at the spa for so long it feels great to let our hair down. We all have boyfriends at home and are starting to miss them . . . and the sex. We're horny and obviously looking it because a group of guys start to surround us. They're obviously on a stag night – American, good-looking, well-dressed, with straight white teeth and lots of money. They offer to buy us drinks and we shrug our shoulders and say 'Why not? We're taken but happy to hang out for a while'.

We have a great time chatting and flirting away, with them buying us champagne cocktails. We sneak outside now and then and have sneaky cigarettes and one of them had some dope, so we had a puff or two on a joint as well. We're all watching the Thai girls dancing and stripping who are incredibly petite and beautiful but the American guys aren't digging them at all. They say they want to see real women with real breasts and a few curves up there on stage and dare us to perform for them.

I'm always up for a dare and two of my friends also say 'Why the hell not!' I'm given the task of asking the manager if we can put on an impromptu strip show and he says yes, they love amateurs and it's great for business. So my friends and I have a little confab and decide we'll strip down to our pants and knickers and that's it. One girl suggests we do a little girl-on-girl teasing to hype the boys up even more.

The guy announces us and the three of us get up on stage. Everyone's going wild because we look like 'good girls' and they know we've never done anything like this before. We're a bit giggly to start with and are pretty rubbish but then we start to really get into it and the Americans are looking hot and bothered which makes us really want to tease them. My friend is already down to her bra and knickers and gyrating about on her heels. She looks quite hot so I go and stand behind her and sort of rub up against her. She presses against me and turns her face and kisses me! I'm a bit shocked but aroused as well. I take off my top and I can see the Americans shouting and cheering and then I slide off my skirt as well, thinking, thank God I have nice underwear on.

My third friend has gone one step further and taken off her bra. Suddenly I want to as well, so I take mine off and then I decide to be really brave and take off my panties as well. My friends do the same and we're all up there naked, dancing and showing off and getting so much attention. The friend who kissed me comes up behind me and she starts kissing my neck and playing with my breasts. Then the other friend kneels in front of me, spreads my legs and licks me teasingly between the legs.

The crowd go absolutely wild. I'm wet and so turned on I can't bear it. I don't mind the girl-on-girl thing but I want a man. I call to one of the American guys to come up on stage and he's there in an instant. We all fall on him. One friend starts to kiss him while the other undoes his shirt. I unzip his jeans and get his penis out and start fellating him in front of everyone. He can't help himself and orgasms immediately. The audience are so excited, but the manager comes to tell us we have to get off the stage because the venue doesn't allow live sex on stage. We reluctantly obey and the audience boos and hisses at him, then we go back to a hotel with the American guys and have fantastic group sex.

THE DECISION

My boyfriend had always gone on and on about my breasts: how pert they are, how big, how men must look at them and admire them wherever I go, all day long. Thing is, men *do* look at them and it gives you confidence when guys are always checking you out. I think that's why I've always thought stripping would be quite fun, rather than nerve-racking. I am a bit of a show-off!

The whole thing started when I confessed my stripping fantasy to my boyfriend. He loved it! He'd make me tell him in detail what I did and what it felt like and what the guys watching were doing. I added more and more elements to the fantasy as time went on. He got most turned on when I said guys were playing with themselves while watching me and trying to climb on the stage. I guess it's the whole 'My girlfriend's so hot, everyone wants her' thing that was behind it all.

He came home one night very excited and told me there was an amateur strip night in a club in East London. He'd printed out all the information and said he thought I should enter. I'd like to say I protested at first and that he had to talk me into it but I'd be lying. I was well up for it! It was in two weeks' time and we went online and registered immediately. Then we went and had amazing sex, just thinking about how hot it would be.

I did loads of research online and got a lot of good tips. I came up with a stage name (Randy Candy – hilarious!) and planned my outfit. I even went and bought some really classy but sexy underwear in strong, bright colours so I'd stand out on stage. I got some hold-up stockings too and practised dancing in different pairs of shoes until I found heels high enough to look good but not so high I'd topple over while stepping out of my clothes. I decided to wear short denim shorts and a tight vest top with my heels to keep it simple: men like that look too.

We never had better sex than the sex we had before the event. My boyfriend usually takes ages to orgasm but all I'd have to do is mention the strip night and he'd be off like a rocket. I was secretly convinced I was going to win because I'd practised a little routine in the mirror and it wasn't half bad. I knew I wouldn't get nervous and drop out at the last minute because I'd already rehearsed the routine in my head a million times while fantasising about it! I figured it was all about timing and not removing everything too soon. I couldn't wait and neither could my boyfriend and we were beside ourselves with excitement when the night finally arrived and we pulled up outside the venue.

THE REALITY

The club was exactly what I'd expected: dark, sticky, grimy, and reeking of stale beer and other smells I didn't want to identify. It was a typical strip club: lots of red, shabby, worn around the edges with stained carpets. The stage was smaller than I'd pictured and the venue itself was smaller than it looked online. The guys watching would be much closer than I'd imagined. This didn't worry me particularly but my boyfriend's face changed the second we walked inside. He hated it.

'This isn't what I imagined. It's so tacky,' he kept saying over and over. It was tacky but it was a strip club, what he did think it was going to be like! This was my first clue he wasn't as cool with it as I was but I was so excited, I just ignored him.

We'd deliberately got there early so we could check it out and have a few drinks. There were probably 30 other people there already and I spotted some girls with their partners or with groups of other girls, looking nervous and talking too loudly and drinking too quickly. I smiled at them and eyed up the competition. A few girls were very pretty but no-one had boobs as big as mine. I pointed this out to my boyfriend who was chugging back a double vodka but all he said was 'Mmm'. I thought he'd launch into his spiel about how no woman in the world had better breasts than me but he'd gone very quiet.

When I asked if he was OK he snapped at me, 'I'm fine. Of course I'm fine. Why wouldn't I be!' He clearly wasn't fine but I didn't know what to do and now I was here, I really wanted to be up on that stage. I was wearing the outfit and had my hair all blown out so it was full and glossy, I'd even had my make-up done and I was already getting some admiring looks. This was what my boyfriend had wanted – me getting lots of attention from men with him able to see it – but he wasn't looking around and when he did see one guy looking at me he glared at him.

I knew I should have taken him by the hand and got the hell out of there but I was buggered if I was backing out. I'd only been with my boyfriend for four months and this had been a fantasy of mine for years. It was blatantly obvious it was about to backfire, though I had no idea just how badly.

The competition was supposed to start at 11pm but it didn't start until much later. I'd been watching how much I drank because I didn't want to make a fool of myself by being on stage swaying around on my heels but my boyfriend was legless. He seemed to be a little chirpier drunk than he had been sober, so I figured he'd just had an attack of the nerves and was fine with the situation now.

At last the night started and the guy called us all up on stage. There were probably a dozen girls and about sixty guys standing around watching us with the odd female friend smiling encouragement. I smiled a lot when they introduced me and when I saw my boyfriend's face in the crowd he gave me a watery smile and a thumbs up sign. The compere gave us a running order and I found out I was number five.

The first girl looked terrified when the music started. Her knees were knocking together, she was so frightened. I wondered if she'd been forced up there by some asshole boyfriend but she started dancing around a bit and the audience were really appreciative and cheering her on so she got more confidence as she got going. She stripped down to nothing and her body was great but she didn't work it well and lacked sex appeal.

The second and third girl had clearly done it before. They had proper routines and seemed almost professional, they were that good. The audience seemed to know them so they were obvious regulars and probably won most of the time. They were definite competition but I had novelty on my side. The men didn't know me and had never seen me naked, so hopefully they'd get more excited. I was so busy watching the girls, I was quite surprised to see my boyfriend had worked his way through the crowd and was now standing right at the front.

I met his eye and smiled but he didn't smile back. He was looking around him quite aggressively and giving filthy looks to the guys cheering the girl on stage.

Next thing, I was being introduced. I walked up the side steps and stood confidently and sexily on stage, smiling broadly. I then made eye contact with a guy in the front row, centre stage, and started doing my routine. I couldn't look at my boyfriend because I knew it would put me off. The crowd loved me. They were applauding like mad and men were shouting out 'Great tits!' and 'Take it off, Randy Candy' and it was exhilarating having all these guys watching me and wanting me. But it's also a little scary seeing a group of men with lust in their eyes and knowing they didn't see me as a real person, just boobs and legs. When I tried to make eye contact with some of them, their eyes would slide away and remain fixed on my breasts or legs or bottom. They didn't want a personal connection with me: maybe men are ashamed of themselves underneath all the bravado?

I didn't feel threatened though because there were quite a few bouncers standing around so I kept going and took off my top to reveal my bra, then slid off my shorts and did a sexy little number taking off my stockings by putting my foot up on a chair on stage, like I'd seen burlesque dancers do. I was turned facing away from the stage, wearing just my G-string and bra, legs spread wide, bottom in the air and about to unhook my bra when I heard my boyfriend yell above the crowd, 'No!'

I heard him but I thought *fuck you, this is my moment and you wanted this. Don't throw a hissy fit now.* I'm extremely competitive and I felt I really had a shot at winning this. I stayed in the same position but turned around and saw my boyfriend trying to get on stage while other guys held him back. The bouncers were marching grimly towards him, ready to kick him out and there was a right old scuffle. A lot of the men were shouting at him and you could see a few were angling for a fight. Meanwhile, the music was still playing and I wasn't quite sure what I was supposed to do – stop, continue or what? It sounds really awful but I was much more concerned about winning the competition than placating my boyfriend, which is of course the absolute opposite to what you're supposed to do in these situations.

He was still shouting at me, 'Stop it, get off the stage' and crying and so horribly drunk, it was awful. But the bouncers literally picked him up and got him out of there so fast, the whole thing was over in mere minutes. The audience turned their attention back to me so I kept going and finished my act – I even managed a huge sexy smile and wink at the end.

The organiser asked me if I wanted to leave because he'd seen what happened but I said no and he said 'Good girl, because you're in with a chance'. He brought me a stiff drink and I necked it down but I still refused to go running out there after my boyfriend. A few of the guys standing nearby started trying to pick me up and I flirted a bit with them but had no intention of leaving with anyone. I watched the rest of the show in a weird mood: I was elated after performing and being the centre of attention but I was really angry with my boyfriend. I didn't know if he'd be waiting for me outside or not but I hoped he'd taken himself off home and passed out. I didn't check my phone.

I didn't win but I did get runner-up and was quite pleased with myself. My boyfriend wasn't outside or at home when I got back, though. It was probably for the best – I was exhausted and in no mood to deal with some drunk, over-emotional guy. He turned up the next afternoon and was furious with me for continuing when it was obvious he didn't want me to. I didn't back down and told him he was the one who'd asked me to do it in the first place. He said he hadn't expected to feel jealous and the whole thing made him realise how much he cared for me. But it had the opposite effect on me. I realised I wasn't that into him at all. I'd never have stayed up there performing if I was. There was an awful scene that ended with him packing up all his stuff and leaving. Not quite the hot sex ending we'd envisaged!

The moral of my story is what I've always secretly thought: you live out fantasies like this with casual boyfriends or when you're young and not that attached to people. Anything that involves other people carries a huge risk of something like this happening. I guess if I'd really liked him, his reaction might have been the catalyst for our relationship to move into something serious.

I'm still glad I did it but don't really have any desire to do it again. It's funny that we'll run the same fantasy in our heads to turn ourselves on over and over for years on end, without ever getting sick of it. But once is usually enough when you take it through to reality. What's happened now is that my original fantasy has been replaced by me reliving the night I actually did it: imagining how I looked up there and how sexy I felt. I add in variations I'd never want to have happened in real life – and I haven't confessed it to any future boyfriends since!

'I slept with three men in one day'

Chelsea, 21, is a PA

THE FANTASY

I've volunteered to take part in an experiment on sexuality, which is being run at a university near me. When I signed up for it, the woman explained that it was 'hands on' and wasn't for the prudish. I told her I was up for anything and she smiled mysteriously at me. So I'm both nervous and excited on the day and have put on super sexy underwear just in case!

The same researcher greets me and explains that the experiment will start soon. I ask her how many people are involved and she says ten others. My tummy flips and I wonder what exactly the experiment is seeking to prove. She says it's to judge how long it takes men to orgasm and my job is to challenge them and try to make it happen quickly. They have to try to resist me for as long as they can. She tells me that's the reason why she chose me: because I'm really sexy and irresistible.

She leaves me to check to see if the men are ready, then returns and leads me into the room. There are ten naked men in there, all standing in a line for me to inspect them. They all have erections and they're all handsome in different ways. She says there's a mix of different nationalities and looks because she wants to see if ethnicity makes a difference. The men are checking me out but they don't say anything. The researcher tells me they're forbidden to speak.

She sits in a corner with her clipboard and a stopwatch to

time and rate them and tells me to start with whoever I want. I take off my dress and stand there in my underwear checking them all out and watching them check me out, deciding who will be first. I settle on a guy who looks Scandinavian. He's all chiselled cheekbones and icy blue eyes. His body is amazing and, most importantly, his penis is huge and also rock hard.

I go and stand in front of him. I can see the other men watching, wondering what I'm going to do and what's going to happen. The woman tells me the men aren't allowed to touch me, I can only touch them. I'm liking this game already.

The man I've chosen looks nervous. I go up to him and start rubbing my body against his. Then I put my arms around his neck and give him a long, deep, kiss with lots of tongue action. He groans and I put my hand down to feel him and his erection is practically touching his tummy. The rest of the men are looking on, enjoying watching us, knowing it's their turn soon. I remove my bra so am just wearing a thong and there's a collective sigh as I expose my breasts for the first time. They're full and pert and I reach to the left of the guy I'm kissing and grab the hand of the guy next to him and put it on my breast. He eagerly feels it, tweaking my nipple. As he continues to fondle my breast, I reach down and give my guy an expert hand job. My grip is firm and relentless and I'm kissing him sexily. He's not expecting it and ejaculates instantly. The woman notes down how long it took him – under two minutes – and nods at me to continue.

I work my way down the line, choosing men at random. I give parts of myself to each one, never the whole thing. Some men get to lick me. Others I'll fellate. The very lucky ones get to penetrate me. None of them last longer than a few minutes: they can't resist my charms or skilful technique. Sometimes I'll let the guy next to the one I'm concentrating on do things, like kiss me or lick me while I'm ravishing the other.

I've managed to seduce all of the men in record time except

for the most handsome of them all. He looks Italian – black glossy hair, gorgeous brown eyes, with skin you want to lick, it's so olive and plump. Unlike the others, he regards me with disdain. He looks almost uninterested and I'm sensing a challenge. He's well-hung but only half erect and looks at me insolently, almost sneering. The other men are spent and looking sheepish because none of them performed terribly well, so they're watching this interplay with interest.

I walk up to Mr Handsome and come unbearably close to him but I don't kiss him or touch him. Instead I maintain eye contact and don't break it while I run my hands over my body, pushing my breasts high so they're an inch from his mouth but not allowing him to lick them. I put a finger inside myself and then make him suck it. He does it but he's pretending not to be turned on, even though his erection is now enormous.

I make him lie down on the floor on his back and I straddle him, gyrating above him on all fours. I'm so close he can feel the heat radiating from my body, but he can't touch me. I can see raw, primitive lust in his eyes and wonder how long he'll last before he breaks the rules. He's not a man who's scared of authority; I can see it in his eyes. I crawl up and over him so his mouth is inches from my genitals. I move tantalisingly close and he strains upward, trying to touch me with his tongue, but I move away again. I laugh and sit up, daring him to do something and suddenly he snaps. In one swift movement, he grabs me and pushes me down and he's on top of me and inside me and thrusting long and hard before the woman's even on her feet and shouting at him that it's not allowed. He can't make the moves, I have to. But he ignores her and so do I because it feels heavenly and just as he bucks and lets loose, I have the hardest, most passionate orgasm I've ever had.

THE DECISION

I've always been a bit of a slut – I say that in a playful sense, not judgemental! I have a high sex drive and am experimental and adventurous by nature, so I'm naturally curious and open in bed as well. My fantasies reflect this and I think this is why I've never lacked attention from men. I like men and *love* sex and they sense it. It shows in the way you walk and smile and move. Women who like sex make eye contact more, are more conscious of their bodies, encourage men to look at them rather than discourage it. I smile and flirt and pay them attention. It's not rocket science to spot someone who'll be good in bed! People give themselves away in all sorts of ways.

The other thing that's important to know about me is that my father cheated constantly on my mother. He's remarried three times since then and cheated on all of his other wives as well. My knee-jerk reaction to his constant infidelity was to be jealous and suspicious of men, thinking they'd all behave the same. I used to grill my boyfriends mercilessly on where they were, who they'd seen, what they were up to. It cost me a lot of relationships and clearly wasn't working. That's when I decided if all men were going to cheat on me (which is what I honestly believed at the time), I might as well get in first. I went from being my mother to my father. Even if I really liked a guy, I'd think nothing of cheating on him. I'm not like that now and loyal as they come, but this was how I ended up sleeping with three different guys in one day.

I had a boyfriend I wasn't that happy with and planned on dumping, and was already seeing another new guy on the side. Neither knew about the other. I also had an ex that I'd see on occasion and invariably end up sleeping with. I looked at my diary for one particular Saturday and realised my boyfriend would be staying over, so I'd have sex with him in the morning, I was seeing my ex for lunch, so would probably have sex with him at his place afterwards, and I was seeing the new guy for dinner that night. I actually hadn't slept with him at this point but I knew he was gagging to. It occurred to me that I could conceivably have sex with three different men on the same day and instead of thinking 'How tacky', the thought of it turned me on. It made me feel powerful and desirable. Looking back, it's also obvious I was punishing men for what my dad did to my mum. Regardless of motivation, the thought of it made me feel incredibly horny and I decided to make it happen.

THE REALITY

I woke up, as usual, to feel my boyfriend's morning erection poking me in the back. The thought that it was the first of three penises that were going to be inside me that day made me instantly wet (I told you I was a slut!). I turned around to face him and his hands were all over me instantly, feeling my breasts, heading straight between my legs. The thing about lovers you've been with a while is that they're trained. They know exactly what you like and how to touch you in the right way. My boyfriend was great in bed – that certainly wasn't the reason I was ditching him – and I was aroused and ready for him to penetrate in minutes. He loved taking me from behind so we could both watch in the mirror opposite the bed, so that's what we did. I looked at myself and thought of what I was about to do and I swear I have never looked sexier than I did in that moment. I looked and felt liberated and formidable. I could feel my boyfriend on the verge of an orgasm so I grabbed his hand and put it between my legs while he was thrusting and felt myself tip over into a strong, potent orgasm. I wondered if I'd have one with all of them as I sometimes don't orgasm with guys even if the sex is really good.

My boyfriend asked what I was up to that day and I told him I was having lunch with a girlfriend and dinner with another friend. He was a bit put out I wasn't spending the weekend with him and I think it was starting to dawn on him that I perhaps wasn't happy. But I didn't want to get into it there and then so fobbed him off and sent him on his way.

I showered and got ready to meet man No 2 for lunch and deliberately wore an outfit I knew he liked: skinny jeans, boots and a tight shirt, topped off with a push-up bra to show off some cleavage. He smiled broadly when I met him at the pub we were having lunch in and the hello kiss he gave me told me all I needed to know: if he was seeing someone it wasn't serious, so sex was definitely on the cards. We polished off a bottle of wine at lunch which made me feel even more up for it, so I suggested we go back to his and the next thing we're on the bed and he's licking me and then inside me and the thought that it was mere hours between sex with him and sex with my boyfriend made for another fierce orgasm. I'd almost told my ex at lunch what my plan was that day because I thought he'd get a kick out of it – we used to have brilliantly filthy sex together. But then I thought about how fragile the male ego is and also didn't want him to think I was a complete whore, so I kept my mouth shut.

We ended up watching a movie afterwards and drinking more wine so I didn't have time to go home before meeting the new guy that night. He'd booked a restaurant in central London and I hoped it wasn't dressy because I was wearing what I'd worn to lunch – and I hadn't had a shower! I can smell when someone's had intercourse and I was tempted not to wash to see if the new guy would notice or say anything. But you couldn't really, could you? No-one would expect that you'd just come from having sex with someone else to a date!

It was date four with him and I knew he was hoping and expecting to come back to mine after dinner. Instead of feeling sated after having had two men and two powerful orgasms earlier that day, I was hornier than ever. The whole way through dinner I felt naughty and flirted outrageously. I went to sit next to him and we shared a dessert. I was feeling him under the table and he had a stonking erection so I kissed him and whispered 'Do you want me tonight?' and he said, 'Fuck yes'. So I took him home and the second we were through the door, he started kissing me passionately. I was tempted not to wash and just go for it because I was intrigued to know if he'd tell something was up, but I bottled it at the last moment and went to the loo and washed.

When I came out, he was already on the bed naked, stroking himself. His erection was pretty impressive, I can tell you. He made love to me like a man who'd just been released from prison and hasn't had a woman in years. He was either really into me or really loved sex: hopefully both. I loved the enthusiasm and how turned on he was. When he was begging to be allowed inside me, I told him I wanted him to take me from behind so we could watch in the mirror. He didn't need persuading and for the second time that day, I watched a man enjoy my body. It was exactly as I thought it would be: incredibly liberating. There wasn't one part of me that thought what I was doing was in any way wrong or slutty or promiscuous. I still don't have any regrets and think of it as a really positive experience even if it's not a story I tell very many people. He came really quickly, understandable given the build-up, but he knew I hadn't and offered to go down on me again. I said no. Not because I didn't think I could have another orgasm but because I was absolutely exhausted with all the wine, sex and rushing around. I slept like a dead person and woke up feeling rather pleased with myself!

'I got a massage with a "happy ending"'

Erika, 25, is the beauty editor of a magazine

THE FANTASY

My best girlfriend is a successful businesswoman who travels the world first-class. She's just found out she has to spend a week in a hotel that's a converted palace in an exotic Eastern location and invites me to keep her company so she doesn't have to dine alone all the time. I've travelled with her before and it's always expenses paid, fantastic restaurants, spa treatments – the lot. I have some time due off work so eagerly accept and before I know it, I'm in first-class drinking champagne on the plane, then a driver is picking me up from the airport and taking me to the hotel, and there she is, looking polished and professional and more than a bit glam, to meet me in the foyer.

We have dinner at the hotel and are treated like royalty, which is sort of what you'd expect staying in a converted palace! We check out the spa treatments on her iPad after dinner and she books a massage for late afternoon the next day. She has to work but she encourages me to go for the half day special with all the extras. She says she's had the full treatment before and thinks I will like it, winking at me when she says this. I look quizzically at her and she says mysteriously, 'You'll see. Just say you want the full treatment when they ask you.'

I'm intrigued and looking forward to four hours of blissful pampering when I turn up to the spa. It's beautifully decorated with oils burning in the dimly lit relaxation rooms and corridors. I'm shown into a large, luxurious room which has a deep, sunken bath, a massage table and a chair for my facial. It's dark and peaceful music drifts through the speakers. I already feel relaxed.

A girl arrives and says she's going to bath and exfoliate me. She asks me to undress and then proceeds to sponge my back and wash me. I'm slightly embarrassed but she assures me that nudity is normal and nothing to be ashamed of. I get out of the bath and lie on the specially warmed stone floor beside it while she rubs an oily gritty mixture that smells like lavender all over my body. She works methodically and rhythmically, working in little circles to exfoliate all the dead skin. I close my eyes and enjoy the sensation. Unlike Western therapists, she's not shy about touching my breasts or bottom and I'm trying not to get horny . . . but not succeeding. A touch is a touch and if you've got your eyes closed and it feels good, it doesn't really matter who's doing it.

I get back into the bath to rinse it all off, then she dries me off with a big, fluffy towel, deliciously rubs moisturiser all over every part of me and invites me to lie face down on the table ready for my massage. I do as I'm told and am so relaxed my body feels welded to the table, but I'm also feeling aroused and energised. I wonder if this is what my friend meant when she winked at me: that it would produce these feelings.

I'm left on my own for about five minutes and nearly drift off to sleep when I hear the door open quietly and the next therapist coming into the room. I smell the different oils being mixed together and breathe in the relaxing scent. I wait for her to warm her hands and that first touch – always the best because you know you've got an hour of pleasure ahead of you. Except it's not a woman's hands I feel but a man's. They're too big and too firm to be female. I start, open my eyes, and half sit up to see who it is. The dishiest man I have ever seen smiles back at me. I gulp.

He's over six foot with broad shoulders and muscular arms.

His skin is olive, his teeth whiter than white and his lips are curved into a smile.

'I'm your masseur,' he says. 'I hope you don't mind that I'm a man.'

'No, God no ... I mean of course not,' I say, immediately wishing I'd put some make-up on and blow-dried my hair, though that would be a bit daft considering I'm here for a facial and massage!

The feeling of leaden limbs disappears immediately and I'm almost tense. I'm completely naked on the massage table and his hands, all oiled-up and strong, are gliding all over my body. Like the girl who bathed and scrubbed me down, they don't avoid the 'intimate' zones, but neither does he focus on them. Instead his fingers knead and pummel and relax my whole body, fingers slipping into my armpits, the crevice of my bottom, kneading the top of my thighs, so close they're almost grazing the lips of my vagina. He works silently and professionally and I relax into it. This is just the way they do things in this country, I think. Half of me is pondering why Westerners are so uptight about nudity and the other half is trying desperately hard not to get visibly turned on by what's happened.

He gets me to turn over. I'm embarrassed because he's going to know how aroused I am if he sees my eyes and he must sense this because he puts some cotton pads soaked in rose water over my eyelids ('To relax me') and a small, light facecloth over the top so the room is black. I relax again. It's better not to have eye contact and watching him work on me would make me feel even sexier. It's warm in the room but I can feel my nipples hardening and myself getting wet. His hands are suddenly massaging my breasts again and I'm mortified because my nipples are so hard. That's when he says, 'Do you want the full treatment?' and I squeak, 'Yes!' I'm desperately hoping it means what I think it means!

I'm not sure what I'm supposed to do, so I just stay where I am and do nothing as he continues massaging my breasts. Except now he's deliberately tweaking my nipples, one hand is on my breast while the other slides down my stomach and rests on my pubic bone. He says, 'Do you want me to?' and I say, 'Yes' and then his fingers are sliding between my lips and both hands are working on me down below.

He inserts two fingers inside me and I'm so wet, it makes a squelching noise but I don't care at this point. His fingers curve upward so they're stimulating the front wall of my vagina and I feel him searching around until he settles on one specific area and strokes it. I've had G-spot stimulation before, but never like this. This is the best, most intense sensation I've ever felt. With his other hand, he expertly circles my clitoris with his thumb. He's practised at stimulating women and skilfully brings me to the best orgasm I've ever had. My hips are pushing frantically up to meet his hands and I come so hard, I'm convinced I've ejaculated fluid. He knows to keep going until the very last contraction stops and then he gently removes his fingers and I hear him discreetly wash his hands in the sink.

I'm wondering what I do now but he says 'Lie back – you have half an hour of massage left to enjoy'. Have I died and gone to heaven? It feels like it. His hands are gliding all over me again, my arms, my legs, my stomach, my neck and it's the best post-orgasmic feeling ever. When he's finished, he squeezes my hand and says goodbye and I hear the door click shut, then he's gone. My facial is next and it's wonderful, however uneventful!

I walk out of my treatment room, wrapped in my robe, dazed and thinking 'Today is one of those days you are very, very happy to be alive' and I see my friend who says drily, 'Someone looks like they've enjoyed themselves'. I wink at her and say, 'You never owe me another birthday or Christmas present as long as you live. That was all of them, rolled into one.'

THE DECISION

I think every female in the world has had the hot masseur fantasy and as a beauty editor I've certainly had lots of massages! I get invited to loads of product launches and cosmetic companies know the more they spoil us, the more we'll push their products in our magazines. The launches are often overseas in stunning resorts and I've been massaged in Italy, France, Spain, Mauritius, Turkey, Singapore and Japan. Not once, sadly, has any masseur ever been anything but professional. I'm sure men get offered 'happy endings' all the time but I don't think women do. Or maybe it's because the massages I get are always in posh hotels. I suspect the more downmarket you go, the higher the chances are of sex being on offer.

This particular trip was for the launch of a new beauty serum, five-star all the way to a resort in Thailand – the home of 'happy endings', if the country's reputation is anything to go by. Perhaps I had this in the back of my mind and was more open to subtle advances. I was also incredibly randy that trip because I'd just started a relationship with my now boyfriend and we were in the hot and horny stage where you're constantly winding each other up with sex-texts and dirty pictures.

THE REALITY

There's nearly always a treatment or two thrown in on these junkets and this was no exception. Except our group was so big this time, the spa couldn't accommodate everyone at the same time. The hotel hired freelance masseuses to give some of us massages in our rooms and I was one of them. I was incredibly amorous because I'd been having phone sex with my boyfriend just before the woman turned up and because she was early I didn't have time to finish masturbating. 'Maybe she'll be hot and do it for you,' my boyfriend said, a tad hopefully, before getting off the phone.

The girl was hot, actually. She was tiny and petite, with long straight hair and a pretty smile. I can see why men go gaga for Thai girls, they're just so feminine. If you were a guy, you'd feel protective – and also you could lift her into all sorts of positions! I hasten to add at this point that I'm not gay or bisexual and have never had any desire at all to be with a woman. The fantasies I have always star men, not women.

She set up the table and told me to get undressed. I asked if I should leave my panties on and she said no, it's easier to massage the buttock cheeks, where all the tension is stored, if I'm naked. I felt a little stirring when she said that. I lay on the table and she got to work. She had tiny hands but boy, did she know how to use them! She was also using her elbows to get right into the knots and it was the perfect combination of pleasure and pain.

She asked if she could massage my breasts and my bottom. She said some Western women didn't like it but it wasn't a full body massage otherwise and that's where all the tension is. I said fine, even though I was a bit worried about what it might do to me in the state I was in!

She started massaging my breasts but in a different kind of way. It was an incredibly subtle shift in technique but noticeable – slower, less kneading, more stroking, more sensual than therapeutic. It was brilliantly done, looking back. If you were completely uninterested in any 'extras', you probably wouldn't even notice how her touch had changed from professional to slightly suggestive. But if you were feeling aroused, you'd sense it immediately.

I did (obviously!) and mentally struggled with what to do next. I wasn't absolutely convinced I'd interpreted it correctly – I was so turned on, it could have been wishful thinking! But I didn't want it to stop and, even though I was a little ashamed, I wanted more. I was practically *throbbing* down there and desperate for her hands to touch me. Anyone's hands would have been welcome at that point! But I didn't know the protocol. Was I supposed to ask if there were 'extras' like they did in movies? What if I got it wrong and she reported me and everyone heard I'd asked for a happy ending! How humiliating would that be?

I decided to do nothing at all and leave it all up to her. She got me to turn over and started massaging my bottom. Again, the touch and technique was different. Her little hands kept working downwards, focusing more on the bit where my buttocks met my upper thighs. Her fingers were getting closer and closer to my vagina and then she let her fingers quickly brush over me. I was so wet, she couldn't help but feel it. I don't know whether I did it instinctively or deliberately, probably a bit of both, but I opened my legs. It was a clear and direct signal and she got it instantly.

'Do you want an extra?', she said, her fingers now trailing provocatively close. *My God, they really do say things like that, it's not just the movies,* was my first thought. Then I panicked about the cost of the extra being put on the bill and the organisers seeing it and knowing what it was. I asked her how much and if I could pay in cash and she said yes, of course. (It was the equivalent of £5!) I said, 'Yes please then', totally embarrassed. The conversation broke the mood a bit and I very nearly told her I'd changed my mind, but again, she was perceptive. She didn't dive straight down there but went back to massaging my breasts and my bottom and by the time her hands slid down, I was practically humping the table.

It was weird when she finally touched me properly. First up, because it was a woman doing it and her hands were so small. Secondly, I was lying face down and the angle wasn't what I was used to. But she knew what she was doing and she was dextrous: it felt like she had about five hands! Fingers slid inside me, others slid between my lips, a thumb worked on my clitoris, another finger slid inside my bottom. The combination was stupendously arousing and I came in under a minute but when I did orgasm, it seemed to go on and on and on.

The second I'd come I was overwhelmed with shame and humiliation. I honestly didn't know how I was going to look her in the eyes. I worried it meant I was secretly gay; I worried it counted as cheating on my boyfriend; I worried she'd tell someone and somehow the other girls on the trip would find out. A billion anxious thoughts poured into the space that had been previously filled with lustful thoughts. It was awful!

The girl put towels on my back to wipe off the oil and I tried to pull myself together. I decided to pretend nothing had happened so I got up off the table the second she finished and was into my robe so fast, it wasn't funny. I hovered in the bedroom while she packed everything up under the guise of finding my wallet. She said 'I am going now', so I came out and gave her twice what she'd quoted for the extra, avoided meeting her eyes and practically pushed her out the door. Once she'd gone I went and had the hottest, longest shower in the world to cleanse myself of the whole thing. It took me about two days to reconcile myself with what I'd done and I never did tell my boyfriend. But then I started to see it for what it was: something incredibly sexy that I could use to masturbate to forever. It's my little secret: a very dirty one that never fails to get me hot.

'I let my lover tie me up and spank me'

Judy, 42, is a university lecturer

THE FANTASY

They'd booked in earlier that afternoon and burst into the lobby of the country hotel laughing too loudly, wobbly and unstable, slightly drunk on wine and each other. The manager, nonetheless, likes them. Exuberant, over-excited, like two young children about to cut the cake for their birthday party, you can't help but be infected by their enthusiasm. He serves them dinner, then coffee, in the front room by the fire. An elderly couple, also guests, play chess a few feet away but these two, in their own world, settle in as though the room is theirs alone.

They order red wine, then cognac, consequently caring even less about the other people. The manager watches, shocked but oddly aroused (at his age!) as the man's hand slides up the woman's thigh, disappearing under her dress, which is hiked high, her legs carelessly a little too open. He watches the man whisper something into her ear then his mouth hover over her neck as if considering whether to kiss or bite. They are doing nothing really, just playing. But simply looking at them makes him feel things he hasn't in years. Her eyes rarely stray from his mouth and she keeps putting her fingers into her own. It is a curiously innocent, childlike gesture that becomes unbearably erotic when she does it. He thinks it is the eye contact between them that does it: it is electric. The man's are on an eternal journey, travelling lazily over her neck, breasts, shoulders, legs. His eyes burn into her flesh, lifting the hairs on her skin, like he is touching her everywhere she feels his gaze. The manager offers them more cognac but instead they wrap their hands around two (more) enormous glasses of red wine, asking, 'Is it OK to take them to the room?' Reluctantly, he agrees. He wants to watch them more.

Once inside their room, the man takes both glasses and puts them down on the table. It's done decisively: drinking time is over for the time being. She starts to walk towards the bed but he pulls her back and slams her against the wall, pins her arms above her head and kisses her deeply, fully, biting a little. Then he draws back and with one hand, roughly pulls her dress down over one shoulder, revealing a bare breast, nipple hard and begging him to lick. The mood has switched rapidly from playful to dangerously sexually-charged. She looks at him, lips parted, breathing hard, and bats her eyelashes but there's insolence and sarcasm in the look she's giving him, like she's daring him to take control. His eyes narrow slightly and he accepts her unspoken challenge.

He starts by hungrily licking and biting her breasts, tongue swirling around her nipples. One hand still pins her against the wall, stopping her from moving. Not that she wants to be anywhere but there. There is nowhere else, ever, that she wants to be. Let real life continue without them. His hand runs over the curves of her body, sliding over the fabric of the dress. He slides it between her legs, still keeping the fabric between their flesh. She is panting, sliding down the wall with wanting him. But he won't touch her properly, won't put his fingers inside or play with her clitoris which is what she wants so, so badly. Nothing is guaranteed with sex with him. Sometimes he just teases her and leaves her in a state of desperate arousal. Other times he makes her climax so many times that she has to beg him to stop.

Abruptly, he lets her go and drags her by the arm to the bed.

She can't bear being clothed and begs him to remove her dress. She could do it herself but knows he is the boss and she likes being in his thrall, obeying him. She's wearing a new push-up bra and G-string and she wants him to see. He orders her to stand still and not move, then he removes her dress, slowly, agonisingly slowly, button by button. It takes an eternity for him to finish and he won't kiss her the whole time, just looks into her eyes, commanding her to be still or he will stop completely. The dress is finally open and then he removes it swiftly, groaning when he sees how beautiful she looks in her underwear.

He sits on the bed and orders her to lie across his lap. She obeys, positioning herself so her bare bottom lies over his crotch. This is a new game for them but they've done it once before. She is so excited about what's about to happen, she feels herself melt with anticipation. He moans when he hears her groan and starts stroking her buttock cheeks with his fingers. She can feel his erection straining through his jeans.

She is close to orgasm already, but he won't start until she's dripping with desire. He deftly removes the G-string and at last his fingers stroke her, feeling the lovely wetness and touching her clitoris which is erect with longing and straining towards him. She feels the sting of his first slap and it nearly sends her over the edge because one of his hands continues to stroke her while the other slaps her buttock cheek. The combination of the gentle but relentless stroking with the short, sharp stabs of pain feels exquisite. The room fades and her world shrinks to just his hands and how they are making her feel.

He ups the pace and the pain level. The spanks become more frequent, harder and he starts to use both hands. One hand dispenses the slap, making her cheeks burn, redden and tingle; the other massages before the pain has a chance to disappear. She wriggles lasciviously. She feels prurient but humiliated at the same time, which is why she loves it. It's forbidden for lovers to hurt each other. It's unacceptable. But pain is one of the strongest sensations she feels and it doesn't diminish, even once she's accustomed to it. His gentle touching of her, no matter how delicious, is eventually screened out by her subconscious. Pain stays in her awareness and that's why she loves it. She is totally 100% present with him when he spanks her.

'Come for me baby, let go,' he whispers to her and she needs no further encouragement. The contractions are fierce and so powerful, she loses consciousness as she surrenders herself to them – and him – completely.

THE DECISION

My fantasies are always in the third person. I think it's because I used to feel ashamed of them. If I pretend it's not me in the fantasy, I can relax and enjoy them without feeling judged. I am a female in her early 40s – the age when many women often manage to rid themselves of the burdens of their past. For me it is the burden of a strict upbringing, parents who made me feel bad for feeling sexual and the awful guilt that comes from being educated in a Catholic school. There, even thinking about something as innocent as touching yourself because it felt nice, is a sin.

I struggled with my sexuality because of these things and was a virgin until 32. But then I met a man who was patient with me and gradually I learnt that sex is a way to express love and desire and something to be embraced, not denied.

I suspect because sex was something 'bad' that I wasn't supposed to want, my fantasies have always included me being dominated by a man. It effectively removes any guilt if you have no choice in the matter. You have no option but to enjoy it. When I finally trusted someone sexually for the first time, I felt brave enough to confide my fantasies to my partner. He was shocked at first, given how shy I was with him initially, but he understood where they came from and didn't judge me for having them. Far from it, he would ask me to describe my fantasies during sex and it made sex even better when I did.

THE REALITY

The first time he spanked me it wasn't planned, though I guess it was inevitable given I'd 'talk dirty' to him about how much I wanted it. We were in our bedroom and he was taking me from behind, when he suddenly reached over and grabbed my hairbrush and used the back of it to hit me on my bottom while he was inside me. It was so unexpected, I jumped and he dropped the hairbrush, immediately pulled out and started apologising. I was saying 'No, no, no, do it again, I loved it,' so he did.

Something inside me snapped and the 'bad girl' who had been locked inside this 'good girl' came out with a vengeance. I felt liberated and asked him to hit me harder and harder. I could feel him swelling inside me and then him coming like it was never ending. It was the hardest he'd ever thrust and the hardest he'd ever come and I loved that I'd made that happen. It made me feel powerful.

Once he stopped, I asked him to put the hairbrush handle inside me and push it in and out while spanking me with his hands. He made me kneel on all fours on the floor (this was part of another fantasy I'd told him about) and he knelt behind me while he did as I asked. I felt so wet and so aroused, the hairbrush handle didn't feel enough, so he took it out and shoved three fingers inside me, all the while spanking my ass and I had the most intense orgasm I have ever had.

It's still our favourite thing to do sexually together, though we vary it. Sometimes, I'll clamp a sizeable vibrator between the top of my thighs while he spanks me – it feels wonderful. Other times he blindfolds me. I like that: it feeds into the 'slave' mentality which turns me on so much. Remove sight and you remove free will.

I haven't told a soul about this darker side of me. My friends still see me as the sweet, naïve innocent I was. My partner adores me even more for it and unlike our other couple friends, the quality and frequency of our sex is increasing over time, not decreasing. I didn't start having sex until I was 32. I've got a lot of catching up to do!

'Going to a swinger's club
saved my marriage'

Nicky, 43, works in PR

THE FANTASY

Applications to join the world's most exclusive sex club are closely vetted. Membership is restricted to young, attractive, charismatic couples or decadent, hedonist, exciting single girls who must first meet strict entry criteria. If you aren't gorgeous, loaded or well connected, don't apply. If you're hot and bi-curious, go to the top of the list. The identity of its members is closely guarded and every party starts with members wearing masks. It's a personal decision to remove it and reveal your true identity as the party gets into full swing. Parties take place in New York penthouses, on board yachts moored in St Tropez and in mysterious mansions in the countryside of Britain. Once inside, members stroll their luxurious surrounds clad in Agent Provocateur underwear and Manolo Blahnik heels, peer into Chanel compacts to reapply gloss smudged from kissing other long-legged beauties and sip champagne from elegant flutes, one eye on the arty erotica projected on state-of-the-art television screens.

It's taken me years to get an invitation but the longed for email finally plops into my inbox. I read it with relish and am even happier to see the next party is not only that weekend but in a fantastic venue I have been to before. It's a warehouse apartment owned by a very well-known and wealthy celebrity. I went there for the launch of one of my friend's fashion labels. It's enormous and spectacularly decorated: huge black and white floor-to-ceiling erotic photographs, loads of glass and stainless steel light fittings. The main living area is all white but all the rooms that lead off it have a different vibrant colour theme. I already know what I'm going to wear because a little birdie told me my application was going to be accepted, so I splashed out on a beautiful velvet corset in a deep purple colour. I will team it with an equally exquisite matching bra and panty set with the same deep purple lace, edged with a gorgeous hot pink. I have sheer hold-up stockings, a velvet choker to wear around my neck and the obligatory skyscraper metallic heels.

I have many lovers but I'm going to the party solo. The fact I will know no-one excites me. My mask is black and I intend to wear it all night. I have no interest in revealing my identity at any point. I want to do lots of very, very naughty things at this party and anonymity is crucial.

When I arrive, I press the buzzer and someone asks me the password. I tell them, push the door and take the lift up to the penthouse. It's 10pm and the party is just getting started. I take a flute of champagne from a waiter's tray and look around me, taking it all in. There are about 100 people in the room. All have masks on, though some brave people have opted for the hand-held version, so you get flashes of their faces because they forget to hold the mask closely all of the time. There are roughly twice as many women to men, but this ratio is deliberate because the club is famous for girl-on-girl. I love watching women make love to each other and already there are women kissing each other everywhere.

The standard of beauty is high: most of the girls look like models but in varying sizes. There are slim girls, voluptuous girls, tall girls, cute girls – the men here are all straight and they are in heaven watching them. Nearly everyone is dressed in underwear and skimpy nothings but there's one girl in a full PVC catsuit with the best body I have ever seen. I mentally earmark her for later. Some of the men have jeans on with naked chests. It's a hot look, especially when you've got bodies like they have. Some of the older men look moneyed: their tans, their suits, their manicured hands and buffed, expensive shoes speak volumes.

The organiser spots me and comes over, realising I am a new member. She explains that there are different areas set aside for different activities. There's a huge round ottoman in the middle of the room and this is the group sex area. Languishing on it are beautiful women, kissing and feeling each other's breasts. One girl, astonishingly pretty, is completely naked. Another girl is lying between her legs, licking her, while another kisses her and a third girl plays with her nipples. It's so erotic, I can hardly tear myself away but the organiser wants to show me more.

She walks me into several different rooms, all with huge TV screens, all playing beautifully-shot erotica. Some films have a BDSM theme (that is, Bondage, Discipline, Sadism, Masochism), others two girls, two men, all possible combinations and sex styles: there's something to suit everyone and it's all tasteful. She explains that some people like the comfort of a bed. People can come into any of these bedrooms and do what they like. Other guests are free to wander in and watch or join in if they like what they see. There's a beautiful man being fellated by a woman while another woman bites his neck. On another bed, a man is spanking a woman with a riding crop. There's a group of four or five people writhing on the bed next to that one. It's hard to tell which limbs belong to whom. They've formed a chain of sucking and fucking and fondling. I want to join in but there's more to see.

The other area is for 'closed' swinging: people who want to be able to do what they like but in private. The doors are lockable and totally private. I can't see any fun in this but the woman explains the club has to cater for people who aren't confident sexually or who get jealous watching their partners have sex with others. We move into the dungeon area where a girl is trussed up and being whipped by a man who looks like he knows what he is doing. He whips her and then caresses the area he's just licked with the whip with his hand. She's begging for more and for him to go harder. A large group are standing watching. All the sex is authentic and so unlike the pathetic performances you see on porn. These are real people who love sex and love either watching or being watched. There's a world of difference. The woman shows me the Jacuzzi and the heated swimming pool, where the condoms, showers and towels are. There's every kind of food you could possibly want and staff to fix you any cocktail you could possibly imagine.

She leaves me and I wander around and feast my eyes on couples, threesomes, foursomes and moresomes. I'm in a high state of arousal. As I walk through the crowd, both women and men touch me and I stop to kiss the ones I really fancy. One guy begs me to let him eat me, so I pull my panties to one side and he gets on his knees right there and then and his tongue feels amazing. I spread my legs wide and some people come to watch and admire. It feels great knowing I am being turned on and am also turning others on.

I wander into the bedroom area and choose a group of people to join. I can't tell who is licking me, touching me, kissing my body. I feel fingers inside me, a vibrator is inserted into my bottom, strangers' hands caress me, someone sticks their fingers in my mouth, then a girl sits on my face while I lick her to orgasm, next there's a penis in my mouth. It's all done slowly and sensually and every touch and feeling is unbelievably hot. I come again and again and don't want it ever to stop. Best of all, I know it doesn't matter that tonight has to end because now I'm a member, there will always be another time, another party, another group of people to watch and to watch me. I expected it to be amazing, but it's surpassed even my high expectations.

THE DECISION

I'd been married for 23 years and my husband was the only man I'd ever slept with. We were one of those couples who met in high school and never broke up. We didn't even have a break! People didn't know whether to envy us or pity us and constantly asked whether we felt ripped off that we'd never slept with anyone else but each other. But we never did feel like that. We had good sex together and loved each other desperately and brought up two great kids.

But after they grew up and left home, something changed. We started arguing when we'd never argued before. Everything my husband did started to annoy me and vice versa. We'd never slept apart before but our arguments became so vicious, he started sleeping in the spare room. The whole thing was strange and confusing and came out of nowhere and nearly knocked the whole marriage over. We took ourselves off to get help and the counsellor was brilliant. She said it was all to do with the kids moving out, us having more time to spend together and instead of doing new things, we went back to doing what we'd done before kids. There was no excitement or newness in our life. We had nothing to look forward to and, for the first time, had started to feel trapped and suffocated. It made sense and we were closer than ever after the therapy.

The therapist suggested we try to inject as many new experiences into our lives as possible so we did. The more new things we tried, the better we felt. We felt alive again – except in the bedroom. If we were being brutally honest, sex hadn't been particularly exciting for the last ten years. It was OK in that we both had orgasms but it was only one step up from masturbating. We decided our sex life needed a boost as well so bought some good sex books and flicked through them. We tried a few things like tying each other up, role play and sharing fantasies – and I found out that one of my husband's fantasises was swinging. I had no idea but far from being turned off or offended by it, I was intrigued. We started looking on swinging websites, and just looking at the pictures and reading the testimonies got us hotter than we had ever been. We did this for a few months but we both wanted to take it further. Twenty-three years into our marriage, both of us having never slept with anyone other than each other, we made the decision to try swinging.

THE REALITY

Back in the sex-mad 70s, couples who fancied a spot of 'swapping' or swinging simply invited all the neighbours over, served large martinis along with the fondue and cheese-and-pineapple canapés and pooled the car keys. Sadly, this isn't an option in today's more moral climate. We discovered swingers meet through personal ads, via the internet, or attend swingers' parties or clubs.

There are lots of clubs to choose from, offering a myriad of experiences. 'Elitist' sex clubs attract the beautiful and rich. I fantasise about going to a club like that but know I'd never get in at my age (or weight!).

The club we chose was impressive though. It sprawled across 6000 square feet of disused warehouse space and boasted a dance floor, with poles and a laser light show, that's three times the size of most London nightclubs. There were several inside and outside bars, five Jacuzzis, a steam room and sauna, a massage area and six themed 'playrooms' – private and lockable for those interested in privacy or very public for those who prefer to play in front of an appreciative audience. There was a dungeon complete with stocks, a whipping bench, a St Andrew's cross (with restraining points for ankles, wrist and waist so willing victims could be tethered spread-eagled) and – *de rigueur* for any self-respecting swinger's club – a sex swing.

Sure, the floor was sticky and the cheap vinyl sofas and stools had more than a smattering of cigarette burns, but they weren't immediately apparent in the deliberately dark lighting. The best thing about it was that the management didn't care what age, class, colour, size or shape its members were. Anyone and everyone was welcome to join. The average member was between 40 and 60, a little overweight, and medium-level attractive. Women wore everything from corsets teamed with stockings, suspenders and thigh-high boots, to PVC mini-dresses, French Maid get-ups and 'naughty nurse' uniforms or just a G-string and nothing else. We thought we'd feel comfortable there because rather than not feel good enough, we felt like we would actually fall into the 'most attractive' category. Things like that are important when you're inexperienced with sex, like we were.

We'd called the club before we went there because we wanted to check it was OK to just come and hang out and watch rather than participate. They said sure and no-one would be pushed into doing anything they didn't like. We were both incredibly excited the first time we went and keen to try everything but we'd read a lot about it and knew we needed to go and take it really slowly and see how it affected us emotionally rather than dive right in. We'd dressed up for it and both looked nice but neither of us had revealing clothes on that first time. We turned up looking like we'd just come from church, looking back, but everyone was so nice to us and really friendly. It was early when we arrived and there weren't that many people there – it was just like being in a nightclub or party to start with. The owners were amazingly helpful and showed us around and it was exactly what we'd imagined. We held hands tightly the whole time and I was so glad we'd decided the first visit was just to watch because I was too nervous to do anything else.

Eventually the place got packed and people were stripping off and kissing each other and having sex – so much seemed to be happening everywhere. We wandered around watching everyone and it was such an eye opener but a little overwhelming. We'd had enough after about two hours and left but we were bubbling with excitement when we got home and had the best sex ever. There were no negatives: neither of us felt jealous or threatened. We just felt energised and ready to explore further.

The second time we went, we had sex with each other while others watched. It felt really odd to start with but then it felt good to be admired. Again, we went home after that and waited to see if either of us felt anything that might threaten our marriage – we'd worked hard to fix our previous problems and there was no way we were going to jeopardise our relationship now. We were absolutely fine and raring to go the following weekend, and that was when we both started having sex with other people. We both kissed other people to start with, while the other one watched. I did have a bit of a wobble watching my husband kiss another woman. It felt too intimate and I still don't like him kissing anyone. He doesn't mind me doing it but he respects my wish that he doesn't do it.

Watching my husband feel another woman's breasts and then go down on her didn't faze me at all. I loved watching how he was getting off on it. It turned me on seeing him experience pleasure and give pleasure, so I gave him permission to have intercourse (with a condom and always with a condom) and he did. He came in about one minute flat but given that was the first time he'd ever had sex with anyone but me and the sexy environment we were in, I figured that was pretty normal!

When it was my turn, I kept watching my husband out of the corner of my eye to be sure he was fine with it. But I could tell he didn't have a problem at all. He said, if anything, he preferred and still prefers watching me having sex with other men than actually having sex with other women. He says it makes him feel like the luckiest man alive to have a wife other men are desperate to sleep with. The guy's penis was bigger than my husband's and much harder so I loved having sex with him but the guy didn't last long (which was probably not a bad thing given my husband hadn't with his woman). We were emotionally and physically exhausted after our first time and felt the need to be alone and close, so took ourselves home and snuggled up and fell asleep in each other's arms.

That was two years ago and we've been swinging regulars ever since. We've tried a few different clubs over the years but we always end up coming back to the original one. We feel safe there, we know people and it's a really good social scene. We have learnt not to tell non-swingers though. We don't feel ashamed or have anything to hide: it's not our hang-up but other people's. We confessed to our closest couple friends and they pretty much ignored us after that. I think it's because the husband looked a little too interested and the wife felt threatened. But I still have nothing but good things to say about swinging. If you approach it the right way, like we did, it can rejuvenate the most tired of sex lives. It's not for everyone, obviously, but it works for us!

'I bedded the man of my dreams and it turned into a nightmare'

Ella, 22, works in advertising

THE FANTASY

It's my birthday and my hot, sexy boss tells me he has a present for me. It's Friday and the rest of the office is going out to lunch and not expected back for a while. I was invited but my boss told me he needed me to assist him on an urgent, last minute project he was working on. I don't mind because I fancy the pants off him and any time in private, just him and me, is fine by me.

We have been playing a little game all morning. I give him glimpses of parts of me he shouldn't see and he pretends not to notice. I undo extra buttons on my top before I go into his office and I lean over and fuss about tidying things on his desk, making sure my breasts – looking good enough to eat in a push-up bra – are right under his nose. Another time, I bring coffee in on a tray and bend over right in front of his desk so he can see I'm wearing stockings and suspenders under my dress and no panties. I spend ages moving things from the tray to the coffee table and can feel him staring, transfixed by what's on display. Nothing is ever said. We behave properly at all times and neither acknowledges our peek-a-boo sex game.

He calls me into his office once everyone has left for lunch and tells me to bring my laptop to take notes. I do as he says but when I walk inside, there's an open bottle of champagne there, two glasses and a beautifully wrapped gift. I hear him shut and lock the door behind me and my tummy flips. I say, 'You shouldn't have' and he says 'Happy Birthday!' and gives me a kiss on the cheek. He pours one glass of champagne only, which is odd, then he sits on his sofa and invites me to sit next to him. I move to pour myself a glass also, thinking he's being rude, but he says, 'We'll only need one glass'. He tells me to tip my head back, then takes a swig of champagne and his mouth covers mine. I don't expect this: we've never touched, let alone kissed! The combination of the heat from his lips and the chilled champagne trickling into my mouth is heaven. I gulp it down greedily and then devour the mouth I've been longing to kiss for years. He asks if I want more and I say yes, meaning I want more kissing, but he swallows more champagne and gives me another effervescent kiss. His mouth moves down my neck and finally, finally I feel his hands cupping my breasts and he kisses the top of them, moaning. His thumbs slip inside my bra, moving over my nipples and they go hard immediately. He pulls back, his breathing ragged, and says, 'Present time!'

But he makes no move to get up to retrieve my present which is on the table across the room, so I stand up to get it. 'No,' he says. 'Not like that. On your hands and knees.' I know he wants me to do this because I have a skirt on and he's seen I have my stockings and suspenders on and no panties. I do as I'm told, loving his domination, and I can feel how wet I am. He must see how wet I am when I crawl over to get my present, so I crawl back the other way so he can see my breasts spilling over my bra and jiggling away.

I get back on the sofa and undo my present. It's a beautiful silver vibrator and it has diamonds on it. 'They're real,' he says and takes it from me and switches it on. Then he puts the vibrator between my legs and lets it buzz against my clitoris. 'Do you like that?' he says. I nod, not able to speak I'm so excited by what's happening.

He tells me to move over to the desk and bend over it. I do as he says and I feel him pull up my skirt to expose my bottom and he groans and tells me how beautiful I look. His fingers expertly circle my clitoris and I am dripping with desire. He pushes his fingers inside me and I push back against them, desperate to have him inside me. There's a pause and I hear him unzip himself and then there's a rock-hard penis pressing against the opening to my vagina, asking to be allowed inside. His lips are against my ear and he says, 'Do you want this?' and I pant 'More than anything' and then he's moving inside me and reaching places previous lovers never have. I feel the vibrator on my clitoris and nipples and his hot, urgent mouth on my neck and back and I let him possess me, body and soul, until we both erupt into fiery orgasms that last forever.

THE DECISION

I was 17 when I got a job as the PA to a hotshot advertising executive. He was in his early 30s, powerful, married and arrogant: a lethal combination for a naïve girl in her first ever paying job. Of course I fell for him. He was gruff and famously rude to people but he was always nice to me and I felt special, like he'd singled me out to be someone he behaved differently with. I had boyfriends during that time but none of the relationships worked out because I was besotted with my boss. It was a complete and utter cliché and it must have been so obvious to anyone looking in. I'd spend half my day staring at him and was at his total beck and call. I wish one of the older women had had the foresight to see what was going on and warn me or give me some advice on how to handle my feelings. But no-one did. I didn't tell my parents and my friends just thought it was amusing.

I'd imagine all sorts of scenarios for him and I – but all had two themes. One was him declaring undying love. The other was him locking the door to his office and ravishing me. I was young but I'd had sex with a long-term boyfriend and slept with two other guys who I had two/three month flings with during the time I worked for him. I liked sex and figured my boss would be far better in bed than guys my own age. He seemed masterful and I imagined him taking charge in bed. He'd flirt with me when no-one else was around and I knew he fancied me because I'd catch him staring at my legs or my breasts when he thought he could get away with it.

I knew he was having problems at home because he started closing the door when his wife was on the phone and it was clear they were arguing. I didn't dare hope they'd split but the 'gossips' soon got wind of his separation. He was withdrawn and even less communicative than usual for a few months but then he started confiding in me and we'd have long chats about how he felt about his separation and how the kids were coping. Finally – three years after I first took the job – he asked me to dinner. It was by far and away the best moment of my entire life. I said yes and we made a date for Saturday night.

THE REALITY

Dinner was awkward. I'd imagined us snuggling up and kissing and probably not eating much, but the restaurant he chose was quite formal and we sat opposite each other. At work, we talked easily but conversation was a bit stilted out of that environment. It didn't concern me too much, I figured we were both a bit edgy: him because he was rusty at 'first dates' and me because I was in awe of him.

We went back to my place afterwards for 'one for the road' (why doesn't anyone say 'Do you want to come back to mine for sex?', it would be a lot more honest!) and in the cab we kissed for the first time. I don't think I have ever been more disappointed in my life! I'd imagined that moment – the first time our lips touched

– every single day for years but never had I imagined it to be sloppy and deeply unpleasant. It was the worst kiss I had ever had. He literally closed his eyes and smacked his lips hard against mine and shoved his tongue inside my mouth immediately – it was stiff as a board and made me gag! It was too wet as well. I felt like he was spitting in my mouth rather than kissing me. Quite apart from his abysmal technique, it *felt* wrong. He didn't taste or smell the way I thought he would. I was flooded with confusion and nothing was going the way I thought it would.

When we got back to mine, I fixed us some drinks and sat down on the sofa. He jumped on me immediately and grabbed my breasts really roughly and started kissing and licking my neck. Who licks people's necks? I think he thought it was really sexy but my breasts just hurt and I just wanted to wipe my neck clean of his saliva. I told him to slow down and that there was no rush and thought, *Christ, you're way older and yet I'm telling you what to do and how to behave?* He stopped and looked a bit put out but seemed OK chatting for a bit. No-one told him what to do at work and yet here I was, telling him what to do sexually. My image of him was fast transforming from silent and sexy to lacking in communication skills and the ability to read people.

He suggested we move into the bedroom ten minutes later. I should have said no and stopped it right there and then but I didn't know how to. Instead, I gritted my teeth, crossed my fingers and hoped for the best. Not quite how I imagined I'd feel at this point! Looking back, it was shocking the way he assumed sex was on the agenda, especially given how young I was.

Once we were in there, he started taking off his clothes. He didn't ask if that was OK or attempt to undress me sexily, he just took off his shirt and then folded it neatly and put it on a chair. Then he sat on the edge of the bed and took off his shoes and socks and arranged them so they were perfectly straight under the chair. Then he took off his jeans and folded them and put them on top of his shirt, then changed his mind and put them underneath the shirt, and then he stood there in his pants, waiting for me to do the same. I'm not sure what was worse: the old man prissy way he undressed – which was totally at odds with his public persona – or what it revealed. In clothes, his body looked quite good. Naked, he was about as appealing as his kissing technique. His skin was pale and pasty and his posture was shocking. His shoulders sloped and slumped forward and he made no attempt to suck in his pot belly which bulged over the top of his pants. He had love handles, no real bum to speak of and skinny legs. No muscle tone anywhere. I'd only seen him in a suit or shirt and trousers and believe me, it was a real shock to the fantasy I'd had for the past few years.

There was even more bad news. He had on tight-fitting boxers and there was the tiniest bulge where his testicles and penis were meant to be. I know some men grow loads when erect but from what I could tell, he *was* erect. There was an erection the size of a marker pen nestling in those boxers – and I had zero desire to go anywhere near it.

I had two choices at this point: go through with it out of politeness or call it quits there and then. I wanted to call it quits, make him disappear and crawl into my bed and nurse my poor, dashed dreams. But this guy was my boss and I got the distinct impression that if I didn't follow through, at worst I'd get the sack, at best the office wasn't going to be a pleasant place for me. He had a big ego so I played it safe, however shocking that sounds. All desire for him had disappeared and I tolerated his clumsy efforts to please me rather than enjoyed them. He took off my clothes, grabbed at my breasts again and tried to put his fingers inside me without any thought as to whether I was aroused or not. He got a condom from his jean pocket and put it on his tiny penis and when he penetrated, I couldn't feel a thing. We had sex missionary style and it was over in about one minute.

The most extraordinary thing of all was that he was pleased

with himself afterwards. I lay there on the bed feeling used and disgusted with myself for having gone through with it. He was suddenly up for chatting and wanting to cuddle and said, 'That was great wasn't it!' I didn't know what to say, so just smiled. He was so clueless about reading emotion, he took it as a yes.

I went into work on Monday and avoided eye contact but he summoned me into his office and told me that, regretfully, he didn't feel able to have a relationship with me because it was too soon after him separating from his wife and he thought it would send a 'bad message' to the staff if he was dating his PA. I was ecstatic but played the part of being wounded. I looked for another job immediately and left about two months later. That was a year ago. It taught me a valuable lesson: I will never again obsess about someone when it's based on nothing but fantasy and projection. The other thing I will never do again is have sex when I don't want to. I'm still furious at myself for that.

'My friend and I swapped boyfriends for a day of sex'

Lauren, 25, works in the media

THE FANTASY

My boyfriend is an architect and he's working on a project just near where I work. I decide to go and visit him and take him some lunch because he's been working so hard. I work at a fashion house and am wearing a short mini-dress which is very retro, I've got my hair piled up in a 60s style and am wearing high wedges. I've got great legs that are still tanned from summer. When I approach the site, the workmen stop what they're doing and whistle and check me out. I smile at them and know they're going to be mighty embarrassed when they realise they're wolf-whistling their boss's girlfriend.

My boyfriend emerges to see what all the fuss is about and lets out a long whistle himself, then comes over and kisses me. The workmen realise who I am but they're far from repentant and one says cheekily, 'You lucky bastard mate. She's gorgeous'. My boyfriend agrees I am indeed and says, 'She's not bad in the sack either' which is really cheeky. They all look interested to know more details but my boyfriend instead grabs me by the hand and takes me into his little office on site. Once inside, his hands slide straight up my dress and roam all over my body. My dress is hiked right up around my waist and I tell him to stop it because the guys working just outside can see everything. He's locked the office door but there's a large window and no blind. He ignores me and starts kissing me and I get that he wants to put on a show for them – and I decide I don't mind at all.

I'm facing the workmen and my boyfriend is facing me. He's kissing me and feeling me up through my dress and asking me all the time, 'What's happening. Have they seen? Are they watching us?' There are three guys out there and I can see they've definitely clocked what's going on but are trying not to look too obviously. This suits me fine. I would have bottled it had they walked over and stared in. This is perfect.

I tell my boyfriend they're watching but pretending not to and he says, 'Great' and makes me put my arms in the air then lifts my dress up and over my head so I'm standing there in my underwear and wedges. He reaches up and takes the clip out of my hair and it tumbles down around my shoulders. The guys outside have turned to face us, moving a little closer so they can see better, but are still pretending to work. They have little work-men shorts on and tool belts around their waists so I can't see if they have erections but if I had to bet a million pounds they were all hard, I reckon I'd be mighty rich right now.

My boyfriend lifts me up onto the workbench. He's kissing me and going absolutely crazy. I know this has been a fantasy of his forever and I'm happy to make him happy. I don't mind: I love to be watched and admired. He leaves on my bra because it hikes my breasts right up and makes them look even fuller than usual but he slides off my panties and then unzips himself and he's harder than I've ever seen him. He licks his fingers and then fingers me, to make sure I'm ready for him, and then he's fucking me. The guys don't come any closer, but they stop working and stand and watch us from a distance. The hottest one looks directly into my eyes as my boyfriend pumps furiously and I see the lust and longing written over his face. He wishes he was doing what my boyfriend is doing, and knowing he wants me so badly launches me into a fantastic orgasm. I am practically convulsing and my boyfriend comes too, making far too much noise.

The second we've both orgasmed, it's like we suddenly see sense. I quickly get dressed and my boyfriend zips himself up and apologises, worrying he took everything too far. I look outside and the men have disappeared so I decide to make a run for it while the coast is clear, kiss my boyfriend goodbye and get the hell out of there. I get back to the office and my workmate asks why I took my hair out and I tell her I just fancied it down again. She looks a bit suss but there's no way I'm telling her I just put on a sex show for my boyfriend's workmates!

THE DECISION

It was a year ago, I was 24 and having the time of my life just hanging out with friends and sleeping with different guys and not taking life too seriously. I felt young and like anything was possible and that I had all the time in the world to grow up. My parents are quite alternative, 'hippy' types I guess, and I grew up in a permissive household where sex was openly discussed and not hidden away. I inherited my parents' high sex drive and am attractive so sex has always been freely available.

My best friend and I ended up dating two guys who were also friends. We were about three months into our relationships and all got on famously. We were always mucking about and dancing with each other's boyfriends and flirting, though in an affectionate rather than sexual way. There wasn't any forethought to us swapping partners, it just happened.

We'd been on the beach one Saturday but it was too hot, so we moved on to a ritzy bar in our favourite hotel which was way too expensive for us but we'd go there now and then for a treat. My boyfriend and I were mucking about kissing and feeling turned on, so I tried talking him into renting a room at the hotel so we could have sex. My friend overheard and said she wanted to do the same and then we looked at each other and said to our boyfriends, 'We don't need two rooms, get one room'. Our reasoning at the time was that we could afford a much better room then but I think we were all feeling in the mood to do something naughty. Our boyfriends agreed it made sense and, luckily, the guy behind the desk knew us all so he gave us the penthouse suite for the price of a superior room if we were out by 8pm that night. That gave us four hours to play.

THE REALITY

The penthouse was stunning: it had a private outside swimming pool, Jacuzzi, sauna, an enormous bed and a great sound system. We sent the boys out to get more beers and put our bikinis on and went in the pool. When the guys came back it was party time. We'd already taken our tops off so we could sunbathe without getting marks and the guys were used to seeing our breasts anyway. But then I took my knickers off and held them up and said whoever catches these gets a kiss. So I guess I started it all!

The guys looked at each other to see what I meant exactly by this and I winked at my friend and she winked back, so I knew it was cool to kiss her boyfriend. I threw them at her guy and he caught them and said, 'You have to kiss me now', so he came over and knelt down by the edge and gave me a kiss that wasn't full on but wasn't just friendly either. Then my friend said, 'Hey, if she's kissing him, I'm kissing you,' and threw her bikini bottoms at my boyfriend, so he came over and they had a little kiss as well.

The guys wanted to go into the Jacuzzi so we ran across, only to be joined by our two naked boyfriends seconds later. You couldn't see under the water but the Jacuzzi wasn't that big and pretty cosy with four people in it. I was suddenly really hot for my friend's guy. My friend was leaning back onto his chest and I could see his hands reached around her, playing with her breasts under the bubbling water, but he was looking at me as he was doing it. The mood had definitely shifted. You could see the boys were well up for swapping partners and taking it further but too scared to suggest it.

I moved over so I was next to my friend and asked what she thought, in a whisper: should we sleep with each other's boyfriend? She laughed and said why not. She'd always fancied my man and I'd always fancied hers.

She was exactly like me with her attitude to sex. We both saw it as fun and didn't complicate it with feelings and emotions. None of us were in love with each other. It was just a nice, fun time in our lives. The sun, the drinks, the laughter – sex seemed like a natural progression of it all. The guys were sitting opposite, looking warily but hopefully at us. I wanted to have sex with my friend's man but I didn't want to do it right in front of my friend and boyfriend – that really would have been weird! So I asked him to come and help me freshen up the drinks. I was naked under the towel and I covered my front but left it open at the back so he could check out my ass as we walked inside. I looked back and saw my friend hadn't wasted any time at all. She'd pounced on my boyfriend and they were snogging away: his hands were all over her.

We headed straight for the bed and lay down and started kissing. Our skin was all cool and damp from the water and we were just the right amount of tipsy. It was open plan so it was private enough but not too intimate. Even though we were all getting off on it, there was still a pretence that it was all a bit of a giggle. He was a fantastic kisser and when he went down on me he was much better than my boyfriend. I came and we went back outside, even though he hadn't. My friend and my boyfriend were all over each other but I could tell they hadn't had intercourse either. When we got in, they got out saying they wanted the bed for a bit.

We decided we'd had enough of the Jacuzzi so went to the pool. He got us more drinks and we mucked about for a bit, then he blew up some lilos and I lay on one as he swam beside me and pushed me around the pool. In the shallower end, he grabbed my legs and pulled me towards his mouth and licked me again. That was hot. The sun was beating down on my body which always makes me feel sexy, the bottom part of me was lovely and cool in the water and his tongue was wonderfully warm. He had his hands under my bum and lifted me out of the water a bit – both the guys were fit and strong – but there was still the sensation of hot and cold and I guessed the pool wasn't completely private so there was the added thrill that people might be watching.

I felt bad for not reciprocating – so far, he'd done stuff to me but I'd done nothing but kiss him – so when we got out and went to lie on the sunbeds, I gave him head and he came in my mouth. About a minute later, the other two emerged so we all got in the pool again and had a few more drinks. It says something about all of us that no-one quizzed each other on what each had done. We just naturally drifted back to our normal pairing and laughed and drank and we were happy and there was no weirdness at all.

We all decided today was a one-off and had to book out of the room soon so we decided we were each allowed 15 minutes more. I suspected (and was right) it was because none of us had actually done the deed and had intercourse yet. My friend and boyfriend disappeared into the main bathroom and I heard the shower running. They shut the door and knowing they wouldn't be out for a while, we ran for the bed and I guided my friend's boyfriend's penis inside me and we shagged for about ten minutes. He was good and didn't try to show off by changing position all the time and he knew to use his fingers on my clitoris while he was inside me. My friend had trained him well!

After that, we checked out, went back to the bar and laughed about what had happened. Then the guys went back to their place (they lived together), I went home and so did my friend. She called me later that night and we had a good old girly gossip about it all and argued over whose boyfriend was better in bed (hers won for oral sex, mine won for intercourse). It was great fun. We were four adventurous people who really liked each other and wanted to explore something new. I don't see anything wrong with what I did and I'd definitely do it again, but only with a guy I didn't love. Him I won't want to share!

'Our longed for threesome ended in disaster'

Olivia, 32, works in finance

THE FANTASY

I'm 18, brunette, big-breasted, with hips and curves – a modern style Sophia Loren, oozing sex appeal. I'm on a skiing holiday with some girlfriends. We've just finished school and this is the treat from our parents for getting good grades. There are three or four girls bunked up in each little chalet but my friend and I lucked out because it's just the two of us in ours. We're so excited unpacking our things: it's the first time we've been allowed away without parental supervision. She produces a bottle of vodka from her suitcase so I go to get some ice and tonic and before long we're nicely tipsy.

We chat for a bit, talking about boys, but then get ready to go out. We're keen to explore the après ski scene and plan on making an impression so put on some sexy clothes. My friend is Scandinavian: blonde, cheekbones you could cut yourself on, pale blue eyes, creamy skin and model tall. She pours herself into a little black dress that clings to her and shows off her breasts – I can see her nipples poking through the sheer fabric. It's not exactly practical, given how freezing it is outside, but she puts her ski coat over the top and pulls on some sheepskin boots, planning to carry her heels and put them on once we're inside the bar. I wear a bright red body-con dress that makes my waist look tiny and my hips look voluptuous – perfect for my hourglass figure. I do the same as my friend and put my ski jacket on top. I joke that we'd be every man's dream for a threesome: the tall blonde and the curvy brunette.

We shed our winter gear once we're inside the bar and all the guys turn to check us out as we walk across the room. There are lots of catcalls. We ignore them and head for the bar: they're mostly posh boys and rugby players and like most girls our age, we consider ourselves far too superior to date guys our own age. We're standing at the bar waiting to get served when I notice a man sitting across from us, on his own at a table, watching us silently. He's older, about 40, and European looking. He's still wearing ski gear and I'm guessing he's come in for a quiet drink after a day on the slopes and the bar got taken over by loud-mouthed students. He's staring at me and I flash him a little smile. Normally guys smile back but he doesn't. He just continues studying me, then his eyes move to my friend and he looks her over as well. It's not just the fact that he's incredibly handsome that makes me instantly fascinated with him; it's the way he refuses to engage with us. As if suddenly bored, he looks away and takes a sip of his beer, looking in the other direction. I turn to my friend to see if she has clocked him too and she's looking as transfixed as I am.

'Wow!' she says, 'Did you see that guy checking us out?'

'I second the "Wow" but he's old enough to be our Dad.'

'Who cares,' says my friend. 'He looks like the hot ski instructor I used to have when I was 15 and I wanted to shag him senseless.'

My friend is more daring than me. She lost her virginity at 16 and has had two boyfriends since then. I'm not a virgin but I'm not as cool about sex as she is. I think it's because she's Scandinavian: they're much more open than the British. Some of the young guys start talking to us so we turn away but every time I look around the stranger is staring at us. My friend nudges me and whispers the same, 'He can't take his eyes off us!' she says delightedly. She's putting on a show, flicking her hair, giving him the eye and making sure he gets a good look at her. I feel slightly competitive and start doing the same. His eyes remain on us but there's not a hint of softness about him. He's aloof but interested, detached but engrossed: it's an intoxicating combination for two 18-year-olds used to men falling all over them and behaving like drunken idiots.

One of the guys we're talking to also notices the man checking us out and asks if we know who he is. We say we have no idea and he tells us he's a former Olympic skier who is now an instructor. Well that explains the arrogance, I think. The guy tells us every girl on the mountain wants to sleep with him but no-one's ever seen him with anyone. Rumour has it he has a model girlfriend who doesn't like skiing so he does the season solo.

It's getting late and the bar is about to shut. My friend makes a spur of the moment decision and says to me, 'Wait here'. She makes a beeline for the man and leans down to whisper into his ear. His eyes are glued to mine while she speaks. He listens, nods once, and then gets up, drains his drink and walks out of the bar without a backward glance.

'Looks like you lucked out there girls,' the young guy says to us. My friend smiles mysteriously and simply says 'We'll see'.

It's too cold to chat on the way back so we cover up and make our way back to our chalet as quickly as possible. My friend immediately rushes around dimming the lights and cleaning the place up a bit. She tells me she asked the man if he wanted to come back to our chalet for a nightcap. I ask her what else she promised but she says 'Nothing', protesting innocence, but I'm suspicious. We've just poured fresh drinks for us, even though we hardly need any more, when there's a discreet knock at the door. My friend grins at me and rushes to open it and then there he is, standing before us – the sexiest man in the world that every woman on the mountain wants to sleep with, in our chalet with us.

He nods at me and asks for a vodka. His voice is low and cold and he has a sexy European accent. He still doesn't smile, just goes to sit on the sofa and looks at us.

'I'm not interested in playing games,' he says finally, 'I want women not girls. I want sex with both of you or I want neither of you. Your choice.'

Holy hell! I look at my friend astonished. Is that what she promised him? A threesome? She looks defiantly at me and says, 'I'm game if she is.' The good girl in me wants to be back in my childhood bedroom, in my pyjamas, hiding under the duvet. But another part of me is so intrigued by him, I'll do just about anything to get to kiss him, let alone sleep with him.

'OK,' I say and wonder what I've let myself in for.

That's when he smiles. A slow, sexy, lazy smile that starts at the corners and spreads across his face. I've never seen anything so erotic in all my life.

'Come here,' he says and we both do exactly what he says, hypnotised by the power he has over us.

He makes us both stand in front of him and then he trails his fingers along our necks, down our arms and over our bodies through our dresses. His face is close to mine but he doesn't kiss me, just runs his hands over my hips, feeling my curves and looking at me. He's wearing tight black jeans and I can see the outline of his erection. He's large and well-hung and I can't help but feel nervous.

I'm a little relieved when he shifts the focus to my friend. He's more daring with her. His fingers graze her nipples through her sheer dress. They are so erect, they're nearly poking a hole through the fabric. I'm too embarrassed to look my friend in the eyes so even when he slips her dress off and starts kissing her shoulders, then her breasts and drops to his knees to kiss her stomach, his tongue lazily licking her belly button while his hands hold her hips, I sneak little looks rather than watch everything. I see his hands pull her panties down and only then do I look to see how she's coping with all this. She has her head tipped back and her eyes closed, and she's loving every second of it. She steps obediently out of her panties and grabs his head and pushes it between her legs. He grabs hold of her wrists and holds her arms to the side while he buries his head into her pubic hair and sniffs. Then he teases her by licking her thighs, her abdomen, then finally, when she's begging him, he licks between her lips and his tongue plays with her clitoris. She's moaning and I think she comes because he stops and gets up, wiping his mouth and looking dangerously turned on. My friend plonks herself on the bed and grabs her drink then watches with interest to see what he's going to do to me.

I'm still fully clothed and shaking with both desire and fear. He tells me to lie on the bed next to my friend. I obey him and then he comes to lie beside me, reaching underneath me to unzip my dress. He pushes it roughly off my shoulders and down over my hips so I'm just in my underwear. He props himself up on one elbow and says to my friend, 'You undress her.' My friend hesitates so he barks at her, 'Now!'

So my friend comes over to me and starts removing my bra and my panties while I have my eyes firmly closed shut. I'm not sure how I feel about her touching me but I get the impression this isn't the first time she's played around with a girl. The man orders her to straddle me and kiss me and she does. It feels weird to feel breasts against breasts but her mouth feels gentle and just like I'd imagine a woman's mouth to feel like with lips that are full and soft.

While we're kissing, the man gets off the bed and I hear him remove his clothes, and his body is amazing. He's incredibly fit and just the right amount of hairy. He stands by the side of the bed watching the two of us and he plays with my friend's breasts with one hand as she's kissing me. She's groaning into my mouth and I want more attention from him too so I turn my head and I'm faced with his gigantic erection, so I wrap my lips around it and take him in my mouth. Now it's him who is groaning. I'm not sure I'm very good at giving head but he seems to love what I'm doing.

'Get behind her and lick her,' he orders my friend, in a husky but no-nonsense voice and 'Move' to me, so I do as I'm told and move myself so I'm still sucking him but my bottom turns towards her. Her hands push me so I'm wide and exposed and I feel her little tongue lapping at the entrance to my bottom and I tilt my back to give her access to my clitoris. All the while, he's got handfuls of my hair in his hands and is holding me in position over his penis. It's incredibly hot but I'm glad I'm drunk because it's all so deliciously overwhelming.

'Neither of you are virgins, right?' he asks and we both say no, we've had sex. He says it's time and he wants to fuck us one by one. My friend begs to be first. He lies on the bed on his back and orders me to move upwards until I'm sitting on his face, facing the wall, then he starts to lick me. He orders my friend to sit on his penis and face the other way, so he can lick me and fuck her at the same time. She cries out loud when he penetrates her because she's not used to a man this big. He thrusts slowly but deeply and powerfully into her, yet licks me gently and relentlessly. I hear her orgasm and he pushes her off and lifts me off his face, turns me around on the bed and takes me from behind.

It's unexpected but I am so horny and ready for him that it doesn't hurt, it just feels amazing. I was about to climax from his tongue and his big, thick, hard penis gets me there. My orgasm is so intense, it feels like the room is spinning as I feel myself contract around him again and again. When he lets go I can feel him pushing deep inside me and pumping furiously until every last drop has been emptied out of him. We lie in a sweaty, tangled mess, limbs intertwined, totally spent and satisfied and my friend and I fall asleep. When we wake later, the man is gone.

THE DECISION

Like lots of girls, I'd experimented with the same sex when I was in my early teens. In my case it was with a girl who wasn't terribly attractive, but had a spectacular set of knockers, even at age 12. She used to come with me to feed my horses. We'd shove a bit of hay in their direction, then settle down for hours of snogging in the bushes. At school, we wouldn't acknowledge each other at all. No-one knew we were friends, let alone friends of Dorothy.

Later, this progressed to role play. We'd lock my bedroom door and she'd pretend to be a travelling salesman, however strange it sounds now! I was the housewife so she would show me her range of saucepans (not kidding), then sort of order me about, undress me and then we'd lie on the bed, kiss passionately and furiously play with each other's breasts. One day she put her tongue down there. I let her for one wildly exciting minute but then pushed her away and we never 'played' again. It was one lick too far and scared the hell out of both of us.

This all happened when I was 14 and I'm now 32. In between then and now, I've often masturbated to fantasies of me with other women and I really like watching lesbian porn and reading erotica with girl-on-girl themes. But it's always 'lipstick lesbian' stuff: all the woman in my fantasies look like supermodels! I have absolutely no desire whatsoever to sleep with butch-looking gay women.

It's also worth noting that I always take a submissive role in my fantasies, whereas in real life I'm strong-willed and don't like being bossed about. I enjoy it in bed though and my lesbian fantasies mainly revolve around the woman doing everything to me or – if it's a threesome – a hot guy ordering us to do rude things to each other. I guess that's why they're called fantasies: we try out roles we wouldn't normally go for in real life.

Like most guys I'd met, my boyfriend of three years had been begging me to have a threesome with him ever since we met. I'd always said no but our sex life had become a bit routine and he was incredibly persuasive. He kept saying it was just what we needed to get us going again and we'd only have do it once because the images would be burnt into our brains forever, for use whenever we felt we needed a sexual lift. When I gave a hint I might finally be relenting he was beside himself!

We took baby steps and I agreed to look online and see if we could find a girl who would be up for it that – crucially – I found attractive. Then we'd take it from there. It was really important to me that she was bisexual not gay. I didn't want anyone 'dykey', but I didn't want her to be straight and a newbie like me either. I wanted her to know what she was doing!

I took my time looking, despite my boyfriend thinking every single girl who replied was perfect, and we tried lots of different websites. Most of the girls who responded to our ad I dismissed immediately, purely on the way the reply was worded. Anyone who couldn't spell properly or sounded too young or coarse, I vetoed. But then we got a response that was nicely written by a woman who sounded well-educated and had a sense of humour. I asked for a photo and she sent one through . . . and she was perfect. Really pretty, slim, in her late 20s with dark hair and a nice sense of style. She said she'd slept with a girl once before with a boyfriend and really liked it but they'd since split and she thought she'd give it a whirl solo with a like-minded couple. So far so good!

We talked on the phone and I liked her voice so we made a date for her to come over the following Saturday night. My boyfriend was so excited; I thought he might spontaneously combust between now and then or have a heart attack! I was looking forward to it as well but not nearly as enthusiastic as he was. It was all he talked about from the moment we started searching.

We talked about safe sex and how much he was going to be involved with touching/kissing her etc. – because full sex was never going to be part of it – but I didn't spell out specifically how I wanted the session to run. I just figured my boyfriend would take a dominant, masterful role since he wanted it so badly. Every fantasy I have ever shared with him about threesomes had him as the boss of it all and he would say 'I'm going to get you to do this and her do that'. This made me feel reassured. I was happy to do it but I didn't want to be the one driving the whole thing in case I lost my nerve.

THE REALITY

Neither of us slept much on the Friday night. I swear my boyfriend jerked off about three times during the night: I could feel his hand working under the covers! I was a tad apprehensive in the morning but not to the point of wanting to call it off. I worried more about things like what the correct etiquette was: should I put out some nibbles? Did we all chat for a bit and then go into the bedroom? What did one do in these situations?

Half an hour before she was due to arrive, we sat down to have a drink together. My boyfriend was jumpy, making really bad jokes and laughing in a weird, high-pitched way. He was obviously a lot more nervous than I was but wouldn't admit it. The woman was meeting us in our flat and when the buzzer went, dead on time, I jumped and suddenly thought, 'Say she's a con woman or bonkers and now she'll know where we live!' Now I know why people meet first in public places! I went cross-eyed trying to scrutinise her through the peep hole but happily she looked just like the photo, so I let her in.

'Hi,' she said, and my boyfriend and I stood in the doorway and sort of beamed at her inanely while she stood there and smiled back. No-one moved for ages. Then she said, 'Should I come in?' and my boyfriend and I both said, 'God! Of course, yes you should come in. How silly of us,' in absolute unison. We couldn't have rehearsed it to sound that synchronised! We felt like idiots and she looked us both up and down more intently, no doubt trying to work out whether we were a weird swinger couple who did everything together, even speak!

I fled to the kitchen to pour us all a drink and left my boyfriend to take her through to the lounge room. I was only gone about three minutes but when I walked in the woman was perched on the edge of the sofa, looking like she wanted to leave, and my boyfriend was sitting opposite her, bright red, staring at her saying nothing. He was behaving like people do when they finally get to meet their favourite celebrity: faced with what he'd longed for, he had stage fright. I figured he'd calm down but he just got worse.

Meanwhile, I'm checking the girl out now she's taken off her coat and can't decide if I fancy her or not! She is terribly pretty but in a very 'nice girl' way. The girls in my fantasy were ruder somehow; classy looking but still naughty and cheeky. This girl looked like she should be working behind a make-up counter and advising on what day cream to wear, not sitting in our lounge offering herself up for group sex!

We chatted stiffly about a few things for about ten minutes but my boyfriend just sat there looking terrified and dumb-struck. She was nice and sweet but this wasn't exactly what I'd imagined happening. Secretly, I wanted to say 'Look, let's just forget the whole thing' but I thought that would be rude.

I suggested taking our drinks into the bedroom, but when we got there my boyfriend just stood looking even more awkward. Apart from our synchronised greeting at the door, he hadn't said a word. His eyes were like saucers and he was sweating. I sent him out to get the wine to top us all up and then said to the girl 'I think he's freaking out a bit. Sorry about this.' She shrugged and said, 'That's OK. My boyfriend was a bit nervous first time too. But it's you I'm more interested in. I can sleep with a guy any time.' This was more like it!

She said, 'Let's get onto the bed and see what happens,' so we sat on the edge of the bed and started kissing. Her lips were really soft and it was totally different to kissing a man. We were kissing when my boyfriend walked back in with the drinks and said, 'Oh. Shit!' We stopped kissing and smiled at him but instead of looking turned on, he looked a bit put out. He said later he felt left out because we'd started without him. I didn't have the heart to say if we'd waited for him to instigate anything, we'd still be sitting in the lounge looking blankly at each other.

My boyfriend said he might just watch for a bit so he went and stood in the corner near the drinks looking agitated. Meanwhile, the girl stood up and took off her clothes. I did the same and the mood changed a bit. I had on quite racy underwear – hers was quite normal. I was a bit disappointed but I liked her taking the lead and by undressing first, it fed more into how I'd imagined this in my head. I glanced over at my boyfriend to see his reaction – surely he'd be liking this part now we were both naked? – but he just gave me a watery, wan smile and gulped nervously.

We lay down on the bed and started kissing again – and that's all we did for ages which, quite frankly, was a bit boring! I tried moving it on a bit by feeling her breasts, which she seemed to like, and putting her hand between my legs but she pulled it away and whispered that she wanted to take it slowly and 'get used to me' first.

Jesus! No wonder men get annoyed with women when they're all raring to go and we make them do more foreplay. After what felt like an eternity, she got my hand and put it between her legs. Again, this wasn't what was supposed to happen. I didn't want to be the one doing everything, I wanted her to do things to me or for my boyfriend to command us to do things to each other.

I half sat up and said to him, 'Honey, come over here and be part of this. Tell me what you'd like to see us do.' I was hoping this might remind him of our dirty fantasy talk and spur him into action but it was not to be. He went white and, still clutching his glass of wine, moved towards the bed like we were standing there with loaded guns pointed at him. The girl sniggered a bit, which didn't really help, but it was hard not to see the funny side. She didn't know that he'd been the one begging me for this: it must have seemed like I'd forced him into it, from her perspective.

I decided to ignore him and at least try to enjoy the experience for what it was: something new I'd always wanted to try. I did what I'd like her to do to me and slid my fingers back and forth between her vaginal lips while playing with her breasts and kissing her. She felt wetter than I thought she'd be and I guessed maybe she was more turned on than she was letting on. Feeling her so aroused did it for me and I was just starting to get all worked up when my boyfriend suddenly appeared by the bed with two wine glasses and asked us if we wanted sips of our wine.

You're fucking kidding me, right? I thought. But at least he'd finally spoken, even if it was to suggest something ridiculous. Women are so polite. We both stopped doing what we were doing and took the glasses of wine, and my boyfriend actually said, 'Cheers!' *Cheers?* Had he gone fucking nuts? Weirdly, she and I said 'Cheers' back and then lay back down on the bed again. The whole thing was surreal and I was verging on the giggles. It was just so *proper*.

I wanted heat and lust and passion and nastiness. Hell, the sex I had at 14 with Ms Big Knockers was hotter than this! I decided to up the stakes and pushed her back on the bed and started going down on her. She tasted salty/sweet: a weird taste but not unpleasant. I licked her for about five minutes and she was moaning and clearly loving it when I felt my boyfriend getting on the bed behind me, naked and standing close enough for me to feel the warmth of his body. Good news but rubbish timing. I didn't want him involved right at this moment because we were finally getting somewhere. But, like a good girlfriend, I stopped and turned around to suck him a little only to find his erection was only half mast.

So I went back to licking the girl, who'd made no attempt to fondle me or get involved with my boyfriend while I gave him head. I think she really wasn't interested in him at all. She liked what I was doing though and making all the right noises and I was thinking, *if she just follows suit and does to me what I'm doing to her, this night might just end in orgasms all round,* when my boyfriend tapped me on the shoulder. I couldn't believe it! I ignored him and kept going but he did it again, more insistently. I stopped and turned around, furious, to ask him what he wanted and he said, 'I'm sorry to interrupt but do you mind putting your finger up her ass while you do that? And I can't see properly.'

I lost it. I mean seriously? I couldn't give two hoots about his fragile bloody male ego at this point. I was fed up with it all and looked him in the eye and said, 'No. Now shut up or sod off.' He looked majorly pissed off and the semi-erection shrivelled to nothing. At this point, I couldn't have cared if *he'd* shrivelled and disappeared into thin air.

Feeling that the moment had passed, I sat back and looked at my boyfriend, who was now sitting in the corner on a chair in a right old huff with his jeans back on. That made me even more annoyed.

'Any other requests? Would you like to have sex with me while she watches?' I asked sarcastically. This had been one of the things he'd most wanted to do but the likelihood of him A) being able to get it up and B) getting the courage up to do it, was zero. Minus zero actually. He replied, predictably, with, 'Fuck you. Fuck both of you!' and walked out of the room slamming the door.

'Ooops,' the girl said and I ranted a bit about how the whole thing was his bloody idea and just because he couldn't handle it, didn't mean he had to ruin it for us. She was very sweet about it and said she understood but she didn't exactly chuck me down on the bed and try to ravage me or anything. The night had started out awkwardly, got worse, got better briefly and could even have romped home at one stage if my dopey boyfriend hadn't tried to intervene. But he had and so we just got up and put our clothes back on and I apologised to her again about it all going wrong. I asked her if she wanted a drink before she left and she said no, then we kissed each other on the cheek and I saw her out.

I can't blame my boyfriend for the whole thing. I'd chosen wrong for a start. My mistake was trying to find someone I liked rather than someone I lusted after. The more overtly sexual girls who replied, the really brazen 'out there' ones I'd sniffed at and called 'slutty', were exactly what I should have gone for. But it's not like I'm going to be repeating this one any time soon! Not with this boyfriend anyway.

When I came back in he was sitting in the kitchen with a big bottle of Scotch beside him. He was angry, hurt, sheepish, embarrassed, humiliated, strung out – you name the negative emotions he was feeling! He said he'd wanted to pull out that morning because he suddenly got worried he wouldn't be able to perform and he was also freaking that I'd prefer having sex with her than sex with him and leave him for another woman. I felt sorry for him and suddenly just exhausted by the experience. I put my arms around him and we cuddled and he cried. The whole thing had left him feeling utterly emasculated and he just couldn't help it. Poor sod. I've also realised that it's really hard sleeping with a woman and not comparing yourself to her the whole time. Did her thighs look bigger than mine? Whose breasts were better? Whose tummy was flatter and more toned? I had to fight the urge to ask my boyfriend his opinion on all our body parts. I don't think our experience is that uncommon. I know other women who've had this happen to them. Men are all talk when it comes to stuff like this and the saying 'Be careful what you wish for' couldn't be truer when it comes to men and threesomes.

'I slept with my husband's best friend'

Jane, 51, works in finance

THE FANTASY

My husband was out of town. He travelled quite a bit but I didn't mind. I quite liked having time alone; I'd always liked my own company. I'd curl up on the sofa and read, play classical music and drink red wine. A whole bottle sometimes, all to myself. It was blissful because my husband didn't drink and didn't really approve of it. I'd eat cheese on toast rather than cook healthy balanced meals. Sometimes, dinner would be a bar of chocolate. I'd watch foreign films my husband despised but moved me to my core. I sometimes invited over a close girlfriend or two and it was always better without our partners. We'd open up and talk honestly. Marriage suits men but women tend to grow weary after a while. We all felt like unpaid maids and mothers rather than desired wives.

My husband's best friend was extremely handsome. Everyone commented on it. They'd say, 'Wow! Lucky you! You get to look at him all the time.' He came over a lot and hung out with my husband, sometimes both of us, occasionally just me. We'd laugh and chat about all kinds of stuff. I saw him so often, I was immune to his looks. Or so I thought.

One night, I'm curled up reading and savouring some 'me time'. My husband is in Dubai on business. It is late – about 11pm – when there is a knock at the door. I open it and he is standing there. The best friend. He looks a bit drunk but then I am a bit tipsy so maybe it is me, not him.

He asks if my husband is home and I tell him he is away on business. I think it odd he doesn't know: they tell each other everything. He feigns surprise (or am I imagining it and he really doesn't know?) and asks if I want to have a nightcap with him. He says he's been on a really bad date and wants to be around friends. I ask him in and he tells me what happened: it is so disastrous that it is funny and soon we are giggling and then roaring with laughter.

The bottle is soon finished so I open another. We talk and laugh some more and it seems the most natural thing in the world to lean back against him and for him to put a friendly arm around me. So I snuggle in and try not to notice how good he smells and how hard and muscular and spectacularly good-looking he is. And perhaps I stare up at him just that little bit too long because next thing I know his mouth is coming towards me and the lips every woman I know wants to kiss are suddenly kissing mine.

I don't even try to fight it. I give in and he's got his hands in my hair, and his mouth feels delicious and we're devouring each other. He pulls back and looks at me, grinning wildly, and says 'I know this is wrong but I've wanted to do this for years'. This is complete news to me. He's so handsome and I'm so, well, ordinary. Why would he want me? I say as much and he lists off about 20 reasons why I am adorable. I melt. We drink more wine and he's hugging me and keeps kissing me. It's wrong, I know, and he knows it too, but he takes me by the hand and leads me to the bedroom.

We stand in the bedroom and he kisses me, gently this time, and then he undresses me slowly, planting soft kisses all over my body before laying me back on the bed. I lie there naked and watch him undress. He tells me I am more beautiful than he ever dared imagine but how can he think so when he is so gloriously good-looking? He lies on top of me and he feels hard and masculine and his chest is hairy, which I love. I run my fingers through it and I can feel his erection pressing into me. I want him so badly so I reach down and grab it and he groans and tells me how much he wants me. I open my legs and then he's inside me and I'm full of him and it feels like nothing I've ever felt before. He shouts out my name and lets go just as I do too.

THE DECISION

I met Jack, my husband's best friend, at the same time that I met my husband. I was 19, young, pretty and not interested in settling down. My husband made a beeline for me, chatting me up ruthlessly, and his friend Jack kept saying, 'Man, leave the poor girl alone. You're practically molesting her.' I fell in love with my husband right there and then and I loved him for twenty years. I'm not sure when I fell out of romantic love with him, it happened slowly and insidiously. I never stopped loving my husband but one day I realised I wasn't *in* love with him any longer. It made me sad. I remember turning 40 and being utterly depressed about it.

I'd always got on with Jack. He was married for a while and I liked his wife as well. We made a great foursome. But it didn't work out between them – I think she was career-focused and didn't like being married. He was upset for a bit when she left but I didn't ever get the impression she was the love of his life.

I don't know when I started to have feelings for Jack. I've always liked him. I do remember him helping my husband do some DIY in the garden one summer and him taking off his shirt. I was walking past the kitchen window and stopped . . . and couldn't stop looking at him. My husband was also shirtless and he just looked soft and pudgy. Jack was ripped. I think that's what made me start to see him differently. Pathetic really. How basic we humans are. It's all so primitive when you think about it. Lust. Love. We think we're in control but we're not.

After that day, I'd find myself staring at Jack whenever I could get away with it. I found myself more and more attracted to him. I couldn't believe I hadn't noticed how handsome he was before. He had beautiful high cheekbones and the angles of his face were fascinating to me. He was so physically fit and really looked after himself. He'd grown more handsome and confident as he got older, not less, and I found the whole package incredibly attractive.

I was so aware of him whenever he was near me. I could feel myself getting flushed when he spoke to me. I must have oozed longing and I'm amazed my husband didn't notice. But you don't notice very much at all when you've been married to the same person for two decades. It's easier to deceive someone close to you than it is someone who isn't.

Jack picked up on it though. I could see him staring back at me, when he didn't think I'd notice. He'd look questioningly at me, as though he was trying to figure out what was going on. Then the eye contact started. We'd hold it for longer than necessary when my husband wasn't watching. One time I remember getting all dressed up for a night in, just because he was coming over. My husband thought I'd made the effort for him and we ended up having sex that night. The whole time I was pretending it was Jack.

This went on for months, maybe even a year, before anything was directly said. I'd fallen in love and lust with Jack by this time. I suspected, though wasn't sure, he had feelings for me as well. I knew he fancied me by the way his eyes travelled over my body when my husband wasn't watching but I dared to hope it would be more than just a sexual thing.

This period was the best: the anticipation, the suspense, the longing. It was bittersweet torture. But nothing had been said and nothing had been acted on so there was no guilt. Of course the fact he was my husband's best friend nudged its way into my fantasies. But I dismissed it. This was just a game, a flirtation, nothing else. Until one morning . . .

My husband left for work and I was just getting ready to leave myself when there was a knock at the front door. I opened it to find Jack standing there on the doorstep. He didn't have to say why he was there, I knew why. I let him in, made a coffee and we sat there, facing each other across the breakfast bar. He said very simply, 'What are we going to do about this?' and I said, 'I don't know' and then he got up, strode across the kitchen and kissed me. I kissed him back and it was awful and wonderful all at once.

He pulled back and said, 'I love you and I've always loved you, do you know that?' and I said 'No, I didn't but how wonderful because I love you too.' He said we needed to have a real conversation about it so we made arrangements to meet the following day – lunchtime – at a hotel in town.

THE REALITY

Affairs are clichéd for a reason. You have to meet in hotel rooms because where else can you spend time together knowing no-one is watching? Being alone with Jack for the very first time, knowing I could touch him, kiss him, make love to him, seemed like the most precious thing in the world. But the sex wasn't the star attraction for me. It was being able to talk to him honestly and tell him how I felt about him.

He got to the hotel first and when he opened the door, we literally fell into each other's arms and were both kissing and crying and laughing simultaneously. It didn't feel strange to be with him, it felt like I'd come home. He said the same thing. We lay on the bed and just talked and talked about how we felt about each other. We couldn't stop kissing and staring into each other's eyes, it was the most romantic thing you could imagine.

We were acutely aware of how much time we had (two hours) yet we didn't actually have sex until about fifteen minutes before we had to leave. All that pent-up lust but the reality was when we finally did it, we were both shy and tentative, so eager to please. It was the worst sex we ever had technically because we were so nervous and clumsy but it was the best sex because it was the first time we got to touch each other, after so long wanting to. He was bigger than I'd expected and I was tense so it actually hurt a bit when he penetrated, but once he started thrusting it felt amazing and he came really quickly. I didn't come but I didn't care.

We lay there entwined and I cried. I felt good but also so bad about what we'd done. We'd talked a lot about our feelings but not about what we were going to do about them. We wanted to focus on the lovely part, how much we loved each other, not the awful part of how we had the power to rip my husband's world apart.

In the weeks afterwards, I felt so bad about what I'd done, it physically hurt. I was flooded with guilt and shame, thinking I was a really bad person. I couldn't look my husband in the eyes and he kept asking me what was wrong. I kept thanking God we hadn't had children. But I also couldn't stop thinking about Jack. It was like a tape on a loop in my head and regardless of where I was or what I was doing, I could feel him, taste him, smell him. I was drunk on him. I didn't just want to do *it* again, I wanted to be with him for life. But how could I do that to my husband? They were best friends! It would be bad enough leaving him but to leave him for the person he would have turned to, to help him through it, was unthinkable.

Meanwhile, Jack was thinking the same thing. He'd call me when it was safe and he was clearly in turmoil. He told me he'd been in love with me for years but didn't dare to dream I'd feel the same. But he respected and adored my husband and couldn't imagine hurting him. Neither of us had any illusions that anyone would be on our side. My husband was well loved by all our friends and my family adored him. We'd not only lose him, we'd be judged by everyone and probably stand to lose a lot of people we loved.

The day we told him was the worst of my entire life. I wouldn't wish it on my worst enemy. I threw up all morning. Jack turned up and my husband greeted him cheerily and then quickly figured something was wrong when we asked him to sit down and said we needed to tell him something. Jack told him very simply that we were in love and wanted to be together. My husband went white and then he went deadly quiet. He looked at his hands and his lap for what seemed like ages, tears falling out of his eyes and dripping onto his hands. He finally looked up and I have never seen such pain in anyone's eyes. It haunts me still. He said, 'How could you?', then ordered us to leave. We were both crying as well and trying to explain but he told us to shut up and get out and so we did.

Jack and I are happily married now but we've paid dearly for that happiness. One or two friends realised we didn't set out to hurt anyone and were kind to us. Most rallied around my husband, didn't return my calls and blanked us if they ran into us. It was horrendous. If I could turn back time, I'm not sure I would follow the same path. I love Jack but it broke both of us and the guilt still sits there on our shoulders, and always will. I wouldn't advise anyone in the same situation to act on it. Bury it. It's not worth the pain and upset.

'I let my rich lover
control me sexually'

Adriana, 26, no profession

THE FANTASY

He says he owns me. I am his property and he controls everything from what I think, to what I feel, to what I do. He made this clear right from the start, when he saw me out with some friends at a bar in New York and decided I was to be his. I remember feeling someone staring at me: it made the hair on my back and arms stand up. I had on a short, silky mini-dress with shoestring straps, in a beautiful grey-blue. I could ball it up in one fist but it cost hundreds. I'm a model so I got it at cost but even then it was way out of my budget. I had on nude high heels which make my legs look like they're never-ending and my skin shimmered with my summer tan. My hair is long, blonde and tousled. I am every man's dream lover and he wants me for himself.

I turned around to see who was watching me and I saw him. I can still see it all so clearly . . . He's on his own, sitting on a sofa, both arms spread out on the back, so he takes up the whole space. His suit jacket is off, shirt sleeves rolled up to show tanned forearms that look strong and dangerous. He has dark hair that's cut short and spiky, masculine features – a defined strong jaw line and commanding nose – topped by startling green eyes framed with long, inky eyelashes. The effect is breathtaking: rugged virility mixed with a touch of almost feminine prettiness. I'm guessing he's in his early 30s but he could be older. I'm also guessing he has always been incredibly handsome and always will be, regardless of age.

He looks like he knows the effect he has on people. He is broad-shouldered and looks wealthy – there is a man in a suit standing nearby and to attention, his hands folded, looking like he's from the secret service. I'm guessing and I'm right that he is his driver and bodyguard. The bar is packed but he sits squarely in the middle of a sofa that seats three. He's claimed it as his and no-one would dare ask him to shove over. He looks me straight in the eyes and the corners of his mouth curve upwards, ever so slightly. I frown at him and toss my hair and turn back to my friends. He is at my elbow alarmingly fast, says 'Excuse me' to my friends who are open-mouthed, and pulls me to one side.

'You don't belong here. You're too beautiful. Let me take you somewhere else,' he says, fixing me with those astonishing eyes. I should play it cool but I don't. I love the directness of his approach. Other men would be laughed at for saying that, but not this man. His gall makes me gulp and blink a little, but I say, 'OK', get my bag, tell my friends he is an old friend and leave with him. The driver/bodyguard person follows three paces behind.

Outside on the street, he nods to his driver to fetch the car. We stand waiting and he looks me up and down, deliberately. He smiles as he does it but there's something disturbing about the way he does it, like he's examining an object, not a human. He lifts up my hair and turns my face to the side, studying it, then walks behind me to look at my back and exposed neck. It's the strangest, sexiest thing that's ever happened to me. It sounds offensive but it was done with admiration and reverence – I felt like a thoroughbred being looked over by a prospective owner.

The car appears. It's a black, sleek Jaguar, beautifully designed, a little sinister – the car and owner are a perfect match. The driver gets out of the car and the man instructs him to meet him back at the apartment. He nods and disappears. He slides into the driver's seat and I get into the front seat beside him. I ask him his name and he says names are irrelevant for what he has in mind for me. I gulp for the second time that evening.

He tells me we are going to his apartment, which has the best view in New York, but first we are stopping somewhere to buy me a present. He takes out his mobile, thumbs through his contact list and hits a button that says 'Lily'. 'I have someone who needs special attention,' he says silkily. 'Can you accommodate her?' She clearly says yes because he smiles into the phone and says, 'See you in five.'

I don't ask where we are going because I know he won't tell me. We pull up outside a small boutique, tucked away in a side street. There's no sign advertising what the shop sells, just a number, and there's no merchandise on display in the window. Instead, there's a large, beautifully-lit black and white photograph. It's of the back view of a girl wearing a tight, black corset, leather G-string and high, spiked heels. Her body is perfect: her ass is high, her legs are smooth and long, her shoulders are muscular. She has a dog collar around her neck with a lead attached to it and her hands are tied behind her back. She's bowing her head but she's turned it slightly to the right, so you can see the side of her face, and her expression is cunning not helpless. It's a powerful image. She looks submissive, vulnerable and ready to be taken, but powerful at the same time. My stomach lurches and I wonder if this is going to be an adventure or the biggest mistake I have ever made.

We approach the door and it magically opens for us. A petite blonde woman welcomes us inside. She kisses the man and says 'Jake, it's nice to see you'. Jake's eyes twinkle and he watches my face as I clock his name. I go from feeling afraid to excited: Jake doesn't sound scary. The obvious conclusion is that we're going to have a threesome but the photograph in the window suggests otherwise. I hope it's the latter.

She leads the way down a corridor and suddenly we're in a large room and I stop in my tracks and say 'Oh!' The room is a BDSM's wet dream. There are whips, all kinds of whips: soft, leather tasselled ones, long, fierce bull whips, floggers and paddles, riding crops and canes. There are handcuffs and ankle cuffs, rope and bondage tape, spiked collars and leads, mouth gags, leather catsuits, corsets, fetish heels, chastity belts and bed restraints. It should be intimidating but it's fascinating.

I want to rush over and touch everything but I sense that I need to wait for permission. Jake smiles when he sees me hesitate. He nods to Lily and says, 'Let's start with some basics', so she takes me by the hand and guides me to the centre of the room. Jake sits in the corner on a stool and studies me.

Lily tells me to strip down to my underwear. I think to myself, This is crazy, I have only just met this guy. But I do it. I like my body and men love my body. Jake narrows his eyes and examines every part of it. He then says, 'I don't like her underwear. Get rid of it'. Lily shrugs and comes over to unhook my bra and slides my panties off. I am breathing hard, a combination of terrified and turned on.

Lily comes back with a corset and G-string: it's identical to the one in the photograph outside. I stand obediently, letting her dress me, like a child being dressed for school. My eyes are fixed on Jake's the whole time. The corset is being tied up so tight I can't breathe. It pushes my breasts high and they spill out of it. I look down and I can see the top half of my nipples showing. She brings over high, fetish heels. They are beautiful enough to wear in public: silver and black leather straps with metallic stiletto heels. I look two feet taller. The wall to the left of me is one enormous mirror. I turn to look at my reflection and am startled. I look like a stranger. I'm an athletic, slim build but now I look curvy and voluptuous. My eyes are glittering back at me.

Jake stands beside me but doesn't touch me. We both regard me in the mirror. 'Cuffs and collar and a whip,' he says quietly to Lily. 'Then you can leave us.' She puts the objects he wants on a small table next to him and leaves quietly. He puts the collar on first then attaches a lead. He tells me to put my hands behind my back and then he puts thick leather handcuffs on and snaps them together with a thick chain. He picks up the whip and trails it around my shoulders, letting it caress my breasts, my thighs, my buttocks.

I am transfixed by my image in the mirror. I have never felt so aroused, so exhilarated and alive. It's like all my senses are on full alert. My insides melt and I feel weak, flooded with desire so potent, I can hardly stand. Jake stands beside me and meets my eyes in the mirror. 'You like?' he says. I nod. Then he steps back and draws his arm back and I feel a sharp sting on my buttocks. It's shocking and intensely painful and adrenaline races through my body. He watches my face to see the reaction and when my head tips back and my mouth opens with pleasure, he does it again. He trails his fingers between my legs to see if I am wet and I am soaking. I want more and I wonder how I ever got through life without feeling like this.

THE DECISION

I met my boyfriend through sugardaddie.com, a website for rich men to find pretty girls and vice versa. My closest friends know that's where I met him because they don't see anything wrong with wanting to date a man who has money, but I know most people do. I find it hypocritical. You're allowed to say you want a man who's good-looking but you're not allowed to admit you want a guy who's rich? Personally, I think going for looks is even more superficial. Looks fade but money means I will be financially secure in my old age. It means if I have children they will be well-educated and not want for anything. I am good-looking, I know how to make men happy and I like looking after them so

I think it's a good trade. Not all rich men are ugly and fat either. There are some very hot banking guys out there. I know the world hates them for being greedy but aren't we all greedy for wealth if we're honest?

For our first date, he took me to a beautiful hotel in Mayfair. I love dressing up and I'd really gone all out. He looked massively impressed when I walked in and I liked him too. He's a trader, tall, not bad looking with a nice smile. He'd ordered the best champagne and gave me a present of a diamond pendant as a 'nice to meet you' gift. I loved it, who wouldn't? We went to dinner and everyone fussed over him. The food was amazing, the wine top shelf. I knew not to sleep with him the first night so waited until date three before having sex with him.

Sex was ordinary the first night but he told me afterwards that he liked 'kinky stuff'. I asked what that meant and he said pushing the limits a little. I said I didn't mind so long as it didn't involve other people. I had a threesome once and found it boring. Two men with egos needing to be stroked was just double the hassle. I just don't think I'm into sex as much as other people are. I don't mind it but I don't crave it. But I know men love it and I'm good at pretending I'm having the time of my life. I beg for men to enter me, touch me, kiss my neck and they fall for it every time.

What *does* make me aroused is watching a man powerless with lust for me. I get off on having power over men. It makes me feel like a sexual superhero. That's why I like letting them do things to me that they've wanted to do to a woman the whole of their life. I like seeing them out of control. These men who run huge corporations, I have brought them to their knees. I am closer to orgasm in that moment, *before* physical contact, than I am when they touch me. This is why my boyfriend and I are so perfectly matched. I have never been more interested in sex than I have been with him.

THE REALITY

The first thing he wanted was to get me to wear a remote control sex toy, an 'egg', when we went out to dinner. He pushed it deep inside me and I went without panties to the restaurant. He picked somewhere deliberately stuffy and formal, the sort of place where everyone speaks in a whisper and you can hear a pin drop. Then he spent the night pressing the button to make the egg vibrate inside me whenever the waiter came near us. I didn't flinch. I carried on conversing, smiling when I was supposed to smile, ordering wine, discussing the menu. He loved it. I felt him under the table and his erection was huge.

The next time we went out, I went without panties again and wore a short, floaty dress. I asked him to choose a posh restaurant with table-to-floor length tablecloths. Then I made sure we were seated in the centre of the restaurant and gave him specific instructions. I made him masturbate me under the table, using one hand, while talking with the sommelier. I actually came that night, something I rarely do, while the sommelier was discussing the difference between two vintages. My face remained the same: I smiled sweetly up at my boyfriend as though admiring his knowledge of wine. He was the one who looked like he was climaxing, not me.

He took me to Agent Provocateur to buy some underwear. He picked it all out and as the sales assistant took it through to me in the dressing room she whispered, 'What an asshole! He didn't even ask you what you liked. Why are you with him?' 'Because he's richer than God,' I said, 'How much does your nice boyfriend make?', and pulled the curtain shut. I put on all the different sets of underwear and took pictures of myself in each one on my mobile and sent them to my boyfriend sitting outside. The pictures got ruder. I sent one with me fingering myself, another playing with my nipples. All this was happening a few feet from where he was sitting talking to the snotty assist-ant. He loved it. So did I.

For our anniversary, he booked us into the most expensive hotel in Paris. He ordered a bath filled with rose petals, had a perfume designed especially for me by a Parisian 'nose', took me shopping in all the designer stores with unlimited funds, then draped a diamond necklace worth about thirty grand around my vagina and licked in between. I came that time too. Wouldn't you?

'I had sex with my hot neighbour . . . and his son'

Megan, 43, is an author

THE FANTASY

Wherever I am in the world, I always go for an early morning run – especially if I'm in a hot country. I'm staying with my father in San Fransisco so I set off that day and follow a well-worn route that I've done many times. I'm wearing running shorts and a sports top and my body is tanned, toned and athletic. My hair is tied back in a ponytail and I've got sunglasses on. I'm jogging past a place with beautiful gardens when I see a man standing there hosing the plants. He has no shirt on, his jeans are low-slung and he's got a washboard stomach, so I slow up to have a proper look. I'm blatantly checking him out when he looks up and sees me. I blush and he smiles and says 'Hi. Great day for a run,' in a sexy American drawl. I figure he's in his late 30s. I smile and say 'Sure is!', wave back and keep running, but the image of his chest stays with me.

On impulse, I decide to jog back the same way. My heart's thumping as I near his place and I realise I'm hoping he'll still be out there – maybe watching for me. He is and the minute he sees me, he walks over to the fence, smiling. I don't know what to say so just stand there but then he grins and says, 'Come in out of the sun and we'll have an iced tea on the balcony.'

He unlatches the gate and a little part of me thinks 'stranger danger', I'm going into a man's house that I don't know. But I'm late 30s, not 13, and think how is this any different to meeting a guy at a bar and going back to his place?

I wait on the terrace, feeling a bit sweaty and thinking running gear isn't entirely what you want to be wearing when you meet a guy. He comes out with the drinks and sits down and I try hard not to stare at his perfect body but don't succeed very well. We start talking about working out and training and then I realise I've been there for ages and my father will worry, so I tell him I need to go. He makes a face and says 'That's a shame. I was enjoying having you here,' and his eyes blatantly travel over my body as I stand up to say goodbye. He takes my hand, pulls me towards him and kisses me straight on the lips, then pulls back and studies me. I look back thinking, 'Holy Shit, that's pretty forward of him'. Then he says, 'I'll see you same time tomorrow. Tell your father you'll be going on a much longer run and not to expect you back for a while. OK?' I know this is a straight out invitation to have sex with him but hear myself saying yes.

I spend the rest of that day and night imagining what could happen. The next day, instead of running gear, I put on some short denim cut-offs and a sexy vest with a gorgeous bra underneath and basically walk to his place (apart from the last little bit) so I'm not all sweaty. He's sitting outside on the terrace waiting for me and gets up the second I appear, hovering a little uncertainly by the gate. He smiles and says hello and his eyes undress me.

We sit outside for a bit but then he says casually, 'Come inside and see the house,' and he takes me by the hand and we go inside. He leads me straight to his bedroom and starts kissing me the second we're in there. He stands back and admires me, then leans in and kisses me hungrily, slipping my top off and groaning when he sees my breasts all pushed up in the bra. I go to lie on the bed but he stops me and continues to undress me while I'm standing, always stopping to stand back to stare at what part he has uncovered. It's unbearably sexy and exciting.

Finally I stand before him completely naked and he pushes me so I fall back on the bed. He grabs my legs and pulls me towards him, then his mouth is upon me and he's licking me everywhere, burying himself into my pussy, licking long and hard like he wants to be inside me. All the while he's making primitive animal noises and I come within about a minute. He gets up and unzips his jeans and frees a hard, long, penis. He holds himself and starts moving his hand up and down the shaft, teasing me. I can't think of anything I want more than him inside me.

I am lying there, waiting for him to penetrate, with my legs spread and nearly dying with desire, when suddenly there's another person in the room. 'Dad?' the guy says. 'Did you ask her?' It's a guy, about 18 years old, and he's a younger, fitter version of the father. He also wears jeans and nothing else and stands in the doorway, not game to come in. He is looking hungrily between my legs and I can see a massive erection straining at his jeans.

I go to cover myself with my hands and say, 'What the fuck?' to the father. But he just grins at me and says, 'This is my son. Handsome isn't he? I was telling him about you and how I was going to have you this morning and he wanted to know if he could watch. He's a virgin and I promised I'd teach him how to be a good lover.'

I should be appalled by this new development. I should get up and grab my clothes and get the hell out of there. I should shout and be indignant and make a scene. But I don't do any of this. What I do is nod and say 'OK, but I think he should watch you lick me because giving a woman good oral sex is by far the best way to please her.'

He smiles, and goes back to licking me. I tell the son to come closer so he can see what's going on. He comes and stands next to us and I tell him he can get undressed if he likes, and hold himself while he watches. He does and his penis is spectacular. I can see how excited he is. I ask him if he's learning anything and he says yes but can he practise on me? I say of course and next thing it's the son between my legs and Dad comes and sits on the bed and pulls me to him so I'm lying between his legs. He plays with my breasts and kisses my neck while his son is between my legs licking me furiously. I come loudly and it seems to last forever but it doesn't satisfy me. The minute it's over I want more.

I turn so I'm on all fours and I ask the father to take me from behind. I get the son to stand in front of me by the bed and I take him in my mouth and fellate him while I'm being fucked by his father. Both of them orgasm quickly and loudly and I'm so turned on by turning them on that I do as well. We collapse in a heap on the bed and they stroke and kiss me until the son gets up and pads off to his room. I get dressed and have coffee with the father and I should feel ashamed but I don't. He says 'If you want more, you know where we are' and I know I will want more and find myself back there many, many times and the sex just gets raunchier and raunchier and I clock up so many orgasms I stop counting.

THE DECISION

One of my best friends is a gay TV presenter who lives in LA. He lives in the hills in an extraordinary house that I'd been longing to visit for years, so when he asked me if I'd like to housesit for a few weeks while he filmed overseas, I jumped at the chance. I was in the middle of writing a book that was particularly challenging and I thought being alone in a big house in the sunshine would both focus and inspire me. I went with entirely pure intentions: to get back in touch with my creative side. I came back having been naughtier than I've ever been in my life!

The house was more isolated than I'd imagined but set in stunning countryside. The mansions were spectacular and my friend's house far grander than he'd let on. It was like something out of a movie: an L-shape design, thick shrubbery and gardens providing privacy from the road, but full length floor-to-ceiling glass on one side, looking out on the pool, Jacuzzi, summer house and rocky cliff face. It was private, though my friend did warn me that one house – perched high above – could see down into the pool area. 'So if you sunbathe or swim naked, just be aware you might have an audience,' he said, laughing. I asked him who lived there and he said the house was often closed up, so he suspected it was the holiday house of someone wealthy.

He left and I quickly settled into an enviable routine. I'd sleep with the blinds open so would wake when sunlight streamed in at the window. Then I'd get up and swim lengths in the pool, have breakfast and read the news online outside by the Jacuzzi, then settle down to write, sitting in the shade. It was heaven.

My view was straight up into the house on the hill from where I was writing, so it didn't take me long to notice that the house was now occupied. I saw the blinds were now open, deckchairs appeared on the balcony and there was a car in the drive. My curiosity was piqued. A few hours later, I looked up to see a man outside on the balcony, leaning against the rail and looking down at me. He was tall and well-built and, from a distance, not bad looking with blondish short hair, a tan and the right amount of wrinkles that hinted he'd led an interesting life. He had sunglasses on, so I didn't know where he was looking, but I decided it would be rude not to wave so I did. He regarded me for a moment or two, then I saw him smile and he waved back. I went back to writing and he went inside.

Over the next day or so, he appeared more and more frequently on the balcony – and I was getting more and more intrigued. Instead of lounging around in sloppy old tracksuit bottoms, I was putting on make-up, blow-drying my hair and wearing sexy bikinis and gorgeous sarongs. I was also turning myself on by conjuring up all sorts of scenarios and excuses to meet him. I wasn't going to resort to borrowing a cup of sugar but I thought running out of wine might be a good excuse.

In the end, he was the one who turned up on my doorstep. I was having a glass of wine and contemplating what to have for dinner when the doorbell went. I knew no-one in LA. My heart thudded and I thought, *Please let it be him!* I opened the door and there he was.

He wasn't quite as good-looking up close but when you're in the middle of nowhere, in gorgeous surroundings and have been pretty much alone for a week, he was up there with George Clooney for me. He introduced himself and – best of all – was holding a bottle of wine. He lifted it in the air and said, 'Hi. I'm your neighbour. I thought I'd say welcome to California.' I invited him in and next thing we're in the garden having a drink together. He tells me he's divorced with one son. I tell him I'm divorced with a daughter. Both are 19. He says marriage didn't suit him, he needs freedom and felt suffocated. I say I completely agree but actually don't at all – I'd love to get married again – and I think it was knowing he wasn't remotely up for having a relationship that made me sexually liberated enough to do what I did. I just thought 'Fuck it. I've been a good girl all my life. Why not see what happens tonight? It's not like I'll ruin a potential relationship by sleeping with him too early'. I'm not into one-night-stands and had never had one. But when we'd finished that bottle of wine and he said yes to my offer to open another, I decided there and then I was going to sleep with him.

THE REALITY

He wasn't exactly difficult to seduce. We'd moved inside and were sitting on the sofa so I just leant across, pulled his face close to mine and kissed him. He leant forward immediately, grabbed my face and kissed me back enthusiastically. He laughed and said, 'I've been wanting to do that from the first time I saw you,' and I said, 'That sounds like a chat up-line if ever I've heard one'. He laughed and said it wasn't but we both knew that's what he'd come down to the house for. Which was fine by me.

I liked that he didn't suggest the bedroom. He undressed me and we had sex on some pillows on the rug in the living room. He was an experienced lover and there was lots of foreplay and a condom produced discreetly and put on in a practised way. Then he got on top of me, positioned himself to penetrate, and said, 'Look at me' before the first thrust. It was incredibly hot.

I was drunk enough to have no inhibitions but not too drunk to switch into paranoid mode once it was over. We had another drink afterwards but it was clear there wasn't going to be a repeat because he said he was leaving the next day. 'My son's coming over and staying on his own in the house for the first time,' he told me. Then he asked if I wouldn't mind if he told his son I was a friendly neighbour in case he got freaked out being up there alone. I said fine though did think at 19, he was more likely to be throwing a party and wishing there were no neighbours!

When he left, I crawled into bed feeling rather pleased with myself and then woke the next day and resumed my routine. I was writing away when I looked up to the house and it was like déjà vu. There was a tall, muscled, blond man leaning on the rail, looking down at me. The son. He didn't look 19 and certainly didn't look like he'd need babysitting – quite the opposite. He waved at me and gave a broad, cheeky smile so I waved back but felt strangely nervous and excited seeing him there. I wondered what his father had told him about me. Did he know we'd slept together? Is that why he was grinning at me like that? Oddly, I didn't feel embarrassed if he did know. I think I *wanted* him to know. It made me feel turned on again! Thing is, when I haven't had sex for a while, having it doesn't just wake up my libido – it comes *roaring* back to life. The sex last night was very good but

I wanted more. Except . . . this guy was 19 – the same age as my daughter! I'd slept with his father the night before! And where did I get off on thinking sex was even on offer? He was a hot 19-year-old and I was a worn out 40-something. I didn't know why I was even thinking these things but for once in my life, I decided not to judge the voices in my head.

I was on tenterhooks that first night and the next, for no reason other than my imagination was going wild, but nothing happened. The son would appear on the balcony and wave and smile but that was it. Until the third night. I'd been watching a movie and polished off most of a bottle of wine. It was about 11pm when the doorbell went. My stomach flipped but I was also a bit annoyed. If it was the son wanting help with something, it was a bit rude to turn up so late!

I opened the door and there he was, very obviously a little drunk, and managing to look sheepish and cocky all at once. He said, 'I've just come back from seeing a friend and saw your light still on so I thought I'd come and say hello.' I was going to point out that neighbours don't usually call in unannounced at 11pm, then decided not to. That was probably early on a Friday night to someone of his age and I'd just come across as prissy and old. So the flash of annoyance disappeared and I asked him to come in. I could tell by his manner that his father had hinted that 'friendly' meant 'hot to trot'. I wasn't sure if he knew I'd slept with him but I did know Daddy knew full well his son would never need 'looking out for', as he put it. Perhaps it was a challenge. I'd told the father that I didn't go around sleeping with strangers but maybe he figured he'd fulfil another popular female fantasy: sleeping with both father and son.

Anyway, I slept with him. Of course. We opened some wine and played some music and he was well-educated, if a little slurry, and bursting with youth so I just figured, why not? I was in another country and no-one knew me so it was the perfect opportunity to get away with something sexually shocking. He took the lead and kissed me and so I took him into the bedroom and, while he didn't have the sexual finesse of his father, his body was obscenely good and what he lacked in experience, he made up for in enthusiasm and stamina. Like father, like son, he left soon after the sex was over – and the next day the house was empty again.

I went through a little period of beating myself up but then decided, what was the problem? I'd practised safe sex, no-one would know and I would tell no-one. The only person I did confess to was my friend who owned the house. He thought it was the sexiest thing he'd ever heard and was only pissed off because I didn't think the father or son were remotely gay and open to a pass from him! Since then I have turned the whole thing into an even naughtier fantasy of having both of them at once, so I'm not exactly riddled with guilt!

'I had a lap dance and ended up a lesbian'

Julia, 38, is an architect

THE FANTASY

The lap dancing club is upmarket and sophisticated. My boyfriend and I have been planning this for weeks and both of us are jittery with excitement. I'm wearing a gorgeous little black dress topped off with high, high heels. My hair is piled high on my head, my lips are pouty in pale pink lipstick, and I've got smudgy, smoky eyes – the look is very Bardot. My man wears a grey suit and white shirt and looks hot and handsome. It's his birthday and tonight is my treat for him.

We're here to choose a girl to give us a private lap dance. It's been his fantasy for ages. Mine as well: I've always loved looking at women. I think their bodies are amazing. We sit at the bar and peruse what – or more accurately who – is on offer. There are so many beautiful girls, it takes us ages to choose. There's a curvy, olive-skinned girl who looks Brazilian. She's sexy and flirtatious and gives the impression she loves what she does. We're blown away by her act: she grabs onto the pole and she's strong and athletic. Her routine is energetic but erotic and her body is perfect: high, rounded breasts, a fleshy, peachy bottom, not an ounce of fat anywhere. But she's soft and womanly, not skeletal.

My boyfriend votes for her but I am transfixed by another girl who stands out from the crowd, not just because she is taller than the other girls – she must be 5ft 11 at least – but because she's aloof and graceful. The other girls are blatant with their advances, lots of eye contact and touching to encourage the men to buy private dances. This girl is cool and manages to look unattainable: quite an achievement when she's a lap dancer and available to anyone who has the cash. The girl has a Farrah Fawcett hairstyle: it's flicked back from her face in an 80s style that suits her perfectly. She is long and lean, wearing a tiny crochet bikini and high, clear Perspex heels. She walks around the club and everyone's eyes follow her, even though the standard of beauty is high and she has lots of competition. She is virtually naked and her body is flawless but her face is even more exquisite. High cheekbones, wide-set eyes, and lips that look bee-stung, full and kissable.

I watch her fascinated for a full half hour. Men look at her but they don't book her for a dance. I think they are intimidated by her: she's too tall and too classy. This is the girl I want. My boyfriend agrees. He's getting off on me watching her. I know he's hoping for some girl-on-girl action but I don't think you're allowed to touch, so that's not going to happen.

She knows I've been watching her and when I beckon her over, she merely arches an eyebrow, smiles and walks our way. She sits down next to me and we start chatting. She's Eastern European and used to live in Prague. We order champagne and she chats away. Up close she's even hotter and I want to kiss her. This is our third bottle of champagne and I feel all giggly and as fizzy as the bubbles. 'Would you like a private dance?' she asks. I nod and my lower abdomen contracts. I feel myself getting wet.

We follow her down the back of the club, watching her perfect bottom as she strolls through the crowd. My boyfriend and I clutch hands and smile inanely at each other. She takes us into an area that has tiny rooms with benches in them. They look like slightly bigger versions of a Catholic confessional booth. We sit down and look at her expectantly, not really knowing what happens next. She smiles and says, 'Sit back and enjoy', stands in front of us, takes off her top and then, unexpectedly, leans forward and kisses me full on the lips. 'You like women?' she asks me and she's got her fingers under my chin so I'm looking straight into those gorgeous blue and grey flecked eyes and I squeak, 'Yes' and my boyfriend draws in a sharp breath. He's incredibly aroused already.

She smiles and says 'Good. So do I', and then she reaches down and takes off her bikini bottoms and stands there before us, completely naked. I didn't think they got naked so I'm a bit shocked. My boyfriend and I are still clutching hands so tightly that my hand is going numb. She turns so she has her back to us and starts gyrating her hips sexily, pushing her bottom towards me so I can see there's a sheen to her. She's turned on. I think she likes me, even though we're paying her. She reaches behind her and holds herself open with her hands so we can see her arse and everything in detail. I didn't expect this. I had no idea it would be this intimate or sexual. Or that she'd be this close. I could stick out my tongue and it would make contact.

I'm suddenly shy about what's expected of me so I turn to look at my boyfriend. His eyes are glazed with lust and he can't take his eyes off her. I should feel jealous but I know it's the interplay between her and me that's arousing him the most. She turns around to give us a front view and dances in front of us, slow and sexily. She plays with her breasts, kneading them, tweaking her nipples. She leans forward and presents them to me, cupping them and literally putting them under my nose. She plays to me the whole time: my boyfriend is sidelined but he doesn't care. She leans forward and kisses me again and then she straddles me so we're face to face and she's perched on my lap, playing with her breasts saying nothing, just looking into my eyes. I look back and want desperately to kiss her and feel her breasts and lick her everywhere but I know we have to play by her rules. I am so turned on by her and the whole experience,

I'm throbbing with want. All too soon the dance finishes. She gives me another kiss on the lips and then, suddenly, it's all over and the tiny bikini is on again. I don't want it to stop and am tempted to pay for another dance immediately but my boyfriend doesn't want to. He wants to go home to have sex. In the cab, he tells me it was the best ten minutes of his life. At home he makes me tell him how turned on I was by her, over and over, while he thrusts long and hard inside me.

THE DECISION

Ironically, it hadn't ever occurred to me to look at another woman in a sexual way until my husband took me to get a lap dance. We were out with friends to dinner, all a bit drunk, and on impulse went into a lap dancing club for a bit of a laugh. The couple we were with got a private dance and my husband begged me to give it a go so we did. I can't say it did much for me. The girl was too plastic: fake breasts, fake arousal, orange tan, five layers of false eyelashes. Trashy. The dance itself did nothing for me but what it *did* do is trigger an erotic dream about how it might have been and that quickly turned into a fantasy I'd regularly masturbate to. I didn't think too much of it: I've fantasised about all sorts of things over the years and this just got added to the list.

About three months after that, I went to a dinner party with my husband at one of my best friend's houses. There were about 12 of us there. My husband and I weren't in the best place in our relationship. We were arguing and I had lost all sexual desire for him – though not desire for sex in general, so I felt in a constant state of sexual arousal that I couldn't satisfy. Perhaps this was a contributory factor to what happened next.

A couple I'd never met before walked in and I was transfixed by the woman. She was the most unusually beautiful woman I had ever seen. Her mother was Brazilian and her father black American and, while her siblings had dark skin her skin was white. Her features looked like what you'd expect from that pairing but her skin was the same colour as mine. It gave her a slightly strange, exotic appearance that I found captivating.

I had never been attracted to a woman before. I hadn't had any 'crushes' or teen same-sex exploration at all. Apart from the lap dance and resulting fantasy, I was about as straight and vanilla as they come. Yet I found myself drawn to this woman in both a romantic and physical sense. I was so confused by not only the feeling but how strong it was. She seemed drawn to me as well and we ended up talking to each other most of the evening. Her husband drifted off to talk to mine and we eventually went and sat outside on our own on the balcony. We it was more than just going out for a cigarette; we wanted to be alone together.

Nothing was said until quite late that night, when it was time to leave. I went outside for a final cigarette, willing with all my heart that she'd take the hint and follow me. And she did. She stood beside me and looked at me and said quietly, 'I don't know how you're going to take this but I really want to see you again. I'm straight but I feel oddly attracted to you. Would you like to have coffee and talk about this?' I asked her later how she knew I felt the same but I think everyone felt the sexual tension between us. It was blatantly obvious this wasn't just two women getting on like a house on fire. My friend who held the party said we barely noticed or acknowledged anyone else that night and only had eyes for each other. The fact we were both married – and to men – made it even more unusual and apparently a few people remarked on it to her.

'I'm straight but I feel the same,' was my reply to her. 'I don't understand what's happening.' She said she didn't either but she gave me her card and invited me to call her if I thought meeting up was a good idea. I pocketed it and said goodbye but honestly didn't know if I'd call her. I have never felt such conflicted emotions – elation, love, guilt, shame, fear, confusion – and in such immense proportions, all at once. My husband, as per usual, was possibly the only person in the room not to notice what had happened. I was quiet but he just assumed I was tired and nothing was said.

I went to sleep thinking maybe I'd imagined the whole thing. We'd consumed a lot of alcohol, after all. But when I woke up, I knew with absolute certainty that I wanted to be with her. Not just for a day or for sex or to have an affair but to live with her as a couple. I didn't wake up and suddenly decide I was a lesbian – it wasn't about loving a woman at all – I simply fell in love with her as a person and her gender was unimportant. People find this the hardest thing to comprehend but I've done research on it and it's not that unusual. I think women are far less hung up on putting labels on their feelings and sexuality than men are.

THE REALITY

I called her at 11am the next day while my husband was playing squash. She answered immediately. I knew from her voice that she felt the same way. It was uncanny. We arranged to have lunch the following day which was a Sunday. My husband didn't bat an eyelid, just said to have fun and he'd enjoy watching films I wasn't interested in. Her husband, I found out later, was annoyed that she'd arranged something on a day they usually spent together but she said she'd already agreed and couldn't back out now. She'd told me the night before that they'd been having problems so I think he was suspicious and had spotted something my husband hadn't.

We met in the bar of a hotel. In typical female fashion, we immediately launched into talking about our feelings. There was no pretence, no games. We drank a bottle of wine and we talked and talked and held hands under the table and laughed and cried and when we couldn't bear not kissing any more, we moved to a sofa near the fire that was more private and kissed for hours. People saw us and we attracted a lot of attention. When was the last time you saw two women in their late 30s, snogging like teenagers in a posh hotel bar? But the clientele were of the same age and most just smiled in our direction. We talked about our marriages, we talked about how we'd never fancied a woman and how weird it was and how soft our lips felt and we talked about how we would leave our husbands so we could be together.

It was absolutely ridiculous when I look back now. Not just leaving for someone I'd only just met but how we both reacted to what happened. Men would never ever react in that way. Can you imagine if our husbands had set eyes on each other and thought, 'Wow! I don't know why but I have feelings for that man!' Their reaction would be repulsion. They'd push the thought away violently, drink more and ignore each other all night.

The next day we both missed work and met at a cheapie chain hotel and spent all day in bed exploring each other. It was the most intensely sensual experience of my life. Women are soft and yielding and everything is tender and gentler. She made me orgasm with her tongue and later her fingers and although the whole experience should have been freakish and surreal, it felt the opposite. It felt normal and right.

We went home and both told our husbands the marriage was over. Neither of us had children; we were both high earners and our marriages weren't in great shape when we met. But I felt awful for hurting my husband: I still loved him terribly, just not in the right way. He was incredibly hurt, which is understandable, and still doesn't speak to me. He says he feels betrayed by my 'pretence at being a "normal" woman'. He doesn't understand this doesn't mean I am lesbian. If things don't work out with her, it wouldn't occur to me to look for another woman to love: I'd look for a man. This is about meeting someone who spoke to me so strongly, it overrode all of society's rules about how I am supposed to behave. I don't think too many people are lucky enough to experience it, so it's not surprising hardly anyone understands.

'I strapped on a penis to become a man'

Alex, 34, is a teacher

THE FANTASY

I'm a prison guard, working in a high-security prison. Most of the inmates are hard-core but there are also white collar criminals who've committed crimes like fraud. Most of the men are unattractive with weathered skin, bad teeth and attitudes to match. They try to get away with things because I'm a woman but I don't hesitate to put them in their place and they quickly learn to show respect.

I have never fancied an inmate. I find those women who befriend prisoners on the internet, then visit and marry them on the outside, to be utterly pathetic. But then a new inmate appears on my block. He's much younger than the rest, mid 20s, and has a vulnerable, sweet air about him. I ask another guard what he did and he says he embezzled funds from where he worked but only because his mother was ill and he needed money for treatment. This still makes him guilty but I feel something I don't feel for the others: pity. I start to sneak him extra treats – it helps that he's handsome – and we start to talk a little. He asks advice on how to keep the other prisoners from making sexual advances. I tell him to keep his head down and not attract attention but secretly think he hasn't got a hope in hell because he's too pretty.

I have to behave a certain way with him because I'm a guard and he's a prisoner. I'm friendlier to him than any of the other inmates but I'm still stern and order him around. But I can tell he looks forward to my shifts and I find myself being drawn to his cell more and more. One night, I ask him how he's going with the other prisoners hassling him for sex and he says it's fine but he needs some sort of sexual outlet. I tell him he's out of order saying something like that to me and that I have to punish him. It's late so the lights are out and the block is quiet and dark as I unlock his cell. I order him to stand when I come in and he does so. He's quivering and I'm not sure if it's with fear or excitement. I tell him to turn around and he feels the cold steel of my handcuffs around his wrists.

I tell him to get down on his knees and face me and he obeys. Then I pull up my skirt and push my panties to one side and command him to lick me. Immediately he pushes his face into my pussy and licks with relish and enthusiasm, burying his tongue inside me. He's been starved of sex and the smell of a woman and I can tell he loves the punishment I'm giving him. I orgasm quickly and push him away, roughly, the second I'm done. I order him to stand up, turn around and not make eye contact and he does as he's told, keeping his eyes lowered the whole time. I undo the cuffs and say I hope he's learnt his lesson. He says he has and it will never happen again.

The next night, as I walk past his cell, he makes eye contact deliberately but then hastily looks away when I stop and approach him. I ask him if he just looked at me and he says 'Yes I did. I am so sorry'. I tell him sorry isn't good enough and unlock the cell. This time I order him to lick my breasts. Over the next few weeks, I command him to lick my breasts, my pussy. He's always handcuffed and always at my mercy. I get him to push his fingers inside me and inside my bottom. Wherever I want to be touched. I never touch him or let him come but on one special occasion, when he was really bad, I undid his fly and pulled out his penis and straddled him, letting him penetrate. He came so fiercely, it felt like a tidal wave erupting inside me. I keep doing this, using him as my sex slave, until

I get bored with it all. He begs me to continue but I've had enough. Besides, there's another new inmate who looks like he needs to be taught a thing or two . . .

THE DECISION

My boyfriend was one of those strong-jawed handsome men that looked a bit like Buzz Lightyear from *Toy Story*, like he should be on a horse, tipping his hat and saying 'Ma'am'. I think that was what made this whole thing so weird for me. I just couldn't equate his obvious masculinity with what happened.

He told me he was quite sexually inexperienced compared to me but keen to explore new things. We'd been going out for about three months when I suggested we played a game where we had to write down 10 new sexual things we wanted to do, then read them out loud to each other. On his list he'd written 'anal'. Rather presumptuously in retrospect, I thought he meant anal sex with me on the receiving end. I sort of smiled and nodded nervously – I've tried anal intercourse and it's not my thing at all but I didn't want to put him off by disagreeing at that early stage. One of his other requests was to go to a sex shop together, so off we went the following weekend on a little excursion to Soho, London.

We wandered around looking at things but he seemed transfixed by these dildos that were revoltingly realistic: all purple veins and flesh coloured and made from that creepy cyberskin. 'We should get one to fulfil that fantasy of mine,' he said, looking hopefully at me. 'OK,' I replied, albeit doubtfully, and picked up the smallest, slimmest one I could see. 'No, that's way too small,' he said and picked up an enormous beast of a thing that looked twice the size of a normal penis. 'Also, doesn't it need to be a strap-on?' he asked.

Two things occurred to me at this point. The first was that he was nowhere near as innocent as he was making out. The second was that I'd got the whole anal thing around the wrong way. He didn't want to anally penetrate *me*, he wanted me to penetrate *him*.

'Is this for you to use on me or me to use on you?' I asked.

'You to use on me,' he said, then looked at me, incredulous, 'God, did you think I wanted to put that inside you? Look at the size of it! You must have been freaking out!'

This I found even more confusing since, as far as I know, men and women are similar size in the bottom department. Why would it be ridiculous to put it up my bottom but not his? He'd clearly done this before! I asked him if he had and he said he hadn't but he did look a bit coy.

Since it was his fantasy, I let him choose and he quickly picked up a strap-on version of the 10 inch one he'd been look-ing at earlier. The second surprise was at the till when he picked up a bottle of something called 'Liquid Gold', otherwise known as poppers (amyl nitrite). I think pretty much everyone knows poppers are the drug of choice for gay men who enjoy anal intercourse because it relaxes the sphincter muscles to allow penetration. My boyfriend was looking less Buzz Lightyear and more Julian Clary by the minute.

THE REALITY

When we got home, he opened a bottle of wine and suggested we take it into the bedroom. Clearly he was keen to try everything out but I didn't quite know how I felt at this point. I was definitely confused by it all – and seriously questioning my boyfriend's sexuality. I kept sifting back through our relationship history for any conversation or suggestion he might be bi. There was part of me that wanted to push this as far as I could, to see how he'd respond, for clues to what was really going on here.

I put the strap-on penis on over my bra and pants (there's a sentence I thought I'd never say) and went and had a look in the mirror to see how I'd look as a man. Hilarious! I felt like a workman with one of those tool belts around their waist and swaggered around the flat, pretending to be a bloke and holding my penis and boasting about how big it was. It was the funniest thing ever . . . except my boyfriend wasn't really laughing, so I figured I'd better stop.

'OK, you get on your hands and knees and I'll get behind you,' I said and he replied, 'No, I want to feel what it's like to be a woman so want to be on my back.' So he lies there on the bed, in the traditional missionary position, and I take the top position, like the bloke. He tells me to push his legs back so I can get to his bottom and he's already lubed up down there, so we each take a sniff of poppers and he says, 'Now!' As gently as I can with my head nearly exploding from the amyl nitrite, in I went. The reward was a squeal. And I do mean a squeal. He didn't grunt or say 'Oh!' or 'Ah!' or moan or (the expected!) 'Owww! What the hell are you doing!' He squealed like a girl!

That put me off completely (not that I was ever really into it, if I'm honest) and, by the way, it wasn't easy thrusting either. I have new respect for men on how much work it is after my strap-on experience! I wasn't very good at it and it's exhausting, so I gave up after a while. He seemed disappointed but I figured I'd been more than accommodating! That image of him lying on his back, with his legs in the air and making that girly noise is burned onto my retina forever. I still find it highly disturbing!

We went back into the living room and I came right out and asked him if he was bisexual or perhaps gay. He didn't seem offended and answered it quite honestly, saying he didn't think so but his boss often asked him if he was and he'd sometimes lie with his head on his boss's lap as he stroked his hair. 'There's nothing sexual in it,' he said. 'We're both straight. It's just sweet.'

I sort of smiled and said, 'Course not' and thought to myself, 'Oh God, you are so gay!'

The next week, my boyfriend went away on holiday with his family and I met up with a gay male friend of mine who was visiting from overseas and told him the whole story. He thought it was the funniest thing he'd ever heard but asked to see the strap-on before officially pronouncing my boyfriend gay. When he saw it, he said, 'Are you serious?' We were both a bit drunk and mucking about and it was safe to say my boyfriend wasn't going to be my boyfriend when he got back.

We were debating what reason to give for wanting to end it and my friend picked up a felt-tip pen and said 'How about this?' then wrote 'For a good time call Mark', followed by his phone number, up the side of the strap-on. I thought it was hysterical at the time, but however hard I tried the next morning, I couldn't get the marker pen off the cyberskin! I'd actually packed up the few things my boyfriend had left at my place and had them in a box by the door. I knew if I didn't include the strap-on, he'd be suspicious, but I couldn't put it back in the box with that written all over it. I didn't want to date him any more but I didn't want to hurt him either.

So I decided to put the strap-on down the rubbish chute and tell him I was so traumatised by the whole thing that I chucked it out. I shoved the box in there but to my horror, it stuck! I got a broom to give it a good shove down but that just made it worse. Now I couldn't reach it! I had visions of having to call our maintenance man, who is about 500 years old, to fish it out but it eventually dislodged itself after I poured hot soapy water down the chute. I was a lather of sweat by the end of it!

My boyfriend came back a few days later and eyed the box of his stuff sitting in the hallway. I think he knew he wasn't coming back to find me overjoyed to see him. He asked if it was because of what we'd done with the strap-on and I said it was part of it but not really. I wished him well and we hugged awkwardly and that was that. After all my trouble, he never even asked me where the strap-on was or what happened to it. I ran into him years later and he was with a girl who he introduced as his fiancée! I still have no idea whether he's straight, gay or bi. Maybe this is the norm and everybody does it and I'm the prude for thinking it's weird!

'I had a threesome with two men and ended up marrying one of them'

Mia, 27, is a travel consultant

THE FANTASY

Perhaps I was the one who started it all by taking off my jacket. My shirt was sheer and my bra even sheerer. I never take my jacket off at work so I'd forgotten how see-through the shirt would be. Both men's eyes gravitated to my breasts immediately. That's when I first started thinking about what happens in movies when people are in this situation: they always end up having sex.

I'm stuck in a lift with two other men. One man is blond, the other dark-haired. The blond man is mid 40s and smartly dressed. The other is mid 30s and also suited and booted but radiates less confidence. I'm guessing both are businessmen given I'm visiting a corporate building. The lift shuddered to a halt about 15 minutes ago. We know we'll be fine because there's CCTV and they announced through the lift intercom that the technician is on his way. We've done the usual chit chat and I'm bored. I'm also quite horny and there's nothing I like more than teasing men.

Perhaps taking off my jacket was subconsciously premeditated. Perhaps it was simply because I was hot. Either way, doing it makes me start fantasising about what might happen if I made a move on one of these men. What would the other do? Join in or ask us to stop? The more I think about it, the more I want to do it. The men are strangers. They don't know me, I don't know them. Where's the harm in some anonymous, no-strings sex?

I look at their hands. The blond is wearing a wedding ring; the other guy isn't. The blond clearly plays around. He has his eyes trained on my nipples and doesn't care that I've clocked it. We're all, somewhat bizarrely, still facing the lift doors. I guess we're expecting them to magically open, even though we've been trapped in here for a while. My eyes slide to the side and meet the blond's. The look he gives me is challenging. He licks his lips and holds my gaze insolently.

I turn my face to look at the other guy, the shy guy. He's also looking at my nipples but more furtively. He sneaks little glances at them then looks down at his shoes. When I meet his eyes, he smiles nervously and says, 'I'm sure it won't be long now. Don't worry'.

I smile slowly and seductively and say, 'I'm not worried. Quite the opposite in fact. Now, if we're going to be locked in here together, how about we have some fun?' Shy guy looks at me confused and gulps but the blond needs no further encouragement. He takes off his jacket and throws it so it covers the CCTV. Good move. Then he steps forward and grabs me and kisses me hard, putting his tongue in my mouth. I kiss him back. He starts biting my neck and his hands are on my breasts in a flash, kneading them and tweaking my nipples through the sheer fabric of my shirt.

The other guy stands there watching us, breathing heavily, not sure what to do. I was right: he's shy and not game to touch me in case he's read the situation wrong. I'm kissing the blond but giving him the eye over his shoulder. My eyes clearly say, 'Don't worry, it's your turn soon.'

The blond unzips my sexy fitted skirt and pulls it down over my hips. Underneath I'm wearing sheer black panties with stockings and suspenders. I like wearing sexy underwear under my corporate clothes because it gives me an edge when I'm dealing with 'alpha men' who think they can intimidate me. All I do is cross my legs and let them glimpse a suspender belt and suddenly they forget their train of thought and lose it completely. Not that I'd ever sleep with any of them but it's a handy trick to have up my sleeve if all else fails when I'm cutting a deal.

My skirt is off and next thing blond guy is sliding off my panties. I tell him to leave my stockings, suspenders and high heels on and get a huge grin in response. He pulls me towards his eager mouth and holds onto my bare buttocks as his tongue dives inside me, finding my erect clitoris and licking noisily. I love noise, it turns me on so much.

I tell shy guy to come and stand behind me which he does instantly. Blond guy is proactive and calling the shots; shy guy clearly needs instruction. I lean back against him and tell him to bite my neck and play with my nipples. He's surprisingly good at it: just the right amount of pressure with both his mouth and his fingers. Meanwhile, the blond guy is still going to town, moaning and licking, and watching him work on me while the second guy tweaks and kisses me, tips me over into my first orgasm. The blond guy keeps licking furiously until I'm done, then stands up, wipes his mouth and looks at me. He doesn't say it but the question hangs in the air: now I've had my orgasm, is the fun over?

'Unzip,' I say, signalling it's not. He grins again, unzips his suit trousers and I immediately fall to my knees and take him into my mouth. I give a hell of a head job and he throws his head back and moans as I pump him up and down with my hand while my warm mouth wraps around his penis, making a snug fit. My tongue swirls around the head. He moves to put his hands on the back of my head to pull me closer, so I'll take more of him in my mouth, but this is my cue to stop. I don't want to waste that glorious erection. I want one of them inside me and the man with the biggest, hardest erection wins.

I turn to shy boy who is still hanging back though clearly excited by the look of the huge bulge in his pants. I turn to face him and order him to show me his penis. I tell him the hardest, biggest man will be the one who gets to fuck me. His eyes slide to the blond guy's crotch. The blond is standing back watching, breathing heavily and jerking himself off. Shy guy's eyes then meet mine and he looks confident as he releases himself. I can see why. I'm impressed! He's thick, long, as hard as a rock and the clear winner.

I turn my back to shy guy, lean forward, lift my bottom and spread myself wide. I am wet and ready and he slides in easily in one stroke. I cry out when I feel him fill me up. I love being licked but nothing compares to having a big, hard penis inside you. Blond guy stands facing me, waving his hard-on somewhat hopefully in front of my face. As shy guy grabs my hips and thrusts deeply inside me, I grab hold of blond guy's penis and expertly fellate him. Within seconds, we're all climaxing in a gloriously sweaty, noisy, writhing sex chain. As shy guy spurts deep inside me and blond guy comes in my mouth, deep contractions start deep within me and spread throughout my body. It's the most erotic, primal, filthiest orgasm I have ever had.

Once we're done, everyone suddenly becomes shy. They zip up and wait politely for me to get myself together and look decent before blond guy removes his jacket from the CCTV camera. Everyone switches into polite mode and pretends nothing happened and we're all relieved when the lift restarts, depositing us safely on the ground floor. The lift technician eyes us all suspiciously but we smile sweetly and pretend to be stressed out by the whole encounter. I shake hands politely with both the men and go on my way back to work feeling satisfied and rather pleased with myself for making the most of a bad situation.

THE DECISION

Travel consultants get a ton of freebies and I spend my life travelling, checking out hotels and resorts for our clients. Our company is high-end and it's a pretty nice job though not great for relationships because I am hardly ever at home. I'm really fit and active so am usually the one in the office who gets nominated for all the sporty holidays or destinations. I don't mind, I love a challenge and jumped at the chance to go to Turkey for a sailing holiday that also included resort stays along the way.

I'm a sexual person and hadn't had any for some months. I have a sex buddy but he's just as busy as I am so I'll often go a few months without sex. I don't like it but that's just the way it is. I remember hoping there would be some other hot guys on the trip and was disappointed when all the consultants met at the airport and I didn't fancy anyone. But when we transferred to the sailing part of the holiday two days later, I remember getting out of the car and seeing the crew of my boat and thinking 'Oh my God!'

The first two guys I set eyes on were gorgeous. They were English but had been working in Turkey as crew for ages. They both had amazing tans and great bodies because sailing is hard work. They were clearly friends because they were both larking about and you could see they both had a great sense of humour. I was by far both the youngest and most attractive of our group, so got cheeky grins and flirty banter from both of them when I got on board.

I figured the three of us would have fun together but didn't think past that even though, like most girls, I'd had fantasies about having more than one man. I've always been way more attracted by the two men/one woman threesome than the two women/one man combo. What's the point of two women? My favourite thing in sex is intercourse. I'm not a huge fan of oral sex so why would I want an extra mouth when I could have an extra penis?

THE REALITY

During the days, we'd sail. At night, we'd stop and sleep at different resorts. I was supposed to mix with the other consultants but they were all either old or dull and I found myself finding excuses to hang out with the boys instead. Over the next few days, we had quite a few laughs and I'd sneak off the second I could from the organised dinners and come and meet them either on the beach or at a local bar afterwards. They were both really flirty with me when I was with them and it was clear both wanted to sleep with me. It became a competition over who was going to win me over, but in a fun rather than serious way.

I definitely got on better with the older guy but the younger guy was cheekier and very, very hot. On the second night before we were due to leave the boats and book into the last resort for my final leg of the trip, they told me they were going to throw me a leaving party at their hotel. When I got there, they took me to the bar and we drank gallons of champagne. When the bar closed, it seemed rude not to go to their room to continue partying. The next day was a free day for me, so I didn't have to be up early and I really liked the attention. They were hot and fun and they were both so complimentary it was a massive ego-boost.

It was obvious by the way the whole thing was handled that they'd planned the threesome and discussed how it would work. Both of them sat beside me on the sofa and the younger guy said, 'Come on, give me a little kiss. You're leaving soon,' and grabbed me and gave me a big tongue kiss. I kissed him back – I was pretty trashed – and then the older guy, sitting on the other side, said, 'That's so unfair. What about me?' and pulled me to him, so I kissed him as well. When we stopped kissing, the young guy grabbed me again and started kissing my neck and feeling my breasts and the older guy put his hands on my hips and pulled me towards him. Next thing, we'd all moved to the bed and both of them were making love to me.

I can't remember feeling either shocked or surprised. Instead, I remember feeling really turned on and not coerced into it. I think I joked that they'd planned it and they grinned and admitted it. It was clear I could say no at any point, though they got my clothes off pretty damn quick so they didn't give me much time to protest. The younger guy was the first one inside me and it felt amazing. He was very hard and thrust really deep and powerfully. I loved it but I was hotter for the older guy, even at that point. I reached for him and he sort of pushed the other guy off and then he was inside me. Their thrusting styles were radically different: his was more of a grinding motion and he kissed me during it while the young guy didn't.

They both took turns, though no-one came (I think we were all too wasted) and I don't know when I stopped enjoying it but it was suddenly all too much. It went from feeling pleasurable and racy to feeling like I was being violated. I started crying – we were all so drunk at this point it was bound to happen – and I remember the older guy pushed the young guy out of the way and told him to stop. Then he cuddled me and said 'It'll be OK, it's fine, I'll look after you'. I remember the young guy saying, 'Shit, is she OK?' They were both nice guys and neither wanted to do anything I didn't want done to me. Up until that point, I'd been very willing!

The younger guy disappeared after that. I think he figured I'd made my choice and I fell asleep crying in the other guy's arms. We woke up the next day at lunchtime and I felt absolutely shocking. It was the worst hangover I've ever had plus I felt ashamed about what I'd done. But he reassured me he wasn't judging me and made me feel a hell of a lot better about everything. Then he said he really liked me and asked if he could keep in contact. I said I'd like that and I realised I actually quite liked him too. But what was the point? Not only was he working in

Turkey and I lived in London, I'd just had a threesome with him and his best mate! Not exactly the perfect circumstances for establishing a relationship! I said a teary goodbye to him and a trifle embarrassed goodbye to his mate and never expected to hear from him again. But he texted the second I'd gone and kept on texting. We Skyped the minute I was back and talked for hours and hours over the next few months.

He asked if he could come to visit and I was so nervous picking him up at the airport. But as soon as I saw him, I relaxed. About three months after that, he threw in his job and came to live with me and we got married eight months ago. No-one knows how we met and his mate wasn't invited to the wedding. He said he can't be friends with him any more because it reminds him of that night. He told me he didn't judge me at all for going along with it but that he feels ashamed about plotting with his friend to seduce me. I know not to remind him I was absolutely a willing victim! We don't talk about it and he hates it if I bring it up. I can't decide if it's cool and amusing that we first got together through a threesome or whether it's positively awful. I do know it's something I certainly won't be telling the grandkids!

'We made a sex tape which nearly put us off sex for life'

Sophie, 28, is an arts student

THE FANTASY

When I arrive on set, the director rushes over to greet me, fawning over how beautiful I look and telling me not to worry that I'm over an hour late. I have won Most Popular Porn Star for the company the last three years running and am their prize asset. So they should be falling all over me given that millions of men worldwide would cut off their right arms to have me for five minutes.

Today's shoot is scheduled to last three hours. That doesn't sound very long but think about the last time you had sex for three hours! Imagine not only doing it, but looking perfect all the way through and enjoying every second. See here's the thing: everyone thinks porn stars don't enjoy having sex, that they're in it for the money or to fund a drug habit. A lot of them are – but the best ones, like me, aren't.

I love sex. I've always loved sex and it was inevitable I'd end up making money from it. I'm good at it and men love me – you don't need to be a career counsellor to figure out porn is a natural fit, pun intended. The first shoot I did, I had to fellate five different men who stood around me in a circle. I made all of them come, even when they weren't supposed to, that's how hot I was. I give the best head job most of these guys have ever had. That's high praise given the competition: the high-earning female porn stars know what they're doing technique-wise, believe me. I like sucking men because I like being adored by men and nothing makes you more irresistible than wrapping your mouth around a guy's penis. Nothing.

Today's shoot involves five other people but I am the star. Two girls will join me for a girly ménage à trois and then I'll be penetrated by two men at once. I know the girls, we've done tons of scenes together and the orgasms are real. The dark-haired girl likes my fingers and tongue together: that gets her off every time. The blonde likes a vibrator and tongue combination and my finger up her cute little butt. The first hour and a half will be pure pleasure and play – and I'm getting paid squillions for it.

Then the boys will get involved. I'm the star, so the other girls get to leave at that point. I'll be just getting warmed up because, as much as I like a bit of pussy, it's men that really get me going because that's what the men watching me online or on-screen want to see. They watch the girls go down on me because all men love to watch a girl get eaten but then they want the main event: penises plunging into my mouth and my vagina. The bit they'll pause and rewind and play over and over again is the camera close-up of a guy moving in and out of me. I've been bleached and waxed and of course had labiaplasty (no self-respecting porn star would ever go on camera without it), so I look real pretty down there. I feel sorry for the women these guys sleep with after watching me. How can they compete with me? I am perfection. My ass is high, my breasts are pert, my stomach is flat and my legs are long. I'm blonde, beautiful and young. I am sexually irresistible. I am the Most Popular Porn Star and the most lusted after woman in the world.

THE DECISION

Miami is reputedly known as the home of models and porn stars but when I booked a holiday there for me and my boyfriend, I didn't realise I'd booked us into a hotel that actually had a modelling agency *in the hotel*! Imagine my horror when we walked into the hotel lobby to check in, only to find it packed with leggy, impossibly gorgeous 16-year-old models. They were all clutching their portfolios and eyeing each other up, making comparisons of who was the prettiest and who had the best body.

I stood and stared, looking quite obviously dismayed, but the desk clerk just chuckled and said, 'They're having a casting – it's not always like this. Besides, you get used to it.' That made me feel marginally better but my boyfriend's gawking did nothing for my ego – it wasn't a promising start to the holiday that was supposed to cement our relationship. But it was sort of funny in a dark sort of way – and even funnier when we came down for lunch the following day to find the lobby packed with young, delicious *male* models. That *was* fun! I made sure I had a good long look at their toned torsos before prodding my boyfriend's belly and saying, 'Don't worry darling, I just love your tummy. It's cute!' That taught him!

Even more entertaining was the view of the pool from our balcony. We never tired of people-watching and this was quite the place to do it! Around 10am, the models would appear to sunbathe, carefully arranging themselves on their towels, ensuring there were lots of free chairs between them and the next girl. They weren't friendly to each other and nearly always came solo.

It was about day two that the porn stars arrived – and they were far more fun! It wasn't hard to spot them – they fit every cliché in the book. Big, fake breasts, high heels worn with their bikinis, women of a dubious age with equally as dubious surgery, fake hair extensions, fake nails, deep throaty voices and attitude galore. They'd settle themselves down with magazines, completely rearrange the pool furniture, click their fingers impatiently to summon the bar staff, talk loudly and stare insolently at any man they didn't know who dared to come near them. The male porn stars had receding hairlines, ponytails, good bodies and tiny swimming trunks with impressive bulges. Seriously, you couldn't have come up with a more formulaic bunch if you'd cast them from a dodgy acting agency.

But they were fabulous to watch. The dreary models did nothing but read books, drink Evian and leave after an hour max. The porn stars were loud and sassy and got louder and sassier as the day wore on. One of the bar staff told us they were filming porn in one of the rooms of the hotel and tended to film in the morning when everyone was fresh (faces and other bits droop when tired and drunk, he said with a wink).

It wasn't quite the romantic escape we'd hoped for. But it was quite something being surrounded by such beauty and the blatant sexuality of the porn stars who loved nothing more than flaunting their stuff and winding up all the poor husbands who hadn't had sex in years. We'd lay bets on which wife would be first to purse her lips and stomp huffily off to the room when hubby stared a second too long at the DDDD breasts and bikini bottoms held together by dental floss.

Apart from initial jealousy pangs, we embraced the whole thing and had the best sex ever in that hotel room the first week. We'd role-play a fantasy where we'd be walking past the hotel room where they were filming the porn. Someone would open the door at that very moment and see us and beg us to help because Long Dong Whatsit and Big Breasted Bertha hadn't turned up and they needed two extra people to take their place. When we were by the pool watching their antics, it had us in fits of giggles. But in private, it got us steamy and sexy and my boyfriend especially loved imagining the scenario while having sex facing the huge mirror in front of the bed. He was behind me so his stomach was hidden and just his shoulders were in view. I was leaning on my forearms so my tummy was hidden by my arms, my breasts flatteringly squashed upwards between my elbows. We should have studied that pose a little more carefully and analysed why we didn't look half bad.

Instead, we rather vainly and naively commented on how good we looked – which is why when my boyfriend came up with the idea of filming ourselves, I agreed. I was a little surprised because he didn't have the best body – rounded shoulders, shocking posture, a huge beer gut and weedy legs (that sounds so unkind but he'd be the first to admit it!). But I figured the models and the porn stars and our little fantasy about starring in a porn movie had overcome his body insecurities. Meanwhile, I was battling with a few of my own. My boyfriend was a real foodie, we'd both given up smoking and I was about a stone over my normal weight. I wasn't feeling too hot either, particularly having to bare my bod beside the perfect and porn-perfect competition by the pool. But if he was game I was and it just so happened he'd bought a new high-tech camera in duty free, so it would be rude not to try it out. Right?

THE REALITY

We decided to film it the next afternoon. We'd had a long, boozy lunch and a swim in the pool and were both feeling brave and fruity. There was a long, low chest of drawers by the side of the bed, so that seemed the obvious place to put the camera and put it on self-timer. We set it to run for ten minutes, thinking that was about right, then jumped into position and basically acted our asses off until the bell went, moaning loudly and sucking our tummies in and being all active when usually we're both lazy and try to just lie there in hope the other one will do all the work. It was a lot of bloody effort, quite frankly, and I think both of us were secretly relieved when the time was up.

We poured a drink and sat on the bed eager to watch the results. The first minute was a bit shocking – we both looked so white and, well, fat really. But just when we started to kiss passionately and it got a little bit interesting, the camera wobbled and then dropped slightly so the view shifted from a side view of us to a view of the wall and our legs from the knee down. I probably don't need to point out that not a lot happens in sex from the knees down. I guess we were flinging ourselves around so much, pretending to be porn stars, one of us knocked the chest of drawers. We both had a giggle but we were secretly peeved. We'd been brilliant and we'd sucked our guts in for a whole ten minutes. We were also slightly freaked by how we'd looked in the beginning minute or two when the camera was on us and spent a lot more time second time around positioning it so it was a more flattering angle – which basically is impossible when you're side on.

My boyfriend decided we needed to use a tripod to put the camera at a different angle and height, so the next half an hour was spent trying to figure out how to put that together. I spent it trowelling on make-up and trying to make my hair look fuller and more tousled. I also decided to wear a sexy bra – basically because I was worried my boobs would look all floppy. My boyfriend rolled his eyes a bit when I emerged and was looking more and more irritated by getting the tripod to stay up but eventually we got it to work and were ready to film.

We were distinctly less enthusiastic second time around and I have to say the overriding emotion flitting across our faces was more grim determination than lust. But no-one could ever accuse either of us of being quitters: we kept going anyway. We'd had another half bottle of wine mucking about with the tripod and gave up on holding our tummies in. The moaning had turned into rather unattractive grunting and it was boiling in the room because we'd shut the sliding window, and forgotten to turn on the air con, and I kept on saying 'Are you hot? Is it really hot in here?' . . . and not hot in the way it was meant to be!

Playing it back was the most humiliating moment of our lives. In our heads, we were two attractive twenty-somethings having hot, dirty, enviable sex. We'd even talked about maybe offering it to an amateur porn site if it was good –though we were both pissed at the time! But neither of us was prepared for the hideous, unspeakably distressing video footage that appeared when we pressed play.

There's a reason why porn stars all have tans, false eyelashes and pumped-up lips. White skin does not photograph well. It looks blue and veiny and blotchy and uneven. The camera light washed us out: I'd loaded on the make-up but looked like I had none on. When there was colour, we looked pink and sweaty and bored . . . but that was the flattering part! It was the wobbling fat that sent us both over the edge. There appeared to be fat everywhere, on every part of our bodies. The hideous lighting found deposits of it under our chins, on our backs, our tummies, our arms and – dear God – the thrusting motion made it wobble and jiggle in the most unbecoming, unattractive way. You wouldn't wish this sex tape on your worst enemy!

We tried to laugh it off and went back down to the pool for a swim, but being surrounded by all those young, ridiculously good-looking people made us even more depressed. We gave up and went for an early dinner but I was so disgusted with how I'd looked on film, I ate nothing but a green salad. My boyfriend did the opposite and pigged out. He said there was no hope so why not eat what he wanted. It was gross! We were both tetchy and bad-tempered and it felt like the holiday was ruined.

Happily, the next day we woke up and the whole thing just seemed funny. Really, *really* funny. We played it again and this time laughed our asses off and saw the funny side. Eventually, we decided just because we didn't look like porn stars didn't mean we didn't fancy the pants off each other and in a way, it was good for us. We'd both always been quite self-conscious in bed because neither of us were that confident of our bodies. Now we'd seen each other at our absolute worst, we gave up worrying about what we looked like and enjoyed sex a lot more because of it. I still wouldn't recommend it though. Unless you're both brown, thin and in a place with *extremely* flattering lighting, knowing what you really look like having sex is a reality most couples could live without!

'I spied on my flatmate having sex with her boyfriend'

Milly, 19, is a junior researcher for
a production company

THE FANTASY

There aren't very many female cab drivers in the city and ninety per cent of the people who get into mine comment on it. Women mostly ask me if I feel safe; men can't help themselves making some sort of quip about women drivers. But once they've got that out of the way, passengers relax and continue on as normal. They chat to their friends, play with their phone or – often the case when you work late at night and in a busy part of the city – each other.

I'm used to drunken couples getting a little carried away in the back of the cab. There's no harm done and so long as they don't start jumping all over the place or – every cabbie's worst fear – vomit, I just look out of the window and ignore them. But I knew the minute this couple got in, something unusual was about to happen. They weren't drunk, it wasn't that late but there was something about the extended eye contact and the piercing eyes the man had. He asked if I'd take them to an address that was a good 45 minutes away and when I agreed, it felt like I'd agreed to a lot more than a cab ride.

They asked for an unusual route – one that took us off the main highways and down deserted streets. The couple sat looking straight ahead, not talking. The girl had her hands folded primly in her lap. She had on a smart coat, gloves, high heels and black stockings and was young and very pretty. The man had on a business suit and expensive looking overcoat. He removed his coat once inside the cab. She kept hers on. They were so quiet, I started to feel a little uneasy – especially since the route they'd chosen was hardly direct.

Then the man said something to the woman, she unfolded her hands and put them, palm down, on the seat on either side of her. He then leant forward and started undoing the buttons on her coat, systematically, taking his time. She didn't move. She just sat passively, looking straight ahead, her hands resting on the seat beside her, allowing him full access. When he'd undone all the buttons, he pushed the coat aside – first one side, then the other – and I gave a little start. The woman was wearing nothing underneath but underwear. Very sexy underwear. A demi-bra with cups that barely covered her, her breasts sitting prettily inside them, half her nipples visible. She had lacy French knickers on with stockings and suspenders. Her expression remained unchanged: she was curiously impassive, even though she was sitting there in the back of a taxi half naked in front of me, the driver.

The man looked in the rear-view mirror when we stopped at some lights and made eye contact. He smiled at me so I dropped my eyes and pretended nothing was going on. Then a car pulled up beside us. Only then did the woman move. She calmly pulled the coat so it covered the sides of her but left the front exposed. Then she met my eyes in the mirror and her mouth curved, just a fraction, upwards. This pacified me somewhat. Whatever kinky game this guy was playing, she was in on it and approved. I wasn't sure what my role was but guessed, rightly, I was merely an observer. They were exhibitionists and I was to be the voyeur.

The car next to us pulled away and I drove a little slower, deliberately not catching up. I knew what they wanted me to do now: create a little private bubble for three, without acknowledging that's what I was doing. The man leant forward again, put a hand on each of the woman's knees and pushed her legs open. I swallowed. Her panties were crotchless so this exposed her completely. Both still staring straight ahead, the man lifted his fingers to his mouth, licked them, and then put his hand in between her legs and started lazily playing with her. I saw her arch towards his hands, just a little, but then she reverted to the 'Nothing's happening' frontward gaze, albeit with parted lips. The man's hand was busy but his head was turned and he looked out of the window nonchalantly.

I, meanwhile, was finding it difficult keeping my eyes on the road which was, of course, their main intention. The woman orgasmed, or at least I think she did. Her mouth opened wider, she shut her eyes for a second or two and her eyelids fluttered. The man's hand slowed and then he took it away altogether. They sat still, companionably, like they'd just finished discussing the weather, then the woman leant over, undid the man's belt and unzipped him. He continued to look out of the window. Her hand snaked inside his trousers and she wrapped her fingers around his penis and pulled out an enormous erection.

It was my second gasp of the evening: even in the half-light it was impressive. The man looked up and caught my eyes, giving me a small, secretive (and one might say) rather smug smile. He then kept looking into the rear-view mirror the entire time his companion jerked him off, her hand pumping up and down the shaft, her palm sliding up and over the head, twisting as she went. I couldn't help but watch as she brought him to a swift climax, but not before she produced a large linen handkerchief for him to ejaculate into. How considerate of them.

Job done for both of them, he casually zipped up his fly and went back to looking out of the window. She did up the buttons on her coat, crossed her legs and looked out of hers. Ten minutes later we arrived at their destination. I was a little shell-shocked by the experience but I have to say, the whole thing was classily done. Truth be told, I'd actually quite enjoyed it. The man paid triple the metered fare, thanked me for being a 'gracious' driver and then the two of them walked off arm in arm, the woman turning to give me a conspiratorial wink before they disappeared into the night.

THE DECISION

I've always shared flats or houses with lots of people, which reduces the intimacy level and makes it easier in lots of ways. But when my best friend suggested we find a place together, it seemed logical and appealing. We were both single, both best mates and excited about having our own place. The first few months after we moved in were brilliant. We had dinner parties and house parties and chilled nights, just the two of us, watching DVDs with takeaway and wine. Perfect!

Then she met her now boyfriend and the dynamic changed. Two single people works well; a couple and a single not so well! I got that she was loved-up and he lived in a shared house, so they got more alone time at our place than his. But it still irked me that he was always there. I felt like an unwelcome intruder in my own home.

The absolute worst thing was constantly walking in on them with their hands all over each other. It was embarrassing – and it highlighted the fact that I wasn't getting any sex! I asked my friend to be a bit more private about the whole thing and only do it behind closed doors but she shrugged and said she wouldn't really care if I walked in because I was her best friend and we talked about sex all the time anyway. In my defence, that is a bit of a green light, isn't it?

THE REALITY

Not long after that conversation, I came back from a party and walked in on the two of them snogging furiously on the sofa. A film was playing, unwatched, on the TV. I rolled my eyes and said, 'For God's sake guys, get a room already!' They laughed and then my flatmate got up and walked unsteadily over to me, gave me a kiss and said, 'I wish you had a boyfriend sweetie, you're so pretty!' I could tell they were both absolutely sloshed. I was tiddly but she was slurry and she always got super affectionate when she was drunk.

I got myself a glass of wine and a cup of tea, went into my room and shut my door. I chilled and read my book for a bit then was about to play some music when I heard moaning sounds coming from the lounge room. I went to put my earphones on but for some reason I paused. They were obviously up to all sorts out there . . . and the only thing between us was a door. That door – my bedroom door – opened into the lounge room.

I knew they were both drunk. I wasn't. They wouldn't be expecting me to watch them but I would have my wits about me. What would happen if I opened the door a tiny bit and had a look at what they were up to? I heard another groan and then the sound of movement on the sofa. I felt really aroused suddenly and put my hand down my knickers to feel. I was wet and horny so I got my vibrator out of the side drawer.

At first I thought I'd just masturbate while listening to them. But when I started doing that, I got hornier and wanted to watch as well. So I decided to push the door open just a little bit. They wouldn't notice and if they did, I could always pretend I thought it was shut. So I got up and turned the door handle really slowly and pushed it open a crack. It seemed to take about ten minutes to perform this simple task. I was paranoid I'd look through the crack and see my friend and her boyfriend standing there with hands on their hips, looking indignant and furious at me. But instead I saw my flatmate lying back with her jumper pushed up and one of her boyfriend's hands kneading a breast while he went down on her. He was facing the other way with his face buried in her crotch, while she had her head back on the sofa with her eyes closed. Bloody hell! Watching oral sex is way more intimate than watching people having intercourse, which is what I'd expected to see. I pulled back automatically, feeling like I was invading their privacy massively (which of course I was!) and felt like a weird pervert. All I needed was a raincoat and I'd be set.

But something made me want to keep looking. I'd watched porn and obviously seen sex on movies and TV shows but watching real people do it, people I knew, was fascinating. There wasn't anything gay about it – I'm not into women at all and find the whole threesome thing with a really good friend pretty gross. I didn't fancy her boyfriend either. What I found riveting was just watching how they had sex. I'm quite a competitive person so I guess I was mentally comparing how I'd look and what I'd be doing with a guy. Also, we'd talked loads about sex and I wanted to see how accurate a picture she'd painted.

I was definitely still aroused but touching myself or using my vibe while watching them would have felt seriously creepy. So I just watched. After she had an orgasm he got up and laid back on the sofa, and she unzipped his pants and returned the favour. I couldn't really see what she was doing but he sure as hell liked it. He didn't take his eyes off her the whole time, which was rather handy for me!

He suddenly told her to stop – I'm guessing because he was about to come and didn't want to. There was a bit of fumbling and then he was on top of her and they were shagging on the sofa. The novelty of watching them had worn off a bit by this point and my first thought was 'Ewww. He hasn't got a condom on and you can bet it's all going to leak out and I've got to sit on that sofa tomorrow!' My second thought was 'Shit! My flatmate is looking straight at me!'

Sure enough, she'd turned her head to the side and was looking directly at my bedroom door. I froze and swear I nearly fainted but thank God I did freeze because after what felt like an eternity, she looked away and started kissing her boyfriend while he humped her. I had three options of what to believe: A) she hadn't seen my door was ajar, B) she'd seen me but decided to deal with me later, C) she saw me and got off on me watching. I made a mental pact with God never to ask anything of him ever again if the answer was A) then I gingerly pushed the door shut with my foot and sat down very, very carefully on the bed. I put my earphones on and pretended all was fine and nothing weird had just happened.

After about ten minutes, I heard footsteps and closed my eyes, bracing myself for a tirade. But they kept going down the hall. The loo light went on and there was a flush soon after then they both took themselves off to bed. I got into mine and wondered if I would be forever scarred by what I had done and never fancy sex ever again. What made me do it? I wasn't even drunk! I hardly slept that night, worried sick about what might happen in the morning. But when I finally did venture out, they were the ones who were sheepish.

'Hi lovely, I hope we didn't keep you up last night with the TV on so loud and ... everything,' my flatmate said. 'I didn't hear a thing,' I replied, 'Put my earphones on and listened to music and then fell fast asleep.' She smiled and looked relieved and exchanged a 'Thank God she didn't hear' look with her boyfriend and that was that. I sent my own 'Thank you God' message to the man upstairs! I don't know how I would have justified what I'd done. A couple of times since I've been tempted to confess and, knowing her, she'd probably think it was funny. But you don't know, do you? I'm not sure I'd think it was funny if my flatmate spied on me. Would you?

'I tried to save my marriage with anal play'

Helen, 42, is a lawyer

THE FANTASY

I'm on holiday in a hotel and lying on a sunbed on my balcony, sunbathing nude. No-one can see me except the people in the next room but they've just checked out because I heard them packing and leaving. I feel drowsy in the sunshine and start to feel sleepy and dreamy. I always get turned on sunbathing nude, so it isn't long before I start playing with myself a little, licking my fingers and lazily stroking myself. I'm just starting to get serious when I feel someone watching me.

I open my eyes and there is a man standing on the balcony next door, facing me, standing still. I have no idea how long he's been there but he has clearly just checked in because he is still in his business suit. He probably walked out onto the terrace to check out the view and instead found me, naked and playing with myself, on the balcony next door! I desperately hope his wife or girlfriend isn't about to come out and join him. It's embarrassing enough just him but it would be doubly embarrassing if his partner saw me as well.

The man is tall and well-built, and his suit is expensive. He has dark hair, olive skin and stubble on a strong jaw. Just my type. I sit up, a bit groggily, and start to apologise. I don't even have my sarong on the balcony to grab so I put my hands over my breasts and pubes. He says, in a smooth, cultured accent I can't place, 'Why apologise? I was enjoying it. Would you like to come over and have a drink with me?' I can't read him because his eyes are hidden under sunglasses but I sense this is a man who is used to being obeyed. I feel my insides contract and my nipples go erect. I like dominant men and being ordered around. This man looks like he's done a thing or two and I'm as horny as hell.

I nod yes and head to go inside but he says, 'No, come this way'.

I walk to the divider and he leans over, picks me up and carries me inside. Holy fuck! This is going to be interesting . . .

I'm expecting him to throw me on the bed, unzip himself and plunge straight into me. But he doesn't. He puts me down in the middle of the room and tells me to stay where I am. I stand obediently, naked in a stranger's room. He then swiftly locks the door, drops his jacket on the chair and undoes his tie. The sunglasses stay on and I love the anonymity. He turns me around so I'm facing the bed and ties my hands together with his tie. Once they're bound, he puts his arms around me and starts squeezing my nipples while kissing my neck. I'm completely naked and he is fully dressed and it's delicious. I try to turn around but he says 'No'. I decide to obey him and that he's not to be messed with.

He orders me to stay facing the way I am and I hear him unzip his suitcase, then he's back and the room goes black. He's blindfolded me. I'm not sure what with but I can't see a thing. I feel so wet, I swear I will come without him even touching me. The whole scenario is just so erotic.

'Step forward' he orders. Then 'Trust me' when he sees my hesitation. His arms guide me as I shuffle forward a bit and find the softness of the bed. I'm lying face-down, blindfolded, my arms tied behind my back and resting in the small of my back. He pulls me down the bed so my feet are on the floor but my body's still on the bed, then he pushes my legs wide apart. My bottom and my pussy are exposed fully to him. A complete stranger and I am completely at his mercy. I can't see but I sense he's still got his shirt and trousers on and I hear rather than see him rummaging around in his suitcase for more things. I expect he's looking for condoms and the next thing I'll feel is him taking me from behind.

But he doesn't. It's not his penis I feel but his fingers, oddly cold and hot at the same time. It's because there's a glob of cold lube on them. It feels wonderful. And his fingers aren't on my clitoris but sliding between my buttock cheeks, grazing the opening to my bottom. His fingers move back and forth, slowly and teasingly. It's the only part of him touching me. I can hear him breathing and it's harsh and hard. He's turned on but he's not getting undressed. I'm nearly sliding off the bed and moaning, straining to move myself against his hand it feels so good.

He gets down on his knees on the floor behind me and holds me in position – legs wide, bottom spread, upper torso face down on the bed – by placing two strong hands under my upper thighs and buttocks. I feel breath then his tongue, sliding between the lips of my vagina, teasing my clitoris. I want to climax and lift my bottom high so his tongue can reach underneath me to get fuller access but he stops, pulls back and I can feel him just looking at me. I moan and beg him not to stop. He obliges and I feel his tongue on me again except this time he's licking my anus, rimming it with his tongue, then he makes his tongue stiff and sticks it inside me, plunging it in and out. No-one's ever done that before but it feels good, really good and so wrong and bad. It's like nothing I have ever experienced. I moan and he asks if I like what he's doing and I answer yes yes yes, God yes.

I hear him squeezing the lube again and then his fingers gently probe where his tongue was. I open up to him and it hurts a little at the start but then he starts moving his finger gently inside, in and out, and then the pain disappears and the feeling is exquisite. I love it. I hear a vibrating noise and with his other hand, he's holding a vibe on my clitoris. The combination of the two sensations – anal and clitoral – makes me orgasm so hard, I feel like I'm going to wet myself. It's so extreme.

'We're not done yet' he says sternly. I feel his fingers inside my bottom again and, amazingly, I'm writhing against his hand even though I've just come. He removes them and I feel oddly empty but then I feel him inserting something else inside me. It feels like a big set of pearls, being pushed inside me, one by one.

'These are anal beads,' he whispers, 'Relax and they won't hurt.'

So I relax and just when I feel on the verge of feeling uncomfortably filled up, he stops and carefully flips me over on the bed. I'm still blindfolded but now face-up, my bottom on the edge of the bed, my legs on the floor, with my hands still tied and above my head. He kneels down and starts lapping between my legs, his tongue expertly manipulating my clitoris until I can feel the waves of orgasm approaching again. The beads inside me press against my vaginal wall so everything feels full and more intense with all the nerve endings on full alert. Just as my body moves into intense orgasmic contractions, he pulls the beads out gently but firmly and, oh, the sensation of the two together is other-worldly. I come and come and it lasts minutes, not seconds, and never seems to stop.

THE DECISION

I'd only been with one other man before I married my husband and that was more a teenage fumble than anything else. I was 22; my husband was exactly double his age. We met through work and it was a nice, if uneventful marriage. We had a child, we worked, we rarely argued and were considerate of each other's needs. To my friends, who seemed to spend their lives with guys who treated them badly, my marriage looked perfect.

Our sex life was routine and dull but I didn't know any different: my libido wasn't high because I'd never developed that side of myself. My parents were strict, my husband was conservative and the predictability of our sex sessions made me feel comforted at first. But once our child reached two, I went back to work and started to gain confidence and that was when I started to change.

I knew I was in trouble about one second after meeting my workmate Sam. He was a partner at the law firm: sexy, worldly, experienced – everything my husband wasn't. He pursued me relentlessly and while sophisticated in other matters, I was hopefully naïve when it came to men. His blatant desire for me made me on edge and wildly excited. I was embarrassed by his obviousness but loved it nonetheless. We started having 'working lunches' that quickly turned into 'working dinners', then we weren't doing any work at all, just chatting and becoming more and more infatuated with each other. I didn't do anything though until we travelled together to another city to service a client.

I knew he'd invited me to do more than assist him workwise and I kissed my husband goodbye, knowing it was the last time I'd be able to look him in the eye without guilt. The 'work' took about an hour and the rest of the time we stayed in the hotel room where, for the first time in my life, I lost myself in lust. My husband had never even undressed me. Sam ripped off my clothes, desperate to touch, feel, lick and bite every inch of me. My husband stuck to the absolute basics. Sam licked me from behind as I crouched on all fours, like an animal. He put fingers in places they'd never been, he buried his face in me and licked me to orgasm again and again, loving it best when I hadn't showered, so he could truly smell me. He said he'd never been with a woman so innocent but so willing to be corrupted, or one who responded so intensely. Sex with him was messy, sweaty and animal. I barely recognised myself in the mirror afterwards. Swollen lips, wild hair and hooded eyes: it didn't look like me. I went home and while my heart still belonged to my husband, my body had been hijacked. It was about that time that I started to have fantasies like the one described: I went from nice girl to 'totally out there girl' in my head all the time.

I loved that I now loved sex. I didn't want it to stop: the genie had been let out of the bottle and it wasn't going back in. But I wasn't in love with Sam and I wanted my marriage to work. I wanted both my husband and great sex and figured if I could be awakened, then so could he.

My husband was a man whose idea of wild sex was doing it on top of the covers, rather than under them. I knew it was a long shot, getting him interested in 'naughty' sex, but I respected him and we had a child together so I felt I owed it to our marriage to at least try.

I sat down with him and told him I loved him but I really wanted to spice things up a little because we were in a rut sexually. He looked uncomfortable but listened. We went through a few sex books together and marked a few things to try. I was instigating everything but I thought he was just shy so I left the books lying about, thinking he might look at them when I wasn't there.

To be fair, I used to be equally as uptight and subdued but my affair with Sam had unleashed a murky, seamy side to me and I was determined to embrace it. I could have just kept on seeing my lover indefinitely but I wanted to create that desire between me and my husband.

THE REALITY

We'd come back from a nice dinner out and so I figured it was as good a time as any to try out the stuff we'd talked about. I changed into some new, saucy underwear and came out of the bathroom, expecting a response. My husband was sitting up in bed reading and looked up and did a double take, but didn't say anything. I tried not to let it put me off and got into bed. He put the book down and turned towards me. My lover Sam loved giving me a running commentary of what he was going to do to me so I tried getting my husband to do the same. I arranged my body provocatively on the bed beside him, kissed him and said 'Tell me what you want to do to me.' I thought that was gentle and non-threatening but he looked at me blankly and after what seemed like 10 minutes, said 'I want to have sex with you?' It was pathetic.

I must have looked annoyed because he started kissing me and I thought things were going OK. He was looking down at what I was wearing so I opened my thighs a little to show him I was wearing panties with a slit in them. They were a tasteful version of crotchless underwear, the idea being we could leave them on during sex. I thought they were sexy but I saw distaste rather than lust cross his face and it made me angry. My husband told me later he hated what I was wearing and didn't know what was expected of him. He said he'd mentally closed his eyes and prayed to God to remove this tacky, nasty woman in this ugly, horrible underwear and return the classy, nice wife he'd loved for the last 10 years. If he'd told me that at the time, perhaps it would have changed things, made me see it from his side more, but he didn't.

When Sam and I did naughty things it was erotic, not seedy, but my own husband was making me feel like I was behaving like a slut. I was also confused because we'd decided together that the way we'd try to become more adventurous was to try out things like talking dirty and role play, which were both fantasies of mine. But he clearly hadn't looked at the books I left for him, judging by how terrified he looked. That also annoyed me. Here I was trying my hardest to make it work and what effort was he making? I know I was cheating but at least the affair had brought things to a head and made me face up to how shitty our sex life really was.

He started kissing me again – I think that's all he could think of to do – and it was awkward and sexless and awful. I wanted to cry rather than have sex. But most of all I just felt overwhelmingly angry, though that seemed to turn me on again in a bit of a nasty way. I think I wanted to show him that I wasn't the scared little person I'd always been in bed; that I'd been liberated. I wanted to show off. So I decided to bypass the dirty talk and go for something far more 'forbidden': anal play. I'd always fantasised about it – I think a lot of really conservative women do, because it's a real taboo still – and I'd done it with Sam and was surprised how much it turned me on.

I pushed him away to stop him kissing me and said 'I want you from behind. But not in the normal way.' He didn't even understand what I meant by that! 'What do you mean, "not in the normal way"?' he asked me. He'd barely been able to muster up an erection but it shrank rapidly when it finally dawned on him what I was suggesting. I hadn't actually had anal intercourse with Sam because he was too big but we'd used fingers and a vibrator, and my husband's penis, even when erect, wasn't as big as the one we'd used. I'm still not sure whether I wanted to shock him into giving proof that he did still fancy me sexually, or shock him into realising I had been with someone else. No-one changes their sexual personality as dramatically as I had without something drastic happening like an affair.

'You want to have anal sex?' he said, making it sound like I wanted him to go into the next room and smother our sleeping child. Again, I felt dirty and punished so I lost it and shouted at him to get with the fucking plot and be a man. It was awful. The old me not only didn't want anal sex, I'd never shout at him or belittle him. I was probably as shocked by my outburst as he was. Things had been strained and stilted but the anger I felt was overwhelming. When I shouted at him, everything drooped. He crumpled into himself and looked bewildered, and I could see why he would be. One minute, he had a happy marriage and a wife who was happy with missionary style sex once a month. The next, for no apparent reason, it was all being called into question.

He told me later – years later when the hurt had eased a little (we still see each other for our child's sake and try to remain friendly) – that he'd figured something had happened to change me, he just didn't know what. It didn't take too much guesswork to work out it had something to do with my new job. But he figured it was a female colleague influencing me and saying he was too old for me and our sex life needed spicing up. It hadn't occurred to him that a man had tempted his wife into actually *doing* any of this stuff I was now saying I wanted to try. He said he knew something had gone wrong with his marriage but he still had immense, unshakeable faith in me to do the right thing by him and the child we'd created. It is a sad fact that the people we think we know the best are often the ones we know the least.

But the way I acted that night and how I'd spoken to him killed the 'my wife would never betray me' innocence he'd been clinging to. He said he knew without a doubt that I'd done this before. I actually *hadn't* had anal intercourse before, but he wasn't far off. He said the more he thought about it, the more he believed it and the rage built and built until suddenly he exploded. I saw the change in his eyes – and his groin. They both went hard. He grabbed me by the hips and shouted at me, 'You want me to do you in the ass? Is that what you want?' Then he turned me over and I could feel his penis pushing against my bottom, trying to ram it inside me.

I'd put some lube by the bed and he grabbed it and poured big globs of it onto my bottom and then he was inside me. I don't know if it was because we'd never done it before and there was so much emotion but when he penetrated me, I climaxed. I guess because it felt so tight, he came too. But it wasn't a nice feeling, that orgasm. It felt wrong and I hated it. A second later, he was slumped over me crying onto my back and I was sobbing into the pillow underneath him.

We both cried for a while and then went out into the kitchen and sat down over cups of coffee where I confessed to my affair. It was pointless lying at that point. He asked if I loved Sam and I said no, which was true, but this only made it worse. My husband was a deeply religious, conservative man. If I had been unfaithful for love, he might have forgiven me. But he couldn't understand and didn't trust lust. I don't think he honestly liked sex that much and seeing this new side of me, a lusty side, offended him. He didn't want to be with someone like that. He was even more disturbed by me having awakened a primitive urge in him as well: he might have hated what we did but he'd still orgasmed from it. In a sense, this is what broke the marriage up – me discovering I loved sex – not me acting on it with someone else.

After that, I quietly went to pack a bag and stayed with a friend for a few nights. I never saw Sam, my lover, after that. I just didn't want to. I sorted out a place to live, my husband and I started divorce proceedings, and I took myself off to see a counsellor and tried to move on. Happily, I am now with a man I love and who loves sex as much as I do. He likes that I'm adventurous and we're still having great sex four years in. I enjoy anal play with him, like I did in my affair, but I'm not interested in trying anal intercourse any more. The whole experience was too traumatic and I think it's put me off for good.

'I turned my husband into my sex slave'

Danielle, 36, works in retail

THE FANTASY

I walk into my harem to choose a man to service me for the evening. I clap my hands to announce my presence and all the men spring to attention and stand in front of me with respectful bowed heads. They have bare chests and wear identical linen trousers that hang low on their hips. They keep to a strict fitness regime and eat super healthily, so all of them are ripped with not an ounce of fat between them and plenty of muscle to go around. There are 10 of them but I have my favourites: there are four that I have a special bond with. They've been with me the longest and I allow them to talk with me when we're in private.

These four look more expectant than the rest but there is one man I have only had once before and he's been in the harem for more than six months. I needed to leave him alone to break his spirit. He arrived too cocky, too sure he would become my favourite. The men are all handsome but he is breathtakingly beautiful. The first and only time I allowed him to pleasure me, he was bold and impertinent. His former mistress had clearly indulged him and he had ideas above his station. I'd ordered him to stop licking me and he blatantly buried his face and continued, relentlessly, so I orgasmed before I was ready. He watched me as I writhed about and that was also forbidden. His eyes challenged me when I was at my most vulnerable. I've

235

ignored him ever since and sure enough, he now looks humbler, more accommodating, less sure of his looks and skills as a lover. He's ready to be taken again.

'You,' I bark. His head snaps up and he looks startled. I'd forgotten just how startlingly blue his eyes were. I order him to follow me into my chambers and to draw me a bath. He does what he's told. I slip into the water naked and it's just the right temperature. I order him to bathe me and he picks up a sponge and begins washing my shoulders and neck with the warm, soapy water. I make him wash my breasts, between my legs and only once do his eyes flick up to meet mine before guiltily sliding away.

Once my bath is done, he wraps me in a big towel and dries me all over. I get him to fetch the body oil and lie face down on the bed for a full body massage. His strong hands glide all over me, kneading and massaging and relaxing me totally. I am putty in his capable hands and I'm confident he is now tamed and completely in my control.

I ask him to stop massaging and start stroking me instead. He lovingly wipes the oil away with a soft towel, leaving my skin silky soft, then his fingers brush so lightly, the touch is barely there. It raises the tiny hairs on my skin and makes goose pimples. It's simultaneously relaxing and stirring.

I want his tongue between my legs and order him to take off his trousers and service me with his mouth. He obeys and I can't stop staring. His penis is the prettiest specimen I have ever seen. It's magnificent: rock hard, straining upwards. A healthy young man's penis, in its prime and begging to be used. But not yet. First his mouth.

He climbs onto the bed and opens my legs wide. I expect him to settle down between them but instead he kneels in front of me, lifts my legs and puts my knees over his shoulders. My bottom is completely off the bed with only my shoulders left on it. He buries his face between my legs and licks me while watching my reaction. He's clever. He's doing what I asked but this is the cunnilingus position of an alpha male wanting to dominate the female. I can see everything he's doing, he can watch me while he's doing it. His eyes are insolent but there's lust dancing behind the insolence. He wants me as much as I want him and I decide I don't care that he hasn't learnt his lesson. I'll deal with that later.

He makes me climax and I do it noisily, and before the contractions have ended he drops me down onto the bed and pulls me by the hips until I'm sitting on top of him and my legs are either side of his hips. He kisses me full on the mouth, another no-no, and plunges inside me, filling me up and hitting all the right places. As he pumps into me, I move seamlessly from one orgasm to the next and when he turns me over and takes me from behind, I know I'm heading for another and another.

THE DECISION

It started innocently enough. I was mucking about with my husband and telling him to behave while we were doing the dishes one day and he said 'Make me'. I grabbed both his hands, put them behind his back and said, 'Watch it because I will!' in a fierce voice and I saw his face change. I know my husband's 'sex face' very well. I've been watching that expression for 12 years and me holding his hands behind his back turned him on big time. Next thing we were kissing and ended up having sex right there and then, up against the kitchen sink. We hadn't done that in years.

'You liked me restraining you and bossing you about, didn't you?' I asked him afterwards. He sheepishly admitted it had been a fantasy of his for ages: to be my sex slave. I thought it was funny to begin with but then I started making up scenarios around that theme to masturbate to. It took us a while to act on them because both of us are quite shy sexually. We have great sex and no complaints on either side but we've never been into role play or talking dirty. Like most couples, the most noise we make in bed is the odd moan or groan.

A few weeks after the kitchen incident, I came up behind him and got both his hands and held them behind his back and whispered into his ear, 'You're in my control now.' I kept one hand around his wrists and reached around with the other to feel him and he was hard within seconds. I played with him for a bit but then ordered him to leave his hands behind his back and made him turn around and kneel in front of me. Then I took my jeans off and said 'Lick me until I tell you to stop'. He's pretty good at giving me oral but having him kneeling there in front of me and not using his hands, was incredibly hot. He was so aroused by me ordering him around, he licked me like a man possessed. I loved it and got off in about a minute.

When I finished, I looked down at him and we were both breathing really hard and his eyes were wild. We smiled at each other and he said, 'My God, that was the hottest sex we've ever had'. I asked him if he liked being my sex slave and he grinned and said he loved it. So I told him that coming Saturday, he was going to be my slave from the moment he woke up to the moment he went to sleep. Every single thing he did was in my control. I swear his face nearly split in two from the grin he gave me. His hand immediately went to his penis but I told him he wasn't allowed to touch himself. He took his hands away and said 'You're the boss' but I knew damn well he had a wank at the thought of it when he took himself off to the loo about three minutes later!

THE REALITY

The planning of the day was almost as good as doing it. I kept thinking of things I wanted to do and was in a permanent state of arousal the whole week before. So was he. He kept asking me what I was going to do with him but I refused to give him any details.

On D-Day, I woke up and rolled over to see my husband already awake and looking at me expectantly. I felt a twinge down there and honestly couldn't remember waking up and being turned on within seconds, except back in the very beginning. He smiled and I smiled back at him but then I got into character and made myself stop. 'Get me a coffee and some toast,' I ordered. 'And don't make eye contact with me unless I ask for it.'

Wow! I'd never ordered anyone around like this and I giggled a bit but it made me feel oddly powerful. My husband went to put on his dressing gown but I said, 'No. Fetch me my breakfast naked.'

He walked out of the room with his erection leading the way.

I made him serve me breakfast in bed and stand obediently beside the bed while I took my time enjoying it and reading the paper. Part of me wanted to laugh but I could see he wanted me to take it seriously so I did. I got up and had a shower and told him he had ten minutes to eat something but if he wasn't back and waiting to service me the second I came out of the shower, there would be trouble.

I took my time and sure enough, he was there, naked with his eyes downcast, standing dutifully outside the door when I returned. I ordered him to get a chair from the kitchen and put it in the centre of the bedroom. He did. I ordered him to go into the closet and get a bag I'd put in there, bring it to me and lay everything inside the bag by the chair. He did as he was told. I had never seen him so hard. His penis looked set to explode! It

239

made me smile to myself but I didn't let him see it. He was right into his role and loving every second of it.

Inside the bag were some worn stockings of mine, nipple clamps, a scarf, lubricant, glass dildos and a butt plug. His eyes widened when he saw the props. We'd never experimented with any toys before, so this alone was risqué for us. I made him sit on the chair and I tied him to it using the stockings. I tied his arms first and then decided to tie his legs as well: one leg to each leg of the chair. Then I tied the scarf around his eyes as a blindfold. He protested and said he wanted to see but I ordered him to be quiet and to only speak when spoken to.

I took my robe off and moved naked around him, letting him smell me. I cupped my breasts and put them under his mouth and ordered him to lick them and bite them. Then I pushed my naked body against him and ordered him to smell and bite whatever I put in front of him. It was incredibly intense and arousing, teasing him like that. I was quite getting into it! I got the nipple clamps and put them on his nipples. He winced: they were only 'beginner' ones but I'd tried them out and they were surprisingly painful. I wasn't sure if he'd like them or not but so far so good.

I took the blindfold off because I wanted him to see me and then I got some lube and started playing with one of the dildos, rubbing it against my clitoris and saying to him, 'You're going to put this inside me but only when I let you'. He nodded and his eyes were on stalks. I then got out my vibrator and sat on the bed opposite him and made myself come while he watched.

Once I did, there was a temptation to stop playing the game because I was satisfied, but I said he'd be my slave for a whole day and was determined to stick with it. I untied him and told him his next job was to go downstairs, do the dishes and then do the ironing: naked. He looked at me with a 'Now you're taking the piss' look but when he opened his mouth to say something, I told him to be quiet and smacked him on the behind. He seemed to like that so I made him go and lie across the bed, face down, then gave him a proper spanking. I hadn't planned on doing that but I liked it and he loved it. I felt a bit sorry for him, not being able to come, so I made him stand in front of me and gave him a quick hand job. He came in about ten seconds, all over the place! We both had a bit of a giggle but then I ordered him to clean it up and he did. What a brilliant idea this was!

While he did the chores, I read and watched a bit of telly. It was weird not having him watch it with me and I tried not to feel guilty while he was working. Then it was lunchtime and the weekend, so I got him to open a bottle of wine and pour me a glass. None for him, obviously. Slaves don't get to drink with their masters! I got another 'Fuck you' expression for that but ignored it.

I thought it would be amusing for me to use him as a human coffee table, so I made him go on all fours and then put my feet up on him. It was an unexpected turn on, so I took off my jeans and did it again naked from the waist down. I asked him if he could smell me and he nodded. He was hard again. I liked the subservience of the pose so I ordered him to stay where he was and went to get the lube and the butt plug and dildos. I came back and lubed up his bottom and pushed the plug inside. He said 'Ow!' but nodded that he was OK once it was inserted and in place. I spanked him again and asked him if having the plug inside made the spanking feel different and he said 'God yes'.

I felt really horny again so I lay back on the sofa and ordered him to get the dildo and lube. Then I made him push the dildo inside me and thrust it in and out. He tried kissing me but I told him that's not allowed. I made him drink wine and then dribble it into my mouth, telling him off for 'accidentally' swallowing some. I desperately wanted him inside me but I wanted him tied up, so I got him to fetch the stockings and chair then tied his hands to the chair again. Then I straddled him and, finally, he got to penetrate me. I went wild! He'd never felt so hard or so big. It felt animal and I loved that we were having raw sex, not 'loving couple' sex. We were polite lovers usually, always asking each other 'Is that OK honey?' This was totally new and I loved that we were both selfishly taking pleasure rather than focused on giving it. This time we both had enormous orgasms and we were spent!

We decided half a day was long enough for him to be a slave so I untied him and we both had some wine and were like two little kids, so excited by the whole thing. We talked about it for ages – how turned on we were, what we liked most about it and why – and we vowed to try more new things. It felt like the sex we'd had at the start and we were so thrilled we'd rediscovered it, albeit a dozen years later. We've done a lot of role play since then and taken turns being 'slaves'. Hard to believe a bit of horsing around in the kitchen could lead to a total revamp of our sex life but it did!

'I slept with my
best friend's boyfriend'

Kate, 38, works in the fashion industry

THE FANTASY

Forbidden people are always the ones who inspire the greatest longing, purely because we know we can't have them. Even being in the same room with him puts every sense on full alert. I am so conscious of him. I can smell him, hear every breath he takes. I try not to stare but when I can I fill my brain with images of him, to keep me going until the next time. I am addicted to him and the addiction needs feeding.

It's worse when it's just the two of us. We behave and nothing is said but I sometimes feel I am going to burst with all the emotion and lust that fills my body, that can't be set free. I busy myself as much as possible. He's in the kitchen, preparing dinner, so I go to my room and gather up some dirty clothes, take them down to the laundry and start putting things into the washing machine, one by one, taking as long as I possibly can. She won't be back for at least an hour, so I need to create space and time away from him. I turn on the machine and lean back against it, close my eyes and imagine what would happen if I opened them and he was there.

And then he is there. He's come in to find me, on impulse it seems, because he's still got a kitchen knife in one hand. 'What are you doing hiding in here?' he asks, standing in front of me and looking at me quizzically, trying to read me. But he knows why. I say nothing, just look back at him and then he puts down the knife and takes a tiny step forward. I grab him and kiss him and dear God, he smells and feels and tastes even more delicious than I'd anticipated. He kisses my neck and my breasts like a man possessed. Buttons pop off my shirt as he rips it open to get at them and I tip my head back and moan.

I'm not fighting it any more and neither is he. I rip open his shirt, my hands roaming all over his chest, and he has just the right amount of hair and feels wonderful. He picks me up and puts me on top of the washing machine and then his hand is between my legs and his fingers are pushing my panties to one side. I am wet and have been ready for him forever. I feel him through his jeans, unbutton him and release his massive erection. He pulls back to look at me and he looks like an animal in the grips of a primal lust and beyond thinking or reason. We don't even stop to take my panties off, he just pushes them roughly aside and then pushes himself inside me as I wrap my legs around his back. I can't believe we're finally doing this, that he's inside me, thrusting powerfully, and we're kissing and it's so unbelievably exciting. I can feel the pressure building and a pull in my lower abdomen and then he's grunting and moaning as he comes and I follow him. I hear someone shouting his name and realise it's me and think we should be quiet, someone might hear us, but at that moment neither of us care.

THE DECISION

My best friend had moved to America about two years earlier and I was absolutely thrilled when I got an email from her saying she'd got engaged. She'd been single for a long time and a lot of her motivation for moving country was to meet new people and hopefully fall in love. I was really happy for her and immediately made plans to come over for the engagement party. I'd just come out of a long-term relationship and didn't relish being around a loved-up couple but she'd been my friend since I was 15. For her, I'd make an exception.

I will never forget the moment I saw her and her fiancé at the airport. I saw her first and thought how amazingly happy she looked. She was standing there, eagerly scanning people coming through customs, searching for me. Her man was standing behind her, hugging her from behind. I smiled at her but her fiancé saw me first and he looked directly at me and smiled. I knew instantly that he had no idea who I was and the smile was an 'I find you attractive' smile, not a 'Hello best friend of my fiancée!' smile. My friend was standing in front and couldn't see the interplay. I wondered if he was a player and this was usual for him, to flirt with strangers literally behind his girlfriend's back, but I didn't get that impression. I just felt a jolt of connection and I think he did too. My friend saw me and broke free and came rushing forward to greet me. He looked shocked and flustered when he realised who he'd smiled at. Nothing had happened other than a smile but something had happened: even before saying hello, we'd acknowledged an attraction between us. Not great when the attraction is between the best friend of the bride-to-be and her prospective husband!

She was crying as we hugged and I smiled at him, tentatively, over her shoulder. He grimaced, acknowledging the awkwardness over what had happened but when officially introduced, gave me a big hug. The second he hugged me I knew I was in deep, deep trouble. The chemistry between us was so strong, I blushed deep crimson. I felt sure my friend would see it, feel it. He was also looking at me too intently, with too much interest. I remember my friend looked from one to the other and frowned, then gave a little shake of her head. She must have been thinking, 'Are those two eyeing each other up? Surely not. This is my best friend and fiancé, I'm imagining things'. But she wasn't.

In the car driving back to her place, all I could think was 'Oh no. Why him? Why him and I?' I don't know what it was about him but he instantly triggered emotions I had never felt for anyone before. I was bowled over by him but it wasn't just down to looks and it didn't feel like just lust. He was pleasant looking rather than jaw-droppingly gorgeous but to me he was perfect. The whole thing felt out of my control even though I was desperately trying to pretend all was fine and talk to my best friend who I adored. She was the last person on earth I would ever want to hurt. What horrid universe would make me fall for her fiancé?

The engagement party was in a week's time and I was in turmoil. My best friend had taken two days off to be with me and all she wanted to do was talk about how much she loved her fiancé and to discuss wedding plans. I put on a brave face but I was dying on the inside. Every time there was the three of us, it was her fiancé and I that dominated the conversation, asking questions about each other. She beamed through the whole thing, remarking on how lovely it was that we both got on so well and were so interested in getting to know each other. Shame overwhelmed me when she said that – even though I'd done nothing, my thoughts weren't pure – and I saw him look away and wondered if he felt the same thing.

I was having daydreams, fantasies, real dreams about him. He'd seeped into every pore, every thought, every second. I fantasised about kissing him, having sex with him, him telling me he loved me. I fantasised that it was me getting married to him, not her. I had no real idea if he felt the same way as I did because nothing had been said. But nothing needed to be said. Every time she left us alone our eyes would bore into each other's and we'd smile manically and everything we couldn't say out loud was being said with our eyes and body language.

THE REALITY

One night, two days before the engagement party, my friend wanted to go to bed early because she had an early meeting the next day. We'd been out to dinner and were in the middle of a rambling conversation about something – the usual nonsensical discussions you have after a bottle or two of wine. Her fiancé went to go to bed with her but she waved him away and told him to stay up late and keep me company. He wasn't working until later the next day and I was on holiday. He made a pretence of hesitating but I knew he'd stay up with me.

We continued the previous conversation for a bit but it was clear we wanted to talk about what was happening. We couldn't talk freely in the house, so he suggested we go for a walk to a nearby lake. It was about 11pm and cold but it was the best idea I'd heard in years. He went up to check my friend was asleep and she was, so we pulled on coats and hats and set off.

It couldn't have been more romantic. We walked through a park to get to the lake and the countryside was breathtakingly beautiful. It was autumn and the trees were a myriad of gorgeous colours, and the sky was clear and littered with stars. We walked in silence for a bit, then a safe distance from the house, he took my hand. I didn't fight it. When we got to the lake, we sat on a bench and he turned to me and said, 'I'm marrying the wrong person. I should be marrying you.' Then he cupped my face in his hands and kissed me.

That kiss was the most bittersweet experience. Feeling his mouth on mine after so much pent-up longing, knowing he was feeling what I was feeling, my heart sang even as my head was telling me how wrong it was. I told him I felt the same way but that we couldn't break my friend's heart. He told me he had loved her but the minute he set eyes on me, he had massive doubts. My head was spinning. I told him how fucked up it would be if we acted on what we were feeling. It wouldn't just mean me losing my best friend; we had a dozen mutual friends who would be horrified and our families were friendly as well. I guess he had less to lose than I did because he was insistent. We kissed again, more passionately this time. I looked at my watch and realised we'd been out for ages and what if she woke up and saw we were gone? He said he didn't care but I did.

We walked back holding hands inside his coat pocket, though the likelihood of running into anyone at that time was low. He begged me to see him after she left for her meeting in the morning and I'm ashamed to admit that I agreed. I didn't sleep very well, obviously, and heard her get up and get ready for work. I felt sick with what was going on but also powerless to stop it. I heard the front door click and her car leave and went to clean my teeth. I didn't honestly expect him to be up but when I came back into the room he was lying on my bed.

And that was that. The next minute we were kissing and then he was touching my breasts and my body, and I have never longed for anything so much or since than having him inside me. I ripped off what I'd been sleeping in and he did the same. Then he was on top of me and inside me and his hands were in my hair and he was saying 'See – we're built for each other. We fit,' and the sex was even better than what I'd imagined even though the whole thing was over in minutes.

But something happened after that. We lay there and waited for our breathing to calm down and every second I lay there in his arms, I was consumed with more and more guilt and remorse. Actually having sex with him made what I was doing real. This was the man my best friend was going to marry! What was I thinking? What sort of awful, disgraceful scumbag of a person was I, lying here in his arms? That was her place, not mine.

I knew I could never face my friend again. I had to get out of there before she came home. Her fiancé sensed my mammoth swing in mood and sat up and asked me if I wanted a cup of tea. I said yes and then got up and had a shower, trying to wash him off me. I don't know when I started crying but I was crying when I came back out and he took one look and said, 'You can't do this, can you?' He tried to cuddle me and kept telling me he loved me but I just felt cold and also thought 'How can he love me when he doesn't even know me?' Whatever spell had been cast had worn off. I started packing my stuff and called a cab for the airport. He looked panicked but I told him I'd tell my friend I had to go back for an emergency, that my mother was ill. He looked relieved and I could tell my reaction had broken the spell for him as well.

He went to his – *their* – room to get ready for work and I was out of there before he came out again. I called my friend on the way and told her my mother was really ill and I'd had to leave. She was desperately concerned and totally understanding. Then I called my mother and told her I was coming back and if my friend called, to pretend she was in hospital. My mother was fabulous. She didn't question. She heard the stress in my voice and said to come straight to her place from the airport. Mum's the only person I told about what happened. She just listened and didn't judge.

I couldn't go to the wedding, so I pretended I was coming and then backed out, pleading work reasons. Thankfully, it wasn't a big church wedding with bridesmaids so not being there wasn't a huge deal. My friend and I have drifted apart since then and hardly email any more. I know she is still married to him and they have a child. She knows something happened I think but she's not game to ask me directly, in case I clarify her worst fears. It's best left how it is with little contact.

'I had sex on a beach as the sun came up'

Shane, 24, is a teacher

THE FANTASY

I'm riding in the woods on my way to go swimming in the lake. Well, that's the excuse I gave. Really, I'm meeting my boyfriend. I've been banned from seeing him by my parents because our families are feuding. Our paths crossed one day when we were both riding and we fell in love. Our mistake was confessing our love and desire to marry. We should have known they'd forbid it because our families have been enemies for centuries, a real Romeo and Juliet scenario. We both promised we'd never see each other again but that could never happen because we aren't just in love, we're soul mates and destined to be together forever.

So we sneak out and snatch whatever time we can at our special meeting place. I tether my horse and go to sit by the lake to wait for him. Three minutes later I hear his horse clopping along the path. I rush to greet him and my heart sings when I see his handsome face. He slips off his horse and gathers me into his arms. I breathe in deeply, filling my nostrils with the scent of him. I look up into his face and kiss his beautiful mouth and we look into each other's eyes, searching for confirmation that our love is still there. I can see by how he looks at me that his family haven't poisoned him against me, however hard they try.

He takes me by the hand and leads me into the woods to our secret place. It's a tiny clearing, flanked by thick trees and undergrowth. No-one knows it's there. It's like Mother Nature created a bed in the middle of the forest, just for us. We find the blanket we leave hidden under a tree, then lie down together and kiss passionately. We haven't seen each other for a week and have limited time: we intend to make the most of it.

His mouth feels hot and feverish as he kisses his way down my neck to my breasts, takes a nipple inside his mouth and sucks it. I arch my back and push my body against him, grinding my pelvis against his. I can feel how hard he is already. He shifts attention from my breasts, sensing my eagerness, lifts up my skirts and removes my panties. He touches me gently and reverently to start, watching my face to check he's doing everything right. He is. I reach down to feel him and he takes this as a cue to unzip himself. I love the feel of him in my hands. I especially love the velvet soft tip of him and rub it around my lips. He groans and pushes me back down so he can enter me. I cry out as he penetrates and squeeze around him as he thrusts gently but persistently, gathering me to him and holding me tightly as we both move towards a shuddering climax.

THE DECISION

I am and always have been a romantic. I have only had sex with someone I am in love with: sex and love are linked and should be linked. I'm religious and shouldn't really be having sex before marriage anyway but I think the church is a little outdated in that regard. My fiancé and I made love about three months in. It was incredibly special and loving and made me love him even more.

I've never been terribly adventurous sexually. I think my fiancé would like me to be a little more outgoing in that department which is why I suggested we act out a long-standing fantasy of mine: to make love on a beach as the sun comes up.

The reason why it appeals to me so much is because it's the perfect blend between romance and sensuality. Being made love to by a man I love and want to stay with forever in such an idyllic location: that's my idea of heaven.

When I told my fiancé this was what I wanted to do, he suggested we make it even more exciting by doing it on our honeymoon. We were going to Thailand and the beaches there are amazing. It was the perfect plan! Our wedding and honeymoon were two months away and I couldn't wait for everything: the ceremony, the honeymoon, being his wife. The sex on the beach part was going to be the icing on the cake!

THE REALITY

Our wedding was everything I have ever dreamed of and more – I couldn't fault one thing. We didn't have sex on our wedding night because I was absolutely shattered, but apparently that's not unusual. We were due to fly out the next day, so we decided our first sex as husband and wife would be fulfilling the beach fantasy. I liked the symbolism of it: sex as the sun came up, the start of a new day, the start of a new life together, possibly even *creating* a new life together!

On the flight over we got lots of treats because we were honeymooners – champagne being one of them – so were quite giggly and smoochy on the flight. It was a two hour transfer to our resort so it was late when we got there but it was worth it. It was spectacular! The honeymoon suite had its own Jacuzzi overlooking the beach and the view was stunning, even at night. It was warm, the staff were friendly and everything was so perfect, I felt like crying!

It was gone midnight but the kitchen was still open so we had dinner in the restaurant, outside on the balcony under the stars. My husband chose a really beautiful bottle of wine and the food was amazing. There were a few other couples still up having cocktails and everyone kept smiling at us, I guess because we were the new guests and also obviously on our honeymoon.

We went back to the room and unpacked and ordered more wine on room service. My husband kept whispering to me that he couldn't wait to get down to the beach and I have to admit, I was excited as well! The sun was due to rise at 6.20am and it was about 4am then, but neither of us were tired. We were buzzing from all that had happened. The wedding, the flight, the resort – it was all fantastic! We got in the Jacuzzi for a bit and larked about and then, before we knew it, it was time to get to the beach.

It was postcard perfect – white sand, crashing waves, the lot. It was still dark but the sky was lightening up fast. We'd taken some towels from the room so lay them on the sand and sat snuggled up together, drinking wine and watching the waves. Then we started kissing and making out. At first, I was nervous people might see us but no-one was up that early so I started to relax.

It felt weird having my breasts touched and kissed, outside in the open air, but I have to admit I liked it! My husband slipped my dress up over my head and next thing I know I'm completely undressed. I made him take his clothes off immediately: I wasn't going to be the only one butt naked in public! Then he was on top of me and we were doing it. I kept wanting to pinch myself that we were really there. I looked up into the sky and I saw the first rays of the sun peeking through and we couldn't have timed it better. Just before he climaxed, my husband whispered that he loved me forever and I closed my eyes and prayed that would be the moment I conceived. I couldn't ever imagine feeling happier. I didn't conceive (our first arrived about 18 months later) but it remains one of the happiest, most amazing experiences of my life.

'I've been having a hot affair for five years'

Mandy, 36, is a business consultant

THE FANTASY

She is newly married. She shouldn't be letting this man do this to her. He spotted her at the conference, made eye contact, saw how she'd blushed but then looked back. A drink at the bar, now she was in his room. Wrong. Bad girl. He's kissing her and she can feel herself getting wet. Her traitorous body is responding to him. She groans as his mouth attaches to a nipple, his fingers disappearing inside her panties. She gasps as he pushes them into her. Hot but wrong. Dirty but delectable. 'You're a dirty little girl,' the man says, 'You love this, don't you? You little slut.'

His words excite her. They make her feel rebellious. Dirty little girl, that's what her parents accused her of being when they caught her with her first boyfriend, who had one hand up her jumper, the other between her legs, when she was 13. Perhaps that's why it is so arousing to be called that now. Slutty. Dirty. Maybe she is both these things. It gives her permission to be both those things.

He goes down on her, sticking his hand up to put his fingers into her mouth. She sucks on them greedily. He licks her then comes up to kiss her, his mouth shiny. When he kisses her, she tastes herself. She tastes salty, aroused.

She reaches down to feel his erection. It makes her feel powerful. I did this, I created this, she thinks. He holds his breath as she closes her fingers around the hardness of him. She makes him stand in front of her then gets down on her knees to unbuckle his belt. She licks a tattoo he has on his hip, winding down to his lower back. He tastes salty, sweaty. Like her. She runs her hands over his fleshy, muscular buttocks. She turns him around and snakes her tongue between them, puts her tongue inside his anus. He groans loudly, calls her a slut again, which makes her do it more.

She stands up and makes him lie on the bed on his back. Then she straddles him, guiding him inside her torturously slowly. Taking her time, inch by inch. Finally, he's buried deep inside her, as deep as he can possibly go, so she makes him stay perfectly still, luxuriating in the feel of him filling her up completely. Then she starts moving on top of him, grinding in slow, sexy circles. He pushes his hips up to meet hers, desperate to thrust deeply inside her. He's watching her face and kneading her breasts as he lifts her by the hips, up and down, up and down. They both watch him disappear inside her. He licks his fingers and plays with her clitoris while he slides in and out. She flexes her pelvic floor muscles, tightening them around him, milking him.

'Oh baby, you're a pro. Say you want this. Tell me you love being fucked by me,' he orders her. She leans forward to whisper in his ear, and their bodies make a squelching nose as they bang together.

'I'm the one fucking you honey,' she says.

THE DECISION

I've been happily married for eleven years and have two children, 8 and 10. Sex with my husband is satisfying and fairly frequent for a couple who've been together over a decade and I love him very much. I am also in love with my lover: a man who is younger than my husband and very different in personality. My husband has no idea I see another man once a week but my lover knows I am married and has no desire to see me more than what we already do. It's an arrangement that works perfectly and, in my opinion, hurts no-one. My husband will never find out because there aren't any texts, emails or letters to find and no friends know my secret.

I met my lover through work but he doesn't work with me – he has his own company. We have a set arrangement: we meet on Wednesday afternoons from 3pm until 6.30pm in his flat. My husband never checks up on me as I'm often out of the office but I always make sure I have appointments written in my diary, just in case he does decide to look. My lover is a worka-holic but religiously slots aside this time for us. Sometimes we'll eat something. Mostly we have wine and chat and have sex, sometimes we'll watch a film together. He's one of my best friends as well as my lover but absolutely no-one in my life knows of his existence and no-one in his life knows of mine. This is why we've got away with it for five years.

I got married at 25 and had little experience with men previ-ous to that. My husband taught me all he knew about sex and I discovered I had a high libido and really enjoyed it. I had no desire at all to sleep around, or leave him and play the field, but when my lover showed obvious interest, I was curious. He was a lot younger than my husband (who is ten years older than me). He was dynamic, creative, driven and ambitious. My husband is kind, loyal, dependable and family orientated. You can see why it works. Between them, they fulfil every need I could possibly have.

He knew I was married but he'd flirt with me when he came in, ask my opinion, and seek me out whenever he visited the office. After six months of this, he finally asked me if I'd like to come to lunch. I said, 'Why not?' and we arranged to meet the following day. I didn't tell anyone at work. I didn't tell my husband. I didn't tell my best friend. I just went to lunch, knowing I wasn't just going to lunch.

He'd chosen a private, romantic restaurant. This wasn't a business lunch and he didn't pretend it was for a moment. He poured champagne and told me he found me incredibly attractive. He said he knew I was married and had kids and he had no interest in 'disturbing' that situation. But if I wanted to explore a relationship with him on the side, he would be incredibly flattered. It sounds very matter-of-fact but I am a matter-of-fact person and this was the perfect pitch.

If he'd professed undying love or been at all sleazy, I would have excused myself and left. But this sounded controllable; put in its proper place before it even started. So I said I was up for trying something and we arranged to meet the following Wednesday at his flat. He didn't touch me at that lunch and only gave a tiny kiss at the end, perfectly appropriate for two friends kissing goodbye. It was obvious right from the start that he had no desire to cause problems or make any scenes. He simply desired me.

I expected to feel guilty seeing my husband that evening but I didn't. If anything, I appreciated him more. I like my husband's personality; he makes me feel loved, supported and accepted unconditionally. On the day I planned to meet my would-be lover, I pulled him to me for a long, deep kiss when he said goodbye. He said 'What was that for?' and I said, 'I just really love you.' He smiled and left, really happy. Even at the start, the affair did positive not negative things for my marriage.

THE REALITY

I drove to his flat at the designated time and when he opened the door, he looked relaxed and excited. I was too – it seemed perfectly natural to be there with him. We had wine, we chatted, and he put a CD on. When he leant forward and kissed me, it didn't feel like the first time he'd kissed me. It sounds odd but I was used to him before he'd even touched me. He kissed differently than my husband, more urgently, with more tongue. My husband probably kissed like that at the beginning but who remembers later on? He undressed me in his living room and took the lead.

It was strange watching another man look at my naked breasts. He ran his hands over them reverently to start, not taking his eyes off them. When I moaned he became more insistent and I liked that better. My husband was gentle with me; I didn't want more of the same. He sensed I liked him being more dominant, so picked me up from the sofa and walked with me in his arms into the bedroom. He threw me on the bed, literally, which made me laugh and then he stood in front of me and undressed. His body was tremendous. My husband's wasn't bad and I liked the softness of his belly against me at night. But my lover was lean and taut. It was all about contrast, right from the start. When people are discovered having affairs and they've chosen a carbon copy of their partner, I always think, *Why would you do that?*

He was naked and hard and ready for me. I felt expectant, excited, *alive*. That was the over riding emotion: I felt *alive*! Any wife with kids will tell you that, as much as you adore your children, they can sap the life out of you with the necessary but relentless routine and monotony of parenthood. I don't resent my kids or husband for making me feel like that – I love being a wife and mother – but this spoke to a part of me that had been buried for a long time.

He was a skilful lover and I admit he wins in the sex stakes – especially in technique. But of course he would. I live with my husband and we have a relationship that involves responsibility. You can't shake that totally when you're in bed. It hovers there and makes sex more meaningful which is both a good and bad thing. My relationship with my lover is pure pleasure. He's an escape for me and I think I am for him. He's had relationships since I've been with him but so far there's no talk of him finishing our affair. I don't know how I'll feel if and when he does. Devastated but resigned is my guess.

I've read several books about affairs, to see if there are other women out there like me. It's not something you admit to people. 'Hi, I'm Mandy. I've got a fantastic husband and two kids at home who love me and a hot young lover who I'm also really into. So you could say I really am having my cake and eating it too!' Somehow I don't think the response to this would be very positive, do you? We are very set in our views as a society. It's clearly spelt out what's acceptable and what's not in marriage. If you're having an affair, you should be riddled with guilt; you must choose between your husband and lover. What I'm doing – having both, not feeling remorseful and refusing to choose – is not acceptable. But I'm happy, my husband is happy, my children are happy and my lover is happy. Where's the problem?

'I put on a naked sex show for the man across the street'

Helen, 30, is a graphic designer

THE FANTASY

I'm in hospital after a knee operation and being sent home the next day. I'm a little high on painkillers when the doctor who did the operation comes to make his rounds. Hopefully he'll give me the all clear to go home because I'm bored senseless in here. The doctor is young and dishy and I'm guessing he's not long out of medical school. I am one of his first operations but I don't doubt he's done a good job. I trust young doctors more than old doctors: they're up on all the new techniques.

As usual, about half a dozen students trail behind him as he makes his rounds, clutching their clipboards and looking adoringly at him. Two of them are women and one in particular is besotted. Her eyes burn with desire for him and even when he points to my knee to explain the procedure, they remain fixed on his face. I don't blame her. He's got the arrogance of the uber-intelligent who are also ruggedly good-looking, a rare and blessed combination. He's flirtatious as well. When he's touching my knee, he turns so his back is to the students and they can't see his face. He makes intense eye contact with me and his eyes deliberately linger on my breasts. I have pyjamas on but I have big breasts and even covered, it's obvious. I smile back innocently enough but I hold his gaze to let him know the breast admiration hasn't gone unnoticed and I'm flattered rather than offended. He smiles and says, 'I'll be back to check on you later'.

He leaves me in a high state of excitement. Did that mean what I think it means? Or did I imagine the whole thing? There's something about the whole doctor/patient dynamic that's deeply sexy. They're in control, you're helpless and your life is in their hands. They can fix you. Most women love to be rescued, even bolshie women like me! I quite liked being 'tamed' by the knee injury. I'm usually so self-sufficient and being forced to rely on others brought out a softer side. I also liked the sexiness of being at someone else's mercy. A hot young doctor's, for instance. It's not like I could get up and run away if he tried anything, is it?

By 10pm, I'd given up any hope of a visit and was grumpily reading my book with a little bed-light, my curtains drawn. The rest of the women on the ward were either reading or asleep. Then I heard quiet footsteps and the curtain was pushed aside and pulled back immediately for full privacy. There he was, standing by the bed, looking down at me with a frown. 'Sorry to disturb you,' he said, in a whisper, 'but I couldn't get away until now. How are you feeling?'

He was still wearing his white coat and acting doctor-like, so I gave him a suitable patient-like response. I said I felt fine, bit of a twinge now and then etc. He asked if he could have another look at my knee so I pushed back the cover. He pulled up the leg of my pyjamas in a slow and sexy way and his fingers examined my knee totally differently to the way he had earlier. His fingers were brisk and professional then, but now he stroked rather than prodded and caressed the skin around it, not going anywhere near the injury at all.

He watched me the whole time, checking my response, alert for anything that might indicate he'd read the situation wrong and I was simply a friendly patient rather than some-one willing to be seduced. I lay there, looking at him, not saying anything but my eyes clearly sent the right signal because he groaned and leant over and kissed me long and hard. He pulled back and put his finger against his mouth, 'Shhhh'. He didn't need to tell me that he could lose his job for doing what he was doing and I absolutely wanted him to keep doing what he was doing, so I nodded eagerly to show I understood.

Have you ever had sex when you couldn't make a sound? Couldn't groan or move a muscle for fear of making the bed creak? Do you know how many noises the body makes when there's complete silence? How noisy lips are when they kiss, bite and lick? How even hands grabbing at breasts make a sliding, connecting noise? How when you're wet, there's a sound when fingers disappear inside you? How when your mouth wraps around a penis, there's a little slurping noise if you do it too greedily?

None of these noises stopped us. We'd occasionally listen to hear if any patients seemed awake (they didn't) or if the nurses had come back from their break (they hadn't) then we'd resume. He turned me gently on my side so my knee was out of harm's way and pulled me to the side of the bed and I stuck my bottom out eagerly. The bed was just the right height: he positioned himself carefully and penetrated me from behind. God, it felt so good, but I couldn't make a sound. Deep thrusting was impossible – it would make way too much noise – so instead he moved his hips in a circular motion and I squeezed my muscles around him, milking him to a climax.

There was nothing but a flimsy curtain separating us from the rest of the ward as we fornicated. One of the nurses could stride over at any moment, fling the curtain back and we'd be busted big time. All of this just made it hotter and I came so hard, I had to put my fists in my mouth to stop myself crying out. I could feel him pulsating inside me as he ejaculated for what seemed like minutes. Then he pulled out and I heard him adjust himself so he was decent and then he gently put me back into sleeping position, covered me up, kissed me and said, 'I think you're healing nicely and ready to go home tomorrow'. The curtain swished and then he was gone. The next morning I wondered if it had all been a dream.

THE DECISION

I've always been an exhibitionist. I'm a born show-off. I'm the person who actually likes playing charades, hogs the mike at Karaoke, stars in all the school plays and is always the first to strip off and skinny dip. I like my body, always have. It's not perfect – not even close to it – but I wasn't like the other girls growing up. I didn't agonise over every little imperfection or extra pound, I just saw all the nice things and the functionality of it all. I liked how it worked, how my heart knew to beat without me having to tell it and how my breasts knew to grow without me telling them that I was a girl not a boy. I found my body incredibly clever as a teenager and still do!

I've never been concerned about being seen naked. I think that comes from having parents who are also comfortable about nudity. I remember seeing my Mum and Dad naked at a really young age. They'd walk from the bathroom to the bedroom naked and it was never a big deal, though we'd always tease each other. I remember stripping off with a girlfriend when I was about 13, to change for a swim, and her looking really shocked and embarrassed when I didn't instantly try to hide behind a towel.

Why are people so scared of others seeing them naked? I mean, I know in the right circumstance it would be dangerous. I'm not about to strip off in the middle of the street or in front of dodgy men in a back alley. But if someone happened to look through the window and the lights were on and they saw me naked, so what? Like I said, I like my body and I'm a show-off. I kind of like people admiring me.

I walk around my flat naked all the time. I live in an apartment block, on the fourth floor. It has big windows that look out onto the flats opposite and there's a busy street below but I'm high up, so people driving past can't see in. The flats opposite can but I think they are owned by people who have them as city flats so they are used infrequently. I sometimes see the odd person going about their business – cooking, washing up or watching TV – but not often. I noticed when the new guy moved in because suddenly there was lots of activity over there. He was home a lot.

This guy's kitchen window faces my lounge room. He cooks a lot and his sink and cupboards and cooking area are close to the window so I could watch him easily. He was in his 20s, average looking, average build. He seemed nice and ordinary. I liked that he had routines. He'd prepare dinner around the same time and go out on Friday and Saturday nights but hardly ever during the week. He'd occasionally have friends over but never a girl on her own. I'd always look for him outside on the street but we never crossed paths.

He first noticed me one evening when I was standing by my window looking out, listening to music and having a glass of wine and daydreaming. He turned on his kitchen light and got himself a beer and unloaded some groceries, then looked over and paused when he saw me standing there. He watched me for a bit then looked away and continued with what he was doing. I wasn't sure if he could see my expression but I could see enough of his face to spot that he was curious. He kept glancing up again to check me out but trying not to. I had on a fitted dress and high heels and was about to go out for dinner. I imagined I looked quite good, silhouetted against the window. The third time he looked up I smiled and gave a little wave. He smiled back and waved and looked pleased. I moved away and left the flat to go out to dinner.

He looked for me then, every night, when he got home. I could see him from another window, though he didn't know that. I'd see him peering across hopefully and have a giggle to myself. I found it amusing and enjoyed coming into view a couple of times a week, pretending to gaze out and not notice him desperate to see me. Other times, I'd look down, look surprised to see him there, and wave again.

The game really began when one night, I went to stand by the window dressed for bed. I was covered in a long T-shirt that skimmed my thighs, but I had nothing on underneath and you could tell I had no bra on and possibly no knickers. I didn't expect him to be there, to be honest, but I saw him walk into his kitchen, without turning on the light, and stand there and watch me, not moving. I'm not sure if he knew I knew he was there or not. But it was sexy the way he stood and watched me. That was how it started . . .

THE REALITY

It turned into a nightly ritual. I'd appear in the window, always around the same time so he'd know when to watch, wearing different things. The night after the T-shirt, I wore sexy little shorts and a vest top. The next night, I wore a short, see-through nightie. I didn't do much, just stood there, sometimes sipping wine, other times a cup of tea, pretending to look out at the city landscape. I liked that he watched me: I'm an exhibitionist remember.

One night, I decided I'd ditch my clothes completely. I had a good look outside first to check no-one in the other flats was home, then I appeared in the window completely naked. This time I didn't pretend not to see him. I looked out until he appeared, standing there alone in his kitchen, the lights off, then I looked down at him. He immediately stepped back, embarrassed at being caught. But I stood where I was and smiled and put a hand up on the windowpane. An acknowledgement I knew he was there, a signal I wanted him there. After a minute or two, he stepped forward. He didn't turn on the light but he lifted his arm and he blew me a kiss, then he put both hands on his heart and I saw a flash of teeth as he grinned at me. I laughed and pressed my body close to the glass to give him one last look then I withdrew, went to bed and masturbated before I went to sleep. I imagined he was doing the same and it made the whole thing even hotter.

I took my time reappearing. I wanted to tease him into thinking he'd never see me again, let alone naked. I made him wait a whole three nights before I reappeared, with clothes on. It was late on a Saturday night. He'd been out but I saw him come home around 10. He'd either had a few beers or was just more confident after seeing me naked because this time he turned the light on, clutched his heart again and made a sad face. He was sad because I was clothed. I smiled at him and flashed my hands, holding up ten fingers to mean 'wait ten minutes'. He got the message. I watched him through the other window and saw him grab a beer from the fridge and sit on the kitchen bench, facing the window, waiting for me.

I took all my clothes off and I got my vibrator from my bedside drawer and a chair from the kitchen. Exactly ten minutes later, I put the chair right near the window, the vibrator on the floor beside it and sat in the chair completely naked. He sat up and instantly stood up, standing as close to the window as he possibly could. I made eye contact with him to be sure he knew I could see him watching me and then I put on a show for him, doing everything I knew he wanted to do to me. I kneaded my breasts and caressed my nipples while he watched me intently. Then I put two fingers inside my mouth and licked them sexily, spread my legs wide so he could see everything and started stroking myself and fingering myself until I was just about to come. I saw him put his beer down and he disappeared for a moment. I knew he'd be taking off his clothes and would reappear naked with his penis in his hand. He didn't disappoint. He looked hot naked, much better with clothes off than clothes on. His penis was long and thin but hard and straining towards his stomach. I liked it. He was stroking himself, and then he started pumping up and down with a loose fist.

I knew he wasn't far off coming and I wanted him to watch me before letting go, so I picked up my vibrator – a slender vibe, not disgustingly big but big enough for him to see what I had in my hand – then I held it on my nipples and my clitoris and slid it in and out. I then put my fingers inside and held it on my clitoris and came really intensely while watching him do the same. He stopped pumping and stood still, the way guys do when they come, and his entire body tensed. About the time I stopped coming, his shoulders slumped and he dropped his hand and leant forward to steady himself on the bench. I blew him a kiss and left him there. I wasn't embarrassed, far from it, I just didn't want him to think I wanted anything more from him because I didn't.

I only did it that once, despite him making begging faces and clutching his heart for repeats whenever he could get my attention. I still stood at the window and I still let him see me naked but I worried other people might watch and while I didn't mind nudity, I didn't relish standing in the local newsagent and wondering why some guy was staring at me funny. Not long after I masturbated for him, he put a sign up on the window that said 'Can I have your phone number?' I smiled but shook my head. I didn't have any desire to meet him in real life. He was cute and sexy and I enjoyed the game but he was too young for me and just not the type I'd go out with.

After a while, I lost interest a bit and he moved out about three months later. I noticed boxes stacked up in his kitchen – he wanted me to know he was leaving, I think – and I waved to him when he appeared to say goodbye. He wrote another sign that said 'You sure no number?' and I shook my head again. He made a sad face, blew me a kiss and that was the last I saw of him. No-one knows what I did apart from one girlfriend. She looked so shocked by the whole thing, I cut the story short and changed the topic. She never brought it up again. I don't think she approved.

Head to Bed: Fancy Making Your Dream Come True?

Depending on which fantasies you've read, your reaction to this will be either 'Yes please!' or 'Are you kidding?' But I bet not one of you has to think for more than a second or two if I ask *which* of your fantasies you'd most like to do in reality.

Most people have their fantasies neatly filed under 'secrecy' categories. Some fantasies (usually those involving bedding a celebrity or the hot guy in the office) we'll readily admit to, especially when we've had a few. Others – usually the darkest, dirtiest ones – we keep intensely guarded, to be enjoyed only in our heads during sex with a partner or masturbation. I'm betting the one that you've just conjured up falls midway: it's saucy but the sort you might confess to an open-minded partner to heat things up, or to see if they're up for actually doing it.

There's usually a point – or a particular partner – in everyone's life, that prompts us to at least consider sharing our favourite fantasy or acting on it. As *Dare* illustrates perfectly, sometimes this results in the most spectacular experience (and orgasm) of your life; other times, well, it's all a bit of a car crash really. This chapter is designed to give you all the information you need to make a sensible decision on whether *your* fantasy would survive the transition from the perfect world of your imagination to the imperfect world of reality.

TO TELL OR NOT TO TELL?

Given that ninety per cent of us fantasise daily, only a small percentage tell our partners about our fantasies, let alone act them out. Why? Because they tend to either involve someone else or our current partners doing something they may not be happy doing. One of the greatest myths about fantasies is that they're suppressed wishes, says Nancy Friday, author of the iconic bestseller of women's fantasies, *My Secret Garden*. Fantasies aren't facts and summoning an erotic image into our heads is usually done purely for sexual entertainment rather than expressing a secret desire to do it. (Even if we do, they rarely take exactly the same form or follow the same script.) But try telling your partner that when you've just confessed you spent Monday daydreaming about having sex with the workmen currently installing your next-door neighbour's kitchen – all six of them, one at a delicious time. In your head, it's sexy. Telling him, it suddenly seems less sexy, more silly. In his head, neither adjective has applied. He's seriously threatened and insulted and knee-jerk reacts by shouting a few choice insults at you.

Think before you speak. Think before you force your partner to tell you his fantasies. Do you *really* want to know the answer? Having manipulated past lovers into doing just that, believe me, they're generally not about you doing something really cool and sexy. They're nearly always about him doing something with someone he'll describe in painstaking detail, ensuring the fantasy is lodged more firmly in your imagination than his – and guaranteed to start rolling the second you even think about having sex with him.

Most of us (definitely me!) don't want to know what our partners conjure up. But is it threatening to the relationship if they fantasise about others regularly while having sex with us? Opinion divides on this one. On one side, there's evidence that fantasies have a purpose in long-term relationships. They help combat the inevitable boredom that creeps in when you're desensitised by sleeping with the same person, all of the time. There are three usual ways of dealing with this inevitable consequence of monogamy: leave and find someone new, have sex on the side, or fantasise. So in this area, fantasies usually help rather than harm. People who fantasise during sex report higher sexual satisfaction and have fewer sex problems – even if the person they're imagining all sorts with *isn't* their partner. Which suggests most fantasies are a playful indulgence and not worthy of the guilt or anxiety we attach to them.

But there's other research that suggests otherwise. If you constantly fantasise about someone you know and interact with repeatedly, it can increase the chances of you following through. The more you think about having sex with them, the more 'real' it becomes and the more attracted you become to that person. British psychotherapist Brett Kahr conducted the largest survey ever on all aspects of fantasies in 2007 (over 19,000 British adults were involved) and in the resulting book, *Sex & The Psyche,* he talks about the 'intra-marital affair': a term he uses to describe sexual fantasies we have about people other than our regular partners. It's the psychological version of the extra-marital affair and he claims that often, an extra-marital affair will be accompanied by, or preceded by, intra-marital affairs within the mind.

PROCEED WITH CAUTION

Even if you're of the opinion that all fantasies are as fluffy and innocent as candy floss when they remain locked inside your heads, handing over the key is tricky business. Sharing fantasies can backfire easily. Tact is essential. Fantasies about people you know are a no-no (for obvious reasons, just keep the sense of the fantasy and the person anonymous). Fantasies about you and your partner doing relatively 'vanilla' things are relatively safe.

Just be aware that what seems a tasty turn-on to you (dragging him by his tie to have sex in the loo at his office party) might sound plain terrifying to him (the boss finds out and he loses his job). Anything which involves sleeping with other people, 'fake rape', some kind of swinging or S & M, needs a great deal of thinking through (don't even think about blurting them out in the heat of the moment unless you're spoiling for a fight – or divorce). Even if you have no desire to act out the fantasy and simply want to share or role-play, he may still find it horribly disturbing (best scenario) or depraved (best get your coat).

It's especially dangerous to share fantasies with people you don't know well (unless they're a one-night-stand and you couldn't give two hoots what he thinks). It's extremely helpful to know his upbringing, religious and moral standpoints. Even better to have an idea of what else he's done, how experienced he is, how adventurous he is and if he's open to new ideas. I wouldn't share any fantasies that weren't entirely mainstream unless I knew the person well enough to be reasonably certain of a nice, non-judgemental reaction. Hell, even when you do know someone, you can't be sure of a positive response. Just because you fancy something and consider it 'normal', it doesn't mean he will too. Even standard male fantasies like threesomes aren't foolproof. The same guy who loves winding you up at the pub in front of his mates ('Come on honey, haven't you always fancied a bit of girl-on-girl action?') will visibly blanch and need to sit down if you offer it up as a birthday treat, muttering, 'Umm, wow, umm, God really? Are you sure, I mean . . .' Never has the saying 'All talk, no action' been more applicable than with fantasies. *Dare* is testament to the fact that some women dare to act them out – and there are lots of reasons why you should – but most people don't act them out because there are also lots of reasons why you shouldn't.

If you do intend to take it through to reality, learn from the mistakes made by some of the women in this book. The overriding message that shouts through nearly all the real-life scenarios is *think it through before doing it*. Reality and fantasy are like night and day – totally different beasts. Think about the fallout and the negative consequences first, then consider the benefits, and it's much more likely to end up a positive, happy experience. Don't kid yourself about potential pitfalls. Generally, if other people are involved consider it risky. If it's just you and your partner less so, but exceptions obviously apply (if your fantasy is having sex outside Buckingham Palace and even better if the Queen's twitching the net curtains, for instance.)

HAVING THE CONVERSATION

Planning on making it a big, fabulous, best-moment-of-his-life type surprise? Unless it's really, really, *really* harmless (like doctors and nurses type harmless), I wouldn't go there. Seriously, what adult really enjoys having things thrown at them when they least expect it? I'd consider it grounds for an instant dumping if my partner threw me a surprise party and didn't get someone to sneakily make sure I'd done my hair and blown a month's salary on one dress and professional make-up on D-day. Don't kid yourself, men are just as vain as we are. Plus half the fun of a fantasy is anticipation, so you lose that as well. More crucially, men aren't as good at thinking on their feet as we are. Thrusting it on him (perhaps literally) doesn't give him any time to think through what he really thinks now it's happening in real life: what to say, do, react. Surprises sound wonderful but often just leave people feeling underprepared, overwhelmed and confused.

So have a conversation first. Here are some tips to help things run smoothly:

- **Timing is everything.** Suddenly deciding to share a fantasy about being ravaged by a dozen buff male models is not going to go down terribly well if he's put on a stone and feeling self-conscious about it. The same goes for sharing anything important when he's come home late from work, tired, irritable and hasn't had a drink yet.

- **Rehearse** what you're going to say beforehand. If you're too shy to say it out loud, write it down and give it to him, reading it over his shoulder while he does.
- **Tailor it to your partner's personality.** Some people react defensively to *any* suggestion of doing anything new at all, let alone sexual requests. Consider using one of the 'sneaky' approaches described on page 277 and be prepared to have convincing comebacks to huffy replies like, 'I was under the misapprehension that you liked having sex with me. Clearly not'. Just talking about a fantasy, let alone doing it, can cause feelings of insecurity and jealousy. Pile on reassurance if it's needed.
- **What's your point?** It's a *very* good idea to tell him what you'd like to do with the fantasy *before* you tell him what it is. Why are you telling him? Are you doing it to talk dirty? Do you want to role-play it? Or do you want to do it? If it's the latter, do you want him to do it with you, simply watch or are you asking for permission to indulge solo? (Remember it doesn't have to be a literal translation for a fantasy to work in 'real life': symbolism is often all that's needed. A threesome could be using a vibrator as the third person to give the sense of two men doing different things simultaneously.)
- **Ask for discretion** – tactfully. 'I know you'll keep this between us because it's very private,' rather than, 'If you tell Jeff, I will cut off your penis when you're asleep'. (If someone shares their fantasies with you, by the way, afford the same courtesy. Yes, it's desperately tempting to steal the floor at that girls' night out by regaling your friends with his fantasy of having you dressed up as a sex-crazed Hobbit. But revealing a fantasy means your partner trusts you. Resist.)
- **If he overreacts** to a mild fantasy, you've inadvertently hit a

sore spot. It might be something he's tried (and has no desire to repeat) or it might trigger memories of a traumatic sexual experience or childhood memory. Stay calm and talk through the possible reasons why, delving delicately into his past. If he absolutely doesn't want to talk about it or go there, back off. Badgering will only make him more obstinate. On that note . . .

- **Don't threaten.** Saying 'Well if you don't want to do it, I'll find someone who does' is sexual and emotional blackmail. If they aren't interested in hearing about or acting out your fantasy, ask them to share one of their own. Or try out another.

SNEAKY WAYS TO SUGGEST SOMETHING SAUCY

- **Have a dream.** Tell him you had an erotic dream (a made-up scenario based around your fantasy) and see what reaction you get. The more detail he asks for, the more interested he is. Ask him if he's ever had an (ahem) 'dream' about anything and once you're both talking, say, 'Hey, I've just had a great idea! Why don't we act them out for a bit of fun!'
- **Rent a film** with a scene which features or resembles your fantasy (you can Google the activity and add the word 'film' for ideas). Watch his face as the scene plays out: does he look captivated or repulsed? If it's the former, pull him to you for a long, deep snog then look him straight in the eye and say seductively, 'I've just had the *best* idea . . .'
- **Buy a book** based on or including your fantasy theme as a present. If he's coy and reserved, let him read it then ask what his favourite bits were when he's done. If he doesn't mention what you were hoping for, ask directly: 'What did you think of the bit where they did X? I thought it was pretty hot!' It's not too much of a leap to then move into a 'You know what would be even hotter? . . .' suggestion. If you're confident he's fearless enough

to handle it, write little notes throughout the book on pages or pictures which particularly appeal to you, before wrapping it up.

ACTING IT OUT

It helps immeasurably if the fantasy you want to act out is a favourite of both of you, rather than just one of you. Especially if it's the first time you've done anything like this. Don't rush into it, even if you're both frothing at the mouth with enthusiasm. Planning the whole thing – working out the scenario together, buying props, deciding where to do it, when, how etc. – is often just as exciting as actually doing it. Don't be surprised if, sometimes, planning ends up being as far as you go. Plenty of fantasies end up being too difficult to act out safely and you both decide it's not worth the bother. Other times, you realise the thrill you were seeking has been satisfied by knowing you could do it if you really wanted to. I wouldn't invest in expensive props for an untried fantasy for that reason and because you don't know if you'll both enjoy it. Most of the time, they aren't necessary. Having said that, the more effort you make planning it, the better it usually is.

If you're role-playing the fantasy, it's usually easiest to play it out at home, using simple props, music and different rooms of your house to suit different scenarios. Just make sure you plan it for when you're not going to be interrupted by visiting in-laws or children wanting cookies and cuddles. But that doesn't mean you can't start the scenario in public. If you're role-playing sex while others watch you, for instance, go to (an appropriate) bar and make out a little. Kiss, try some furtive touching of breasts (and maybe more under the table) before going home to act out the main event. Before the role play starts, check how serious you're both going to take it. Does it matter if you don't stay 'in character'? Or will you (or they) consider the illusion shattered if you don't? If you end up being overtaken by laughter rather than lust, just keep going. (It sometimes helps to fast forward to the really naughty part to push past the giggles.)

If you're planning on actually **acting out the fantasy** you'll need to also work out an agreed 'stop now' signal. The safe word should be something which isn't likely to come up in the conversation you're likely to have during the fantasy re-enactment. 'Orange' is better than 'Harder', for instance. Talking it through is imperative: be as specific as you possibly can about what's allowed and what isn't. Set rules. Get your partner to repeat back to you what they think the rules are and vice versa so it's crystal clear what's acceptable and what's not.

Finally, always remember your relationship is more important than the experience – even if it is bloody fantastic. Don't embarrass each other by constantly asking if you're OK but do watch closely for any giveaway body language signals that hint they're pretending to enjoy it rather than genuinely happy. (If it involves other people and you'd be too embarrassed to stop proceedings by saying a word, work out a clear gesture you can make more subtly. It might be as simple as a peace sign.) At the first hint of anyone getting upset, angry or just turned off by what's happening, stop and break for a private chat. If they don't want to continue, don't. Be prepared to console and comfort them for as long as they need if it's left them feeling unnerved and insecure.

WHEN IS FANTASISING DANGEROUS?

Sorry to go all heavy on you when you're possibly in the middle of a naughty romp through your imagination and have just flicked to the back out of curiosity, but a few things do need to be addressed. Like safety. If someone shares a weird or violent fantasy very early on, proceed with extreme caution. Christian Grey gets away with it in *Fifty Shades of Grey* but it's a book. Made up. What works out marvellously in fiction can be quite another story in reality. Trust your instincts. Tell a friend and ask for a second opinion if you're not sure. Same goes with acting out fantasies with strangers. Meet in a public place first. Don't get too drunk or high. If you get a bad feeling, don't go there. If at all possible, tell another friend where you are and get them to check in later.

But what if it's *you* that's scaring *you*? Are fantasies that are disturbing in content anything to worry about? The answer is mostly no. I'd say the majority of therapists would agree with me that the fantasies in this book are entirely normal. Saucy, yes. A sign of mental instability, no. Humans have always been attracted to the dark side of themselves. It's why we're fixated on crime shows and horror films. But just because we'll happily switch on *Dexter*, a show about a sexy serial killer who works as a blood splatter expert for the FBI, it doesn't mean we want to cover our own bedrooms with plastic and perform revenge killings before cleaning our teeth and turning in. It's the same with fantasies. We'll often picture ourselves in scenarios completely contrary to our core personality. That's sort of the point: a lot of the turn on is to give the forbidden, 'dirty' side of us – the murky part that we'd never dream of showing in real life – a chance to play without being judged.

But, in some instances, sadistic fantasies can serve as stepping stones to sadistic behaviour. Psychotherapist Brett Kahr concluded that some fantasies can damage us by reinforcing self-destructive patterns of behaviour and thought. It's true. Deviant fantasies *can* be an indicator of true sexual deviancy but the fantasies are invariably coupled with real-life symptoms as well. So long as you can distinguish between fantasy and reality and have no desire to take it through to real life, there isn't usually a problem.

You could, however, be headed for trouble of a different kind if you can *only* get aroused and climax by imagining one particular fantasy. This is the head equivalent of a fetish – when a person *needs* a particular object (like their lover wearing rubber) during sex in order to achieve sexual satisfaction. Note the emphasis on the word 'need' rather than 'want'. It's one thing to be playfully begging him to play Tarzan, quite another not being interested at all unless there's a loin cloth handy.

If anything at all concerns you about any aspect of fantasising and your fears aren't allayed by what I've written, please seek professional advice. A good sex therapist will be able to advise you properly.

What Does Your Fantasy
Say About You?

Analysing fantasies is a bit like dream analysis: it's more about the individual interpretation than generalised concepts. Dreaming of performing on stage is a positive dream for some; for others it would qualify as an anxiety dream. Let your instincts guide you on what rings true and what doesn't but here are common themes that tend to apply for most of us.

Anal sex: The rectum is packed with super-charged nerve endings and nice girls wouldn't dream of doing it. Need I say more? A lot of women would like to investigate this under-explored hot zone but don't dare ask. Fantasising about it is the next best thing.

Being forced to have sex: The 'safe rape' fantasy can also hark back to the 'good-girl' hang up: if someone overpowers us, we can relax and submit because we have no choice. Some people, ridiculously, try to use it as 'proof' that women secretly want to be raped. That's a bit like saying if you like watching horror films, you secretly want to be a killer or be killed. Fantasy rape isn't usually painful, violent or frightening. We're in complete control of it – which is the complete opposite to rape in real life.

Being irresistible: Even the most modest people wish to be desirable – it's a universal need to want people to find you attractive. But what if you were *so* attractive, people really couldn't help themselves? What if they were literally falling at your feet, begging you to let them kiss you, touch you, have sex with you?

As females, we're well aware beauty is a prime commodity, and to be worshipped for it makes us very valuable indeed. Being adored also rather handily removes responsibility for what follows: you're being seduced by people who are desperate to possess you, how could a girl resist? Because society frowns on women who instigate sexual encounters, our subconscious tries to find ways to make it 'acceptable' and this is one of them. Sometimes, recurring fantasies of being irresistible mean there's an unconscious fear that in reality the opposite is true. In this case, it can reflect low self-esteem and fears of sexual inadequacy. In most, it's simply a healthy outlet for the recurring dream of going to bed as ourselves and waking up as a supermodel.

Bondage fantasies: No prizes for guessing this one is about power. One person has it, the other doesn't, and we're attracted to both for different reasons. Stripped of it, we are completely at the mercy of someone else, absolving us of responsibility. This means we're 'forced' to enjoy whatever the other person does to us. If you're a people-pleaser and usually the 'giver', this makes it impossible to reciprocate. If we're the ones in control, we're given permission to be completely selfish.

Dominating men or using them as sex slaves: A classic control fantasy which is all about rebelling against having to be a 'nice girl'. They're particularly popular with women who are shy and undemanding in real life. The desire to be the boss and be in control isn't exclusive to men but being sexually aggressive is seen as a male trait. Lots of women are worried they won't be seen as feminine if they act dominant during sex but our imagination (thank God) isn't bound by the same rules which dictate society. We might choose to 'behave' during waking hours but in our dreams and our fantasies, our forceful, domineering sides are given freedom. We don't wait to be given 'permission' but take what we want, when we want it, without apology. The goal isn't to humiliate our lover, it's to give us a total sense of control.

Forbidden people: It's often a replay of what actually happened with a particularly desirable ex (we tend to marry for love not sex); or, if someone new, the grass-is-greener philosophy at play. The more forbidden the person (our partner's best friend, someone's father, the boss), the more powerful the fantasy. The 'we want what we can't have' syndrome is especially potent in sex.

Your partner watching you have sex with another man: You're insatiable – he alone can't satisfy you. The person who craves sex more is seen as more sexually powerful, so this is a power fantasy as well. It also hints at the urge to show off: we can only see so much when we're having sex with someone because you're necessarily physically close. Watching from a distance, he gets to see how good you really look.

Joining the 'mile high club': Joining the 'mile high club' and having sex in the loo on a plane is a common fantasy – and one plenty of people take through to reality. There's a strong element of exhibitionism in this fantasy even though you're essentially having sex in private. Just like having sex in a tent, you're getting up to all sorts with the general public a mere hair's breadth away. Unlike a tent, the chance of being caught in this fantasy is high, which means the sex has to be fast and no frills. This is an excuse to indulge in sex which is lust-driven rather than emotion-driven, which is why we'll often do it with strangers. Women, too, want sex for sex sake with handsome strangers – well, in our dreams anyway.

Receiving or giving oral sex: Oral sex is seen as more intimate than intercourse simply because it involves licking our most private and (because we excrete matter from them) 'dirty' bits. Worshipping them in fantasies therefore represents true sexual acceptance. Then there's the fact that both sexes have frequent and intense orgasms from oral sex. Being good at it can be a power dream; receiving it from someone who can't get enough makes us impossibly ravishing.

Romantic: No real surprises with this one: these fantasies are had by women who are more motivated by love than sex and tend to be sexually conservative. Even if we can't do it in reality, most of us can separate sex and love in our imaginations. Women who only have romantic fantasies tend not to be able to.

Seducing a virgin: The first person we have sex with is guaranteed to always be remembered, so high achievers and those who enjoy being the centre of attention may enjoy this fantasy. If someone's never done something before, we not only get to teach them everything we know – putting us in a superior sexual position – they probably won't criticise our technique. So it may mean you feel sexually inadequate. Corrupting innocence is also a strong theme here: it's forbidden, so highly appealing.

Sex in public or semi-public: This one's about people admiring us – usually, onlookers are so impressed by our sexual skills, they'd cut off a limb to swap places with the person we're having sex with. It's also illegal so can mean you're quite rebellious.

Sex with a stranger: If you don't know them and never will, you can let loose without fear of being judged. If they don't know you, you can become someone else. It is sex stripped of all emotion, purely physical. Often the stranger will be faceless (it all happens in the dark where we can't make out their features or they come up from behind us). Eye contact means intimacy, avoiding it is another way to ensure it satisfies the raw, primitive side of us we may mask in real life.

Sex with someone much younger or older: Plumped skin, high energy, bodies at their prime and minds unburdened by the scars of life: youth has always been appealing. Having sex with someone much younger than us is an ego-boost: we've still 'got it' to be able to attract them. Sex with someone older works on the same principle. We see older people as wiser, richer, more intelligent, worldly and sophisticated. Then there are Daddy issues: women who consistently fantasise about older men or date them in real life can sometimes be working through issues with their own father. We try to fix what's happened in the past by recreating it, with a different ending, in the present.

Spanking fantasies: Mildly sadomasochistic, spanking is a common fantasy with biological undertones. Aggression is common in the animal world – some female animals only ovulate if the male bites them – and humans have also long linked pain and pleasure. Arousal is all about increased blood flow and spanking increases blood flow to erogenous zones like the buttocks and genitals. Wanting to be spanked can also originate from guilt: we need to be punished for liking something we shouldn't (sex).

Stripping: Stripping is a particularly popular female fantasy because it involves exposing ourselves provocatively and teasing – which is something women do consciously or unconsciously a lot anyway! A low-cut top, a slit skirt – we're used to flashing parts of our flesh and getting admiring glances for doing so. Narcissism and exhibitionism are a basic part of life: we need to be 'seen' by other people in order to feel important. 'The look-ing glass effect' is seeing ourselves reflected in other people's eyes: the more adoringly they look at us, the more adorable we feel. Strippers involve the audience in their own narcissism – they want to be looked at. Happily, plenty of men are more than willing to oblige; in fact, most of the men who frequent strip clubs are voyeurs as all they want to do is look rather than touch. Neither the stripper nor the audience necessarily want sex with the other – simply performing or watching the performance is enough. Flaunting gives us a sense of power, and power is always sexy. Exposing our naked body to cheers and applause in our fantasies also helps calm our fear of our body not being good enough in real life. In reality, we might be short, stocky and rather rounded; in our fantasies we have legs which stretch from here to heaven, breasts so pert they practically point upwards and a tummy so flat, it's concave. Some therapists claim 'show-off' fantasies hint at an Oedipal complex: as a little girl we learnt being a tease in childhood got us Daddy's attention, stealing it from Mum. I say in most cases, that's a load of rubbish.

Talking dirty: It's 'unladylike' to swear or talk in a vulgar fashion about sex, which is why this fantasy tends to appeal to women who are relatively innocent the rest of the time. Usually, the fantasy centres around being the Mummy-approved girl-next-door outside the bedroom, a wanton woman when in it.

Threesomes, swinging and group sex: One of the most common fantasies for both sexes, in female fantasies women tend to be the undisputed star of any group sex session and nearly always on the receiving end. For men, it's more about being able to satisfy more than one woman. A heady blend of exhibitionism, voyeurism, bi-curiosity (if there's the same sex involved) and humans longing for excess (if one person feels good, more must feel better).

Trying something you haven't: Most of us are far more daring in our heads than in our beds – particularly women. It's all to do with being judged or seen as 'slutty'. If we're planning on trying something new out in reality, fantasising about it is a great way of rehearsing. It's a mental practice session.

Watching others have sex: Countless surveys have shown women are as turned on by erotic images as men are, so it makes sense that we're also just as voyeuristic. Women are far more 'porn-friendly' – able to enjoy watching it solo or with partners – than society would have you believe. Watching people have sex in real life is even more fascinating because it makes for more realistic comparisons. We all love to think we're great in bed and watching other people means we can see how we rate on the 'best lover' chart. It also hints at sexual confidence – you could teach people a thing or two! There's a narcissistic thread as well: we can't see ourselves having sex, so by watching others we imagine how we might look in the same scenario.

Women with women: 'It's as common for women to have sexual fantasies about other women as it is rare for men to have fantasies about other men,' says Nancy Friday. Women are far less haunted by the social taboo of being gay, probably because society is far less homophobic about gay women than it is gay men. Most women who fantasise about other women aren't gay or bisexual. Simply thinking about something does not mean you're gay. If you find you're also fancying women in real life or feel you're trapped in the wrong body, these are far more pertinent issues. A few bi-curious encounters, are, as the name suggests, more about sexual curiosity than anything else.

Therapists and
Sex Therapists

http://www.itsgoodtotalk.org.uk/therapists/
Counselling and psychotherapy

www.relate.org.uk
Counselling and sex therapy

http://www.bps.org.uk/psychology-public/find-psychologist/
find-psychologist
British Psychological Society

http://www.cosrt.org.uk/therapist_listings.asp
College of Sexual and Relationship Therapists

Acknowledgements

Dare is a departure from my usual self-help books because it's based on real life rather than research. So the people who should be thanked first for my 15th book (!) are the adventurous, fearless, go-getting women who shared their most intimate experiences with me. I don't think I have ever been so entertained hearing your stories or had so much fun writing a book! Thank you for your honesty and trust. This book is yours, not mine.

This is also my first book with publishers Hodder & Stoughton. As an author, I couldn't wish for a nicer team to work with but I am especially indebted to Rowena Webb for recognising that a book about sexual fantasies can be both sexy *and* funny, and Maddy Price who has been ridiculously kind, perceptive and encouraging.

Vicki McIvor, my agent and wonderful friend, thank you for being so constantly and relentlessly positive and never, ever losing faith. Thanks also to Richard Longhurst and Neal Slateford at Lovehoney, who not only produce my fabulous product range but also support all my projects and are so much fun to work with.

To my family and friends: I hope you know (but will remind you anyway) I not only desperately love but appreciate you. Whenever I write a book, I disappear for months on end. Your patience and support reminds me that life really does exist away from a laptop! Heartfelt thanks and drinks are on me!

An invitation from the publisher

Join us at www.hodder.co.uk, or follow us
on Twitter @hodderbooks to be a part of
our community of people who love the very
best in books and reading.

Whether you want to discover more about a book
or an author, watch trailers and interviews, have the
chance to win early limited editions, or simply browse
our expert readers' selection of the very best books,
we think you'll find what you're looking for.

And if you don't, that's the place to tell us what's missing.

We love what we do, and we'd love you to be a part of it.

www.hodder.co.uk

@hodderbooks

HodderBooks

HodderBooks